The Forgiving Air

Understanding Environmental Change

Richard C. J. Somerville

SO-CFU-931

UNIVERSITY OF CALIFORNIA PRESS

Berkeley / Los Angeles / London

The publisher gratefully acknowledges permission to use "Song for
the Rainy Season" from *The Complete Poems 1927–1979* by Elizabeth
Bishop. Copyright © 1979, 1983 by Alice Helen Methfessel.
Reprinted by permission of Farrar, Straus & Giroux, Inc.

Gro Harlem Brundtland's remarks quoted herein are reprinted with
permission from *One Earth, One Future: Our Changing Global
Environment*. Copyright 1990 by the National Academy of Sciences.
Courtesy of the National Academy Press, Washington, D.C.

The material on p. 92 herein is cited with permission from *Climate
Change*, The IPPC Scientific Assessment (1990), World
Meteorological Organization; the information cited is quoted
from the Executive Summary of Chapter V (p. 135).

University of California Press
Berkeley and Los Angeles, California

University of California Press
London, England

First Paperback Printing 1998

Library of Congress Cataloging-in-Publication Data

Somerville, Richard.
    The forgiving air : understanding environmental change /
Richard C. J. Somerville.
        p.   cm.
    Includes bibliographical references and index.
    ISBN 0-520-21388-2 (pbk : alk. paper)
    1. Ozone layer depletion—Environmental aspects.   2. Climatic
changes—Environmental aspects.   3. Greenhouse effect,
Atmospheric—Environmental aspects.   4. Acid rain—
Environmental aspects.   5. Air—Pollution—Environmental
aspects.   I. Title.
QC879.7.S66   1996
363.73'92—dc20   95-18974
                                                       CIP

Printed in the United States of America

9 8 7 6 5 4 3 2 1

The paper used in this publication meets the minimum requirements of
American National Standard for Information Sciences—Permanence of
Paper for Printed Library Materials, ANSI Z39.48-1984. ∞

The Forgiving Air

To my mother

Song for the Rainy Season

Hidden, oh hidden
in the high fog
the house we live in,
beneath the magnetic rock,
rain-, rainbow-ridden,
where blood-black
bromelias, lichens,
owls, and the lint
of the waterfalls cling,
familiar, unbidden.

In a dim age
of water
the brook sings loud
from a rib cage
of giant fern; vapor
climbs up the thick growth
effortlessly, turns back,
holding them both,
house and rock,
in a private cloud.

At night, on the roof,
blind drops crawl
and the ordinary brown
owl gives us proof
he can count:
five times—always five—
he stamps and takes off
after the fat frogs that,

shrilling for love,
clamber and mount.

House, open house
to the white dew
and the milk-white sunrise
kind to the eyes,
to membership
of silver fish, mouse,
bookworms,
big moths; with a wall
for the mildew's
ignorant map;

darkened and tarnished
by the warm touch
of the warm breath,
maculate, cherished,
rejoice! For a later
era will differ.
(O difference that kills,
or intimidates, much
of all our small shadowy
life!) Without water

the great rock will stare
unmagnetized, bare,
no longer wearing
rainbows or rain,
the forgiving air
and the high fog gone;
the owls will move on
and the several
waterfalls shrivel
in the steady sun.

—Elizabeth Bishop

Sítio da Alcobaçinha
Fazenda Samambaia
Petrópolis

CONTENTS

PREFACE TO THE
PAPERBACK EDITION

In the two years since this book was written, the science of global change has steadily advanced, while also growing more important to public policy. On the research frontier, recent measurements in the stratosphere have shown a dramatic slowing in the rate of increase of chemicals that attack the Earth's protective ozone layer. The measured amounts of some of these chemicals have actually begun to decrease. These observational data confirm the success of international agreements designed to phase out the manufacturing of ozone-depleting substances. They provide reason for optimism that humankind, when confronted with serious global environmental problems, is capable of acting rationally and cooperatively for the benefit of all life on Earth. They offer hope that in a few decades natural processes may restore the ozone layer to something approaching its pristine state earlier in this century, before people inadvertently tampered with it.

However, not all the news from the ozone layer is good. Significant loss of stratospheric ozone has been detected over much of the Earth, less severe than the dramatic loss in the ozone hole over Antarctica to be sure, but still worrisome. Not all countries have complied with their treaty commitments to suspend production of the offending chemicals. An international black market has developed in several of these substances, which can be produced easily and profitably. Despite overwhelming scientific evidence of the harmful character of these chemicals, some individuals still remain unconvinced. The struggle for the health of the ozone layer is not yet over.

The prospect of significant human influence on global climate continues to motivate both the research agenda of the scientific community and the political agenda of governments great and small. The computer simulations of climate discussed in this book have broadened in scope to include additional aspects of the climate system, including processes whose importance have only recently become widely recognized. For example, many scientists are now engaged in research to understand more completely the role of sulfate aerosols on climate. These tiny particles, emitted into the atmosphere from the smokestacks of the major industrial nations, are thought to provide a partial screen, shielding the Earth's surface from sunlight.

A naturally occurring analogue may have been the 1991 eruption of Mount Pinatubo, the Philippine volcano, which led to a noticeable global cooling during 1992–93. Volcanic aerosols eventually leave the atmosphere, but humans produce a continuous supply of industrial aerosols, which may be responsible for partially counteracting the human-caused increase in the greenhouse effect. Aerosols are also thought to have significant potential influences on clouds—and hence on cloud-climate feedback processes—and they may influence ozone depletion as well. The multiple roles of aerosols demonstrate the interconnectedness of different processes in the complex system which is our Earth—a linkage that occurs between many topics explored in the book.

The ocean, too, has recently provided dramatic evidence of its key role in the climate system. In mid-1997, surface temperature measurements in the eastern tropical Pacific Ocean showed the characteristic signature of an El Niño event, with waters off the west coast of South America more than 5 degrees Celsius (9 degrees Fahrenheit) warmer than the long-term climatological norms for the same season. Scientists had predicted this event as early as the fall of 1996, although its intensity came as something of a surprise. This El Niño may well rival or surpass the 1982–83 event for the title of "El Niño of the Century." Such events are known to produce worldwide disruptions of normal weather patterns, including severe floods and droughts, with massive economic consequences. El Niños are a consequence of complex interactions between the atmosphere and the ocean. Their frequency and intensity may well change if the global climate becomes warmer, but the state of the science today is too immature to allow us to characterize the nature of such a change. This field is another area of active research internationally.

Scientists and non-scientists alike have been fascinated by the reactions of industries and governments to the prospect of human-caused climate change. A series of international conferences and agreements, starting with the "Earth Summit" in Rio in 1992, has moved many nations to propose treaties limiting emissions of carbon dioxide and other gases that contribute to the greenhouse effect. Different nations have reacted in very different ways to the scientific and political factors that bear on this issue. For example, among the countries most concerned about the possible consequences of global warming are the small island nations, which feel their very existence threatened by the prospect of rising sea levels. Powerful economic forces also find their interests strongly affected, often in conflicting manners. For example, oil companies, like oil-producing nations, fear a reduction in demand for their products. On the other hand, reinsurance companies, chastened by large losses due to recent major hurricanes, are concerned that a warmer world may bring with it changes in the long-term climatology of hurricanes, on which their actuarial calculations are based, and hence increased business risk.

Scientists continue to search in the observational climate records for indications that our planet either is or is not changing in ways that are both distinguishable from natural variability and attributable to human causes. This difficult and important effort is a major focus of current research and will certainly remain so in the future. In December 1995 the Intergovernmental Panel on Climate Change (IPCC) issued yet another report in their series, which began with the 1990 report discussed in this book. As with previous IPCC reports, the 1995 document is a massive and wide-ranging summary of research with contributions from more than 2,000 scientists. The most celebrated statement in the report attracted considerable attention from the popular press because it edged closer to a flat statement that people are indeed changing the climate. The actual language, which had been negotiated at some length, was, "The balance of evidence suggests that there is a discernible human influence on global climate." It seems clear that the science of global change will occupy a central place in international affairs for many years to come.

I have taken advantage of the new edition to correct some misprints and outright mistakes. For pointing out errors and omissions in the clothbound edition, I am grateful to John Katzenberger, Stephen

Schwartz, and Stephen Warren. I appreciate the wisdom and energy of Suzanne Samuel of the University of California Press, who has expertly guided both me and this version of the book through the publication process. Finally, it is a special pleasure to thank my wife, Sylvia Bal Somerville, for providing the photograph on the cover of this edition. This gift beautifully symbolizes our collaborative life together.

Richard Somerville
September 1997

PREFACE

This book is about global change. It focuses on several of the great environmental issues of our time, the various atmospheric phenomena presented by the ozone hole, by changes in the greenhouse effect, and by acid rain and air pollution. Each of these phenomena is complex, but they all share a common cause: ourselves. We're still learning about the capacity of the planetary environment to absorb the by-products of modern civilization, but the plain truth is that we've already harmed the Earth, and especially the atmosphere, by using it as an all-purpose dump. It's therefore in our best interests to learn all we can about "the forgiving air," because we're less likely to do serious and irreversible damage to our environment if we understand it better. It may have already forgiven much, but it's unreasonable to expect it to forgive without limit.

I write about these issues from the perspective of a scientist who does atmospheric research. I am convinced that everyone who is interested in global-change issues can and should become familiar with the remarkable story of the science that underlies them. I think that science has much to contribute to the making of wise public policy, and that an informed citizen of the Earth can and should be scientifically literate. Indeed, I firmly believe that the best reason to learn about science is not that some of us might want to be trained as scientists, but rather to ensure that every educated person is equipped to deal intelligently with a world in which the role of science is increasingly critical. Furthermore, I think scientists have an obligation to participate in this kind of general education and to relate their research to it.

Albert Einstein said it best, in a 1931 address to the student body at the California Institute of Technology: "It is not enough that you should understand about applied science in order that your work may increase man's blessings. Concern for man himself and his fate must always form the chief interest of all technical endeavors . . . in order that the creations of our mind shall be a blessing and not a curse to mankind. Never forget this in the midst of your diagrams and equations."

Science need not be intimidating and inaccessible. My aim in writing this book has been to humanize the science underlying environmental issues. Because every aware citizen of the Earth has a legitimate interest in these issues, my intended audience is not scientists, but all people. No technical training or scientific background is required to read this book. In particular, there is no mathematics in it at all. Instead, the book is full of anecdotes and other information about the scientists whose research has advanced our understanding.

Many excellent books deal with the environment, and I have included an extensive annotated bibliography as a guide to this literature. This book differs from nearly all of those listed there in focusing almost exclusively on science, not on politics or ideology or advocacy or other important aspects of environmental concerns. As an active researcher in this field myself, I have taken the view that the most appropriate contribution I can make to informing a wide public is to provide an account of the relevant science that is accurate, balanced, concise, up-to-date, and reader-friendly. Moreover, I have chosen to limit the scope of the book to planetary atmospheric issues of great global significance, such as the destruction of part of the stratospheric ozone layer and the emergence of climate changes caused by an increase in the greenhouse effect. Many other environmental problems are also important, of course, but the reader who wants to learn more about toxic waste dumps or oil-tanker spills must look elsewhere.

This book is about science, so I want to say something about scientific language. Because scientists are used to dealing in statistical concepts, they differentiate carefully between terms like *mean* and *median*. But most people don't, because there's no need to be so precise in everyday conversational usage. Scientists do often talk in that ultra-accurate jargon, without realizing that those same words have other connotations. As a reality check, I sometimes run my own writing by'my mother, a perceptive critic and a fine writer. Once I gave her a paper that employed a phrase like: "the mean concentrations of chlorine for zonal mean conditions in the winter mean stratosphere." She said, "It sounds so nasty, Richard, to use the word *mean* all the time!"

So I have tried to reduce the jargon here to an absolute minimum. Technical terms will be introduced one at a time as needed, and defined where they first occur. A Glossary of these and a few related terms is included in the back of the book. And again, there are no equations at all. It should be possible to write about science in plain English, though asking a scientist to do that is a little like asking a cat to bark.

I am grateful to Dean Abrahamson, John Firor, and Cheri Morrow, three dedicated scientist-educators, for encouraging me to write about global-change science and for critically reading an earlier version of the manuscript. I also thank Susan Joy Hassol, a fine science writer whose deep environmental knowledge made her an ideal editor for this work. She selflessly went over the entire text with me and also helped compile the Glossary. Additionally, I thank Ken Bergman, Beth Chertock, Catherine Gautier, Jack Kaye, Wendelin Montciel, Claire Parkinson, Mollie Somerville, Geoff Vallis, and an anonymous reviewer for their helpful comments.

This book originated in lectures that I gave in 1991 and 1992 in Project COPE (Change on Planet Earth), at the University of California, San Diego (UCSD), a program that taught elementary- and middle-school teachers about the interdisciplinary science of global change. For their generous contributions to the success of Project COPE, I thank Barbara Edwards, Cara Feeney, Stacia Kozlowski, Carol Radford, Paul Saltman, Dale Teschler, Dotty Valdez, Cheri Koss Waldo, and Mary Walshok. I owe a special debt of gratitude to P. A. Moore, who, jointly with me, first developed the concept of Project COPE, and to Phil Lauder, who edited the original manuscript. I am also grateful to the teachers who participated in Project COPE. Their stimulating questions and comments helped to guide and shape my lectures. Conscientious and enthusiastic, these teachers were a pleasure to have as students. I envy *their* students.

For administrative help and wise counsel, I am indebted to Carolyn Baxter, who for over 15 years has faultlessly run my office at Scripps Institution of Oceanography, UCSD. Cindy Clark, Chuck Colgan, and Jill Ives of Scripps also provided invaluable assistance.

Scripps Institution of Oceanography is among the foremost centers in the world for research in the science of the Earth, and I have been educated and stimulated by innumerable discussions with my colleagues there. Much of the research described in this book, in fact, is due to Scripps scientists, including Charles David Keeling, Walter Munk, Veerabhadran Ramanathan, and the late Roger Revelle, all of whom I cite by name. I am grateful to them all. Those among the Scripps graduate students, postdoctoral fellows, research staff members, and scientific visitors, past and present, who have worked most closely with me over the years have generously educated me through our collaborations, and I am especially indebted to Nelson Byrne, Beth Chertock, Maria Filonczuk, Robert Frouin, Catherine Gautier, Sam Iacobellis, Shirley Isakari, Noah Knowles, Wan-Ho Lee, Fausto Malvagi, Peter Norris, Lorraine Remer, John Roads, David Rogers, Yolande Serra, Geoff Vallis, and Duane Waliser.

I thank Jean-Claude André, Jean-Pierre Chalon, and Jean-Paul Zahn, my hosts during a sabbatical year in Toulouse, France, that afforded me the tranquillity and perspective to plan much of the material that eventually appeared in the lectures of Project COPE and in this book.

Elizabeth Knoll, Michelle Nordon, and Stephanie Emerson, my editors at the University of California Press, have encouraged me throughout, and the book is much improved because of their advice. An expert copy editor, Bill Carver, found hundreds of ways to make the manuscript better.

My wife, Sylvia Bal Somerville, provided thoughtful criticism throughout the course of writing and revising. She and our sons, Alexander and Anatol, have shown infinite forbearance when I have stolen work time from family time. Their steadfast support and love have made this book possible.

Project COPE was administered by UCSD Extension and was supported by a grant from the U.S. Department of Education. I also wish to acknowledge the agencies and organizations that sponsor my own research, on which I have drawn freely for material for this book. These include the National Aeronautics and Space Administration (Grants NAG5-236 and NAG5-2238), the National Oceanic and Atmospheric Administration (Grant NA90AA-D-CP526), the National Science Foundation (Grant ATM91-14109), the U.S. Department of Energy (Grant DE-FG03-90ER61061), Digital Equipment Corporation (Grant 1243), the California Space Institute (Grant CS-67-94), and the University of California Institutional Collaborative Research Program.

1

INTRODUCTION

The Forgiving Air, a brief line from a powerful poem, is a great poet's characterization of an environment of rich fecundity, sustaining an abundant mosaic of life, an environment that is at once beautiful, fragile, ephemeral, and mutable. Elizabeth Bishop's "Song for the Rainy Season" is set in Brazil, in the town where she lived, Petrópolis, which is in the mountains about 60 miles inland from Rio de Janeiro, close to the Tropic of Capricorn. The poem reminds us not only that climate can vary, but that it does so spectacularly every year, as the seasons change. In Petrópolis, as elsewhere in the tropics, the contrast between the dry and rainy seasons can be especially dramatic. For me, that contrast is an apt metaphor for the global changes that people may inadvertently cause by affecting our planetary environment. As the poet warns us, "a later era will differ."

It might be a great comfort to us all if our planet and its climate were constant and unchangeable. They're not. They've been changing naturally for as long as the Earth has existed. Today, however, the people on the planet are collectively such a potent force that their influence on the global environment has begun to rival that of Mother Nature herself. This is in fact a unique moment in human history. We—all of us—have begun to affect the Earth on a global scale. We have of course been affecting the planet in our own neighborhoods for a long time. People were dying of smog-induced illness in London centuries ago. But now there are so many of us—nearly six billion, and more all the time—and we use Earth's resources so profligately that we can alter not just our own neighborhoods but the character of the entire planet. We thus live in a remarkable time, one that can come along only once in human history. That moment hadn't yet been reached even in our grandparents' generation, but it's upon us now. So it's no coincidence that the topics we'll focus on in this book are all occurring at the same time.

The ozone hole, the dramatic depletion of stratospheric ozone over Antarctica, is one of them. It's a fascinating story, and its outcome is not yet known. But it's not the only important aspect of global change. The greenhouse effect, acid rain, and air pollution are others, and the list continues.

We'll begin with the ozone hole. Then we'll take up the greenhouse effect, perhaps the paradigm problem of global change. The prospect of increasing the greenhouse effect, and thus altering Earth's climate, worldwide, illustrates many of the most important and characteristic features of global-change problems. Climate change is international in scope, it occurs slowly over many decades, and there is no simple way to retard or reverse it. Later we'll move on to such topics as urban smog and acid rain.

Two themes will recur throughout this book. One, which I've already mentioned, is the issue of our having become so numerous as a species—and our industries, lifestyles, and energy usages having accordingly changed so dramatically—that we, the human race, have begun to affect the planet in ways that we hadn't expected, ways that are global in scale.

The second general theme is the role of science in all this. I've chosen to talk about the ways in which we're affecting the planet on a global scale because they involve some of the most exciting, most promising, and most relevant science that's being done today. The topics I'm going to spend most of the time on concern everybody: they're in the headlines, they're on television, and they excite people.

Today, in the graduate schools where scientists are educated, a different kind of student is coming to study environmental science. Students who might at one time have chosen to study astronomy or quantum mechanics are instead choosing careers in Earth science. They're motivated by the fact that science on these topics has planetary ramifications. These students are as passionate about their research as they are about our stewardship of the world. They're interested in doing science that's relevant to the environment and to the planet.

Science is inherently unpredictable and often surprising. The story of the ozone hole, which we'll examine shortly, illustrates this well. Ozone is a gas that occurs naturally in small quantities in the region of the upper atmosphere called the stratosphere. Ozone has been studied by scientists for many years as a more or less abstract research problem. That is, some of them were interested in ozone simply for the sake of gaining more knowledge, not necessarily because they were worried about the possibility of destruction of the ozone layer or even the loss of a small fraction of the stratospheric ozone. As we shall see, the fact that these scientists were interested in ozone for its own sake led to a remarkable and completely unexpected discovery of paramount importance.

Basic research is often that way. An investigation carried out with no particular application in mind, a modest little foray into the unknown, often turns out to be tremendously important in ways nobody could have foreseen. A classic example is the work of Albert Einstein, which revolutionized physics. Nobody knew in advance that Einstein was going to do anything important. He was completely unknown to the world of science. He did his first breakthrough research, the work that led to a Nobel Prize and worldwide fame, entirely on his own while earning a living as a minor official in a patent office in Switzerland. His only motivation was insatiable curiosity; his only resource, his brain. The theory of relativity didn't emerge from a famous university, or even a mediocre one, but from a patent office!

Thus, whenever an unscrupulous or misguided journalist or politician grabs a headline or a soundbite by making fun of a science project with a silly-sounding name, real scientists cringe, because they know that nearly all of the most important accomplishments in science, including those that have led to great benefits for humanity, are founded on basic research. The obscure project of one unknown scientist today, which may seem silly or inconsequential, especially to a nonspecialist, can have major implications tomorrow.

Of course, not all basic research leads to wonderful and important results. Sometimes, projects yield nothing at all. More often than not, the chain of events that does lead to an application is long indeed, the later events almost imperceptibly linked to the founding events, and the genealogy of a discovery can therefore be hard to trace. Science, especially basic research, is thus chancy and inefficient by its very nature. When we pay for it—whether we are members of Congress or ordinary taxpayers—we need to recognize that fact explicitly. Appropriating money to support research is a form of investing in the future, and all investments entail risk. We can and should be very careful when we choose which science we will support, but we ought to face squarely the reality that some of what we're funding will turn out to be pathbreaking, some will not, and it's absolutely impossible to be sure in advance which is which.

2

THE OZONE HOLE

Our story starts high in the atmosphere, in the cold, dry region called the stratosphere. On the average, the atmosphere becomes gradually colder with increasing altitude. The atmospheric temperature at sea level, averaged over the entire Earth, is about 15 degrees Celsius, or 59 degrees Fahrenheit. As altitude increases, the temperature falls by about 6.5 degrees Celsius for each 1,000 meters in elevation (or about 3.6 degrees Fahrenheit for every 1,000 feet in elevation). Thus, if we stand at the summit of Mt. Everest, which is about 29,000 feet, or 9 kilometers, in altitude, the temperature is colder by some 59 Celsius degrees or 104 Fahrenheit degrees than at sea level. At this height, more than two-thirds of the materials making up the atmosphere are below us.

If we were somehow to leave the summit of Mt. Everest and rise even higher, the temperature would continue to decrease, until, at an altitude of about 11 kilometers (or 36,000 feet, or 7 miles), the temperature would first stop decreasing and then begin to increase with further gains in elevation. At the altitude where the temperature stops decreasing with elevation, we would be entering the stratosphere. The region below us, called the troposphere (from the Greek word for "overturning," because this region of air is kept well mixed by rising and falling air currents), contains all of our familiar weather and all human beings, except those temporarily in high-flying aircraft or spacecraft. The stratosphere, which extends up to an altitude of about 50 kilometers, or 30 miles, is cold, barren, and inhospitable. Yet it's essential to our well-being, because it's home to the ozone layer.

Ozone is a form of oxygen. Ozone, chemical symbol O_3, has three atoms of oxygen in every molecule. A molecule is simply an assemblage of atoms held together by chemical forces. An atom is a tiny particle, the smallest unit of an element that can participate in a chemical reaction. Most gases in the atmosphere occur in the form of molecules containing two or more atoms. Ordinary oxygen, a gas that's common in the atmosphere, is O_2, with just two oxygen atoms per molecule. The O_2 form of oxygen is a million times more plentiful than ozone. Oxygen is the second most plentiful gas in the atmosphere. Most of the atmosphere consists of nitrogen; nearly all of the rest of it is oxygen. The two gases together constitute about 99% of the dry atmosphere. (It's helpful to speak in terms of the dry atmosphere, the part that's not water, because the concentration of water vapor is highly variable.) Ozone is actually very rare—there's hardly any of it, compared to the enormous amounts of ordinary oxygen in the atmosphere. Yet, ozone is critically important, as we'll see, because of its remarkable ability to shield people and other living things from ultraviolet radiation, a component of sunlight that's harmful.

Whether ozone is helpful or harmful to us depends on where it is in the atmosphere. We'll come back to the harmful ozone later when we discuss smog; for now, suffice it to say that ozone in the lower troposphere, near the surface of the Earth, is an ingredient in photochemical smog. It irritates the lungs, it harms plants, and it's a major part of the concern about air quality in many urban areas. But the ozone we talk about when we talk about the ozone layer, and the ozone hole, is in the stratosphere, far above the Earth's surface. The ozone layer is not a thin sheet like a rubber blanket. Instead, there's a range of altitudes, making up a region in the stratosphere, where ozone is slightly more plentiful than it is elsewhere. But even in this region, ozone is one of the rarest molecules. If you imagine a picture of how ozone is distributed with height, the peak in this picture—the altitude at which ozone is most plentiful—would be at about 25 kilometers, or 16 miles above sea level. So, when we talk about the ozone layer, we're talking about a rather deep stratospheric region, high above ground level. Even at those heights, the atmosphere is still composed mainly of nitrogen and ordinary oxygen, the latter with two oxygen atoms in each molecule. Ozone, with three atoms per molecule, is still a minor component, but it's more plentiful in the lower stratosphere than it is near the surface.

Ozone has been present for billions of years. It appears to have been essential to the formation and evolution of life on Earth, because of its role in shielding the surface of the planet from harmful ultraviolet solar radiation. There apparently was no life on the continents before there was an ozone layer. Deep in the sea, early forms of life may have been protected by the water above.

Ozone concentration, the amount of ozone per unit of volume, also varies with latitude, or distance from the Equator. Ozone in the tropics, near the Equator, is typically much less concentrated than that at middle latitudes, between the Equator and the poles. Ozone concentration also changes with the seasons. In absorbing the sun's ultraviolet radiation and in using energy from this radiation to power chemical reactions, ozone also affects the temperature of the stratosphere. In fact, the increase of temperature with altitude in the stratosphere, noted above, is largely due to ozone.

Ozone occurs in the atmosphere because certain types of sunlight are able to break up the molecules of ordinary oxygen and leave free, single oxygen atoms floating around. These free atoms (chemical symbol O) sometimes combine with the ordinary oxygen molecules (O_2) to form ozone (O_3). There's a complicated chain of chemical reactions going on all the time in the stratosphere, in the course of which ozone is constantly being formed and also constantly being destroyed. In the absence of other reactions involving other chemicals, there's an equilibrium, so that the average ozone concentration doesn't change very much. The much-publicized story of the ozone hole is the story of how people have inadvertently and unsuspectingly tampered with that equilibrium.

Ozone is produced and destroyed at all altitudes, but its concentration varies, because ozone is moved about by winds as well as because of the chemical processes that produce and destroy it. Although the maximum concentration of ozone is found within the region we call the ozone layer, even there its concentration is only a few parts per million. So if you sampled a bucket full of molecules from the atmosphere in the ozone layer, only a few of them, typically ten or fewer molecules per million, would be ozone molecules. If you brought all the ozone in the atmosphere down to the surface, it could be contained in a layer about 3 millimeters thick. (A millimeter is about the thickness of the wire used in a paper clip; an inch is about 25 millimeters.)

In spite of how few ozone molecules there are in the ozone layer, they serve a vital function. Were it not for these ozone molecules, harmful radiation would reach the surface of the Earth. For human beings, the most serious immediate consequences would probably be damage to the skin. Skin cancer is very closely related to dosage of ultraviolet (UV) radiation. Some wavelengths of UV radiation are more harmful than others, and ozone absorbs almost all of these especially dangerous wavelengths of radiation. If you like to speculate, you might consider that perhaps one reason why we and other living things have evolved in the way we have is because we had the good fortune to do so in an environment that was sheltered from harmful UV light, thanks to ozone. Thus, in our atmosphere, a few molecules per million have the remarkable property of shielding the whole lower atmosphere from UV radiation from the Sun.

The UV that we worry about most causes skin cancer, including malignant melanoma, a type of skin cancer that can be fatal if left untreated. UV has other effects, too. It causes premature aging of the skin, and it damages the eyes. It's thought to be connected to the formation of cataracts and may also cause damage to the retina. In addition, UV can suppress the human immune system, and it can injure other animals and plant life as well.

Our eyes are sensitive to the broad spectrum of colors in the rainbow—red, orange, yellow, green, blue, indigo, violet. But there are also colors we can't see: the colors on the other side of red, called infrared, and the colors on the other side of violet, called ultraviolet. If we had better eyes, we could see many more colors. Perhaps we wouldn't think of them as colors but simply different kinds of light. It's the ultraviolet light, the same light that causes skin cancer and cataracts, that breaks oxygen molecules apart. You can think of the process as one in which a small quantity of sunlight, called a photon, is absorbed by an oxygen molecule. The energy from the photon of ultraviolet sunlight is what breaks the molecule apart.

A solitary atom of oxygen, chemical symbol O, is rare because it's highly reactive chemically and, therefore, tends to combine with other molecules. Thus, oxygen atoms don't remain alone for long. By contrast, the everyday oxygen molecule, O_2, is not very reactive, so it's plentiful rather than rare.

An ozone molecule, as we've said, contains three oxygen atoms, chemical symbol O_3. Why is there any ozone at all? Ozone occurs because ordinary oxygen (O_2) is sensitive to sunlight, and sometimes breaks apart in a process called photodissociation, which is jargon for the breaking up of molecules due to absorption of solar radiation. The chemical reaction is one in which an ordinary molecule of oxygen, in the presence of ultraviolet sunlight, breaks up into two free atoms of oxygen. The process occurs high in the atmosphere. Here's how we write the reaction:

$$O_2 + \text{ultraviolet radiation} \rightarrow O + O$$

Notice that the reaction expresses a balance, in the sense that there are two oxygen atoms on the left of the arrow and two on the right. Oxygen atoms are not created or destroyed. Instead, they're simply rearranged. Some of the oxygen atoms that result from this photodissociation reaction soon recombine with ozone to form new oxygen molecules. The relevant reaction is:

$$O + O_3 \rightarrow 2O_2$$

The meaning of this reaction is that one free oxygen atom combines with one ozone molecule to produce two oxygen molecules. Again, there is a balance, with four oxygen atoms on both the left and the right sides, but in different combinations.

Not every oxygen atom from every oxygen molecule that gets broken up recombines. Still, an equilibrium is established between the breaking up of oxygen molecules into atoms and the recombining of the atoms into oxygen molecules.

Every now and then, on some occasions, a free oxygen atom, the product of photodissociation, will combine with an oxygen molecule to form ozone, O_3. We write the reaction like this:

$$O + O_2 + M \rightarrow O_3 + M$$

The "M" in this reaction is another molecule. Don't even think about it. Leaving it there mysteriously reminds us that what we're doing is exploring this subject at a level that's not as deep as we could. M is called a mediator or "third-body" molecule. For now it will suffice to say that the presence of the M molecule is one of the special circumstances required for the ozone-forming reaction to take place.

We've just said that ozone forms typically in the atmosphere when the oxygen molecule combines with an oxygen atom, the lone atom having come from the dissociation process. This raises an interesting question: Why doesn't the oxygen in the atmosphere end up being all ozone? If every now and then we get an oxygen atom and an oxygen molecule combining in the presence of a third-body molecule to form ozone, why doesn't the atmosphere, as time goes on, contain less and less ordinary oxygen and more and more ozone? Why isn't there more ozone this year than last year, much more now than a billion years ago?

Because ozone can also be destroyed. The same ultraviolet radiation that causes the oxygen molecule to break apart can photodissociate the ozone molecule, breaking it apart into its components, ordinary oxygen and the lone oxygen atom:

$$O_3 + \text{ultraviolet radiation} \rightarrow O_2 + O$$

Alternatively, the ozone molecule can combine with an oxygen atom to form two oxygen molecules, in the same reaction we saw earlier:

$$O + O_3 \rightarrow O_2 + O_2$$

Again, notice that in all these reactions the total number of oxygen atoms involved must remain the same. In the last reaction, we started out with four atoms of oxygen, three from the ozone molecule and one from the single atom, and we ended up with four again, in the form of two ordinary oxygen molecules.

If we left the atmosphere alone, all of these reactions would go on continually at each of their various rates, depending on how much sunlight there was, what the temperature was, whether the third-body molecules were present, and what other chemical compounds were around, because these ozone and oxygen molecules and atoms combine with other things besides themselves. In the real atmosphere, there are lots of other things going on too.

In general, taking all that into account, you could imagine the atmosphere reaching equilibrium, a situation in which the total amounts of ozone and oxygen do not change. Indeed, it seems to do that. There's much more ordinary oxygen, even in the stratosphere, than there is of this relatively rare gas, ozone. Photodissociation, powered by the energy from sunlight, produces about a gigaton of ozone per year. A gigaton is one billion tons. Thus, although ozone is a relatively rare constituent of the atmosphere, there's still a lot of it, because the atmosphere is so vast.

In the atmosphere, the ozone is nearly all in the stratosphere. There are about three gigatons of it in the atmosphere right now. Ozone is always being created and destroyed: many gigatons are created each year, and many gigatons are also destroyed, through the processes we've just discussed. But as you can see, you can change the amount of ozone that's there, either by producing more or by finding a way to destroy it faster than it's produced.

It's interesting that, from the point of view of people and other living things, there's both good ozone and bad ozone. Good ozone and bad ozone are the very same molecule, O_3; they differ only in location in the atmosphere. Ozone in the stratosphere is good, because it shields us from ultraviolet radiation, in part because it's absorbing this ultraviolet radiation—destroying itself to save us, so to speak. Then there's the bad ozone, down here at the bottom of the atmosphere where we have to breathe it. It too absorbs ultraviolet radiation, but it also hurts plants, hurts your eyes, attacks many materials, and is poisonous if you breathe enough of it. That's why we worry about ozone in the lower atmosphere, particularly as a constituent of smog.

To further discuss ozone amounts, it helps to use a mathematical-shorthand notation called powers of 10. This is simply a technique for writing large numbers in a compact form. Ten with a superscript 1, or 10^1, is shorthand for 10 itself. Ten with a superscript 2, 10^2, is 10 times 10, which is 100. Ten with a superscript 3, 10^3, means 1,000. You can see that the superscript, called an exponent, represents the number of zeros after the one. So the rule is, if you want to write a power of 10 the long way, the usual way, write a 1 and then as many zeros as are in the exponent. But you don't have to stick to powers of 10; you can write any number at all in this notation. For example, if you want to write 2,000, it's 2×10^3. If you want to write 2,690, it's 2.69×10^3. If you want to write 26.9 quadrillion, you can write that as 2.69×10^{16}, or 269 and 14 zeros. That last number is pronounced, "two point six nine times ten to the sixteenth."

I have a deep purpose for wanting you to know about this number 2.69×10^{16}. It relates to something called the Dobson unit, named after Gordon Dobson, an Oxford physicist who was a pioneer in studies of atmospheric ozone. In 1926, Dobson designed a simple instrument to measure stratospheric ozone amounts from the ground, and it was he who created the first global ozone-monitoring network, locating his instruments throughout the world. The instrument, called a spectro-photometer, works by measuring solar radiation in different wavelengths. With knowledge of the radiation-absorbing properties of gases like ozone, these observations can be converted into measurements of ozone amounts.

If there happen to be 2.69×10^{16} molecules of ozone in the atmospheric column above a particular square centimeter of the surface of the Earth, then the abundance of ozone in that column is said to be 1 Dobson unit, or 1 DU. But the typical ozone concentration in the atmosphere is much greater than 1 DU. In fact, an average column of atmosphere above 1 square centimeter of the surface contains several hundred times more than 2.69×10^{16} molecules of ozone. Thus, the average concentration of ozone in the Earth's atmosphere is several hundred DU. In general, ozone is most abundant at high latitudes, near the poles, and least abundant in the tropics, near the Equator. Scientists measure this abundance by the number of ozone molecules in an imaginary column, expressed in DU. A typical average value of ozone abundance is around 250 DU near the Equator, rising to above 300 DU in the middle latitudes. Values above 400 DU can occur near the poles.

In fact, the total number of molecules of ozone on the planet is about 4×10^{37}, which is four with 37 zeros after it—a very large number.

Nonetheless, ozone is rare. If you counted all the molecules of *everything* in the air—remember, it's 99% nitrogen and ordinary oxygen—you'd come up with about 10^{44} molecules. This is a great deal more than the number of ozone molecules. The rule for multiplying powers of ten is to add the exponents. For example, 10^{38} times 1 million (which is 10^{6}) equals 10^{44}, because 38 + 6 = 44. Thus, 10^{44} (the number of molecules in the atmosphere) is more than a million times greater than 4×10^{37} (the number of molecules of ozone), so there are more than a million molecules of air (nitrogen, oxygen, etc.) for every molecule of ozone. To put it another way, the concentration of ozone in the atmosphere is less than one part per million.

So, when we talk about the ozone "hole," that's really a figure of speech. It's not as if there were a rubber sheet of ozone floating around in the stratosphere and somebody tore it or punched a hole in it. The term is used to dramatize the thinning of something that's naturally very rare. When we talk about the concentration of ozone over Antarctica falling from 300 Dobson units down to only 150 Dobson units, we mean half of it is gone. What once was one part per million has become one part per two million.

There is less ozone in the stratosphere today than there was a few decades ago, due in part to the inventiveness of one industrious scientist, Thomas Midgley, Jr. Born in 1889 in Beaver Falls, Pennsylvania, Midgley grew up in Columbus, Ohio, and studied mechanical engineering at Cornell University. Though his greatest achievements were in industrial chemistry, as a chemist he was largely self-taught. At the age of 33, while working at General Motors Research Corporation, he discovered the value of tetraethyl lead as a gasoline additive. This substance substantially raised the octane rating of gasoline, so that compression ratios in automobile engines could be higher and automobiles could thus be more powerful. It was a remarkable invention and a great spur to the fledgling auto industry.

Only much later did we learn that lead in gasoline, in paint, and in other substances has a deleterious effect when it gets out into the environment. Lead has now been banned from many applications, for this very reason. Many countries today require catalytic converters in the exhaust systems of cars to facilitate reactions that destroy the harmful pollutants in the exhaust gases. If lead gets on the catalytic converter, the catalyst becomes less efficient in helping the reactions. So to help the catalytic converter do its job, we have switched to unleaded gasoline. The story of lead in gasoline has many parallels with that of the chemicals that cause the ozone hole. What initially appeared to be a technological breakthrough, with many benefits to humankind, later turned out to have unanticipated side effects that were so severe that they outweighed the benefits.

Having succeeded with tetraethyl lead, Midgley became a hero at General Motors, and he was put to work to develop a safe refrigerant. The chemicals previously used in refrigerators—sulfur dioxide, ammonia, and methyl chloride—were toxic or flammable or both. Refrigeration was dangerous. In 1928, Midgley invented a class of chemicals called chlorofluorocarbons. (We'll return to this class of chemicals later, to examine in some detail what they are, and to learn something about their chemistry.)

Chlorofluorocarbons, or CFCs, are miracle chemicals. They're nontoxic and noncorrosive. Chemically, they're almost inert; that is, they tend not to react with anything. They make superb refrigerants, and it turns out that they have many other industrial uses as well. They're solvents for cleaning parts in the electronics industry, including circuit boards like those that go into computers and television sets. They serve as the cooling fluid in most existing automobile air conditioners. Millions of tons of CFCs have been produced. Du Pont and other companies made many millions of dollars manufacturing them. Commercially, CFCs have been a great success.

But—and this is a big "but"—they destroy ozone. For that reason, they're now being banned, by international agreement.

So Thomas Midgley, Jr., an authentic superstar of industrial chemistry, developed at least two substances that had tremendous practical value. He made a lot of money for his employers, but, unbeknownst to him or anyone else at the time, his inventions turned out to be terribly dangerous when released in large quantities into the environment. Both tetraethyl lead and chlorofluorocarbons are being banned, and we may live to see the day when nobody makes either of them anymore. Meanwhile, they're out there.

Midgley, by all accounts, was an energetic, gregarious, cheerful man. His accomplishments earned him many honors, including election to the presidency of the American Chemical Society, a remarkable odyssey for a man with no formal education in chemistry. But in 1940, he was diagnosed with polio. As his health deteriorated, he grew despondent, and in 1944 he committed suicide. Even in death, the inventive Midgley was ingenious. He had rigged up a harness to help himself get out of bed, and he intentionally strangled himself in it. It was a tragic and sad end to the life of a remarkable scientist, but at least he was spared the knowledge that his inventions have brought the environment great harm.

The CFC industry flourished for decades. And then, 30 years after Midgley's death, CFCs were implicated in ozone destruction. Two chemists at the University of California, Irvine, were analyzing stratospheric ozone and its sensitivity to other chemicals that might be found in the stratosphere. Mario Molina and Sherwood Rowland, in a paper published in 1974, theorized about the existence and nature of a special molecule, called a catalyst, that might be important in the chemistry of ozone destruction.

A catalyst is a substance that stimulates a chemical reaction, whether by enabling it or accelerating it, without itself being changed. In Rowland and Molina's theory, an ozone molecule combines with another molecule, the catalyst, in such a way that the ozone is broken up into two entities, an ordinary oxygen molecule and the leftover oxygen atom (the third atom from the ozone molecule), which combines with the catalyst. If we call the catalyst X, the reaction looks like this:

$$O_3 + X \rightarrow OX + O_2$$

Chlorine (chemical symbol Cl) works well as a catalyst in this reaction:

$$O_3 + Cl \rightarrow ClO + O_2$$

But things don't stop there. If they stopped there, the chlorine wouldn't be called a catalyst, because it wouldn't be emerging unchanged. It started out not connected to anything, but now it is combined with an oxygen atom to form chlorine monoxide (ClO).

The next thing that happens is that the ClO molecule combines with a free oxygen atom. The result is a molecule of ordinary oxygen, and the Cl atom is freed up again, like this:

$$O + ClO \rightarrow O_2 + Cl$$

Where might the oxygen atom (O) come from? One source is the photodissociation of ozone described earlier:

$$O_3 + \text{ultraviolet radiation} \rightarrow O_2 + O$$

These last three reactions constitute a typical catalytic cycle. If we sum them up, we get:

$$2O_3 \rightarrow 3O_2$$

We started out with two ozone molecules and ended up with three ordinary oxygen molecules. We needed the chlorine molecule to form the intermediate compound ClO, but only temporarily, because the ClO molecule itself was soon broken up. That's why Cl is called the catalyst; it escapes unscathed.

Incidentally, you can't just take two ozone molecules, an O_3 and an O_3, and expect them to break up into three O_2's:

$$O_3 + O_3 \rightarrow O_2 + O_2 + O_2$$

That would seem to be a possible reaction; you've got six atoms in the two ozone molecules on the left and six atoms in the three ordinary oxygen molecules on the right, so it's balanced. But this reaction doesn't happen. Ozone molecules are stable; they don't spontaneously break up. But in the presence of a special molecule—a catalyst—one of the ozone molecules can break up to form a molecule of regular oxygen.

The third, leftover oxygen atom then combines with the catalyst, temporarily, and the molecule thus formed effectively combines with another ozone molecule to produce two oxygen molecules, leaving the catalyst just as it started out.

Thus, although this last simple reaction doesn't occur, nevertheless, in the presence of the catalyst, something equivalent does. We start out with two ozone molecules and we end up with three oxygen molecules. In the process, we first create and then destroy the molecule involving the catalyst. And in the process, we destroy ozone.

Certain molecules work especially well as catalysts. For the reaction above, one of these is chlorine. A single chlorine atom can go through this cycle thousands of times before it finally combines more permanently with something else. The chlorine atom encounters an ozone molecule, breaks it up, temporarily forms a molecule of chlorine monoxide (chlorine and oxygen), then breaks up that molecule in the presence of another ozone molecule to form two more oxygen molecules and free up the chlorine atom. Then the chlorine atom does all this again and again and again.

Chlorine can combine with other things, but the enormous power of this reaction, the frightening aspect of it, is that one chlorine atom can go through this catalytic cycle repeatedly. You don't need a brand-new chlorine atom to start it off. An individual chlorine atom, which just a few seconds ago went through this cycle and destroyed two ozone molecules, can next destroy two more ozone molecules, then two more and two more and so on. So if you add chlorine to the stratosphere, you create the potential for destroying great amounts of ozone very quickly. A typical chlorine atom can apparently go through this destructive catalytic cycle some 1,000 to 10,000 times before something else happens to it.

Scientists had been studying catalytic cycles for ozone destruction for a long time, but the role of CFCs was not recognized until the theoretical breakthrough by Molina and Rowland. Other scientists had concentrated on chemistry involving nitrogen oxides from the exhausts of a hypothetical fleet of supersonic aircraft. Chlorine was also considered, but the main source of chlorine was thought to be exhaust from the space shuttle. Molina and Rowland realized that CFCs could provide the chlorine that would serve as the catalyst that could destroy atmospheric ozone. They recognized that the CFCs Midgley had invented in

1928, which had been continually accumulating in the atmosphere ever since, were slowly making their way into the stratosphere.

In hindsight, it's clear that what Midgley did, quite inadvertently, when he invented chlorofluorocarbons was to create a highly efficient way to transport chlorine up into the stratosphere. CFCs, the simple molecules composed of chlorine and carbon atoms, or chlorine, fluorine, and carbon atoms, are chemically almost inert. That's why they're so good for refrigerants. That's how Midgley made his employers at General Motors rich. The new miracle refrigerants displayed none of the disadvantages of their predecessors. Thomas Midgley had invented a substance that's impervious to almost everything—until it gets up into the stratosphere. There, unfortunately, conditions are just right for ultraviolet radiation to break apart the CFC molecules and free up chlorine atoms.

CFCs are really fairly simple molecules, just slightly more complicated than ozone and oxygen. Chemically, they resemble methane, the main component of natural gas. Methane, as its chemical symbol CH_4 indicates, has one atom of carbon and four atoms of hydrogen. CFC molecules are like methane molecules, but with each hydrogen atom replaced by either a chlorine atom or a fluorine atom.

There are several different CFC molecules, none of which occurs naturally. You wouldn't find CFCs anywhere in the atmosphere if people hadn't put them there. How do they get there? CFCs enter the atmosphere when old refrigerators are discarded and eventually leak, when the refrigerant in automobile air conditioners is replenished and the job is done carelessly, with no attempt to capture and recycle the CFCs, or when the insulation in refrigerators, which also contains chlorofluorocarbons, breaks down. Although CFC molecules are even rarer than ozone, there are millions of tons of them in the atmosphere now. Their concentrations are measured in parts per billion, not parts per million as in the case of ozone, but the atmosphere is so immense that just a few of these molecules in a sea of oxygen and nitrogen molecules are still millions of tons.

One of the chlorofluorocarbons, CFC-11, not only is used as a refrigerant but was for a long time the preferred propellant in aerosol spray cans. In the United States, aerosol spray cans containing Freon were banned in the late 1970s. CFC-11 was the Freon in those spray cans. (Freon, incidentally, is a trade name used by Du Pont; it's easier to say than "chlorofluorocarbon eleven.") Another chlorofluorocarbon, CFC-12, has been used in aerosols, refrigerants, and air conditioners.

CFC-113 is a solvent, used especially in the electronics industry for cleaning circuit boards. These are the main CFCs. In the 1980s, they were being produced at the rate of several hundred thousand tons per year. Closely related compounds called halons are used in fire extinguishers.

All of these compounds are now known to cause ozone depletion, the destruction of ozone in the stratosphere. CFC-11, in particular, is responsible for nearly half of the observed ozone depletion. CFC-12 and CFC-113 are the two next most important of these compounds. Because CFCs are very useful and are the foundation of a substantial industry, the world has not acted as fast as it might have to ban their production. At one point, Professor Rowland was chagrined at the slow pace of the international effort to outlaw CFCs. "What's the use of having developed a science well enough to make predictions," he said, "if in the end all we're willing to do is stand around and wait for them to come true?"

In 1974, when Molina and Rowland wrote about the potential for ozone destruction, it was pure theory. It was intelligent conjecture, a scientific hypothesis they thought up as theoretical chemists using their knowledge of chemistry to figure out how the compounds involved would behave under the physical conditions of the stratosphere.

For a long time following their publication, Molina and Rowland's speculations were considered mere scientific theorizing and were ignored or disparaged by many people—including, as you might imagine, the industry that very profitably made the chlorofluorocarbons. These people discussed the subject in much the same terms that some elements of the tobacco industry have adopted in speaking about the possible health effects of tobacco smoking. You can have a lot of statistical evidence that links cigarettes and cancer, but in the absence of more conclusive "proof," there is still room for interested parties to deny a cause-and-effect relationship.

Eventually, of course, more and more people became convinced that smoking leads to lung cancer, and the consciousness of nearly everyone has now been raised. Today you can't smoke on a domestic airplane flight in the United States, or in many airports, restaurants, and other public places. Bans on smoking are also being legislated in other countries.

Similarly, in the case of CFCs, the evidence became more and more persuasive. Following the lead of Molina and Rowland, other scientists developed more theories, conducted more laboratory experiments, and became more and more convinced that CFCs might in fact be reducing the amount of ozone in the stratosphere. Still, during the 1970s, fragmentary evidence and conflicting viewpoints abounded in the scientific community, and even more so in the popular press. Furthermore, there was no incontrovertible evidence to show conclusively that CFCs actually do deplete stratospheric ozone. That evidence came to light in the 1980s, from a most unlikely place.

Dramatic proof that ozone depletion actually occurred was found in Antarctica. The discoverers were a group headed by a British scientist named Joseph Farman, who had traveled to Antarctica, in the southern winter, to a terribly desolate place called Halley Bay, to measure ozone. Again, this was pure research, performed not so much to prove or disprove Molina and Rowland, or anyone else, but because Farman and his colleagues, like many other scientists, were using Antarctica as a great outdoor laboratory to observe a number of processes that can go on in the environment. In fact, Farman and his group, members of the British Antarctic Survey, had been measuring ozone from Halley Bay for nearly 25 years. Their basic instrument was the spectrophotometer invented in 1926 by Gordon Dobson, a design that had survived essentially unaltered for more than half a century. In truth, the longevity of the instrument symbolized much about the field of ozone measurement: it was a rather dull scientific backwater, populated by a handful of devotees like Farman. All that was about to change.

In 1981, Farman noticed something most unusual during the spring, which starts in late September in the Southern Hemisphere. At the beginning of spring, the ozone amounts over Halley Bay in Antarctica decreased sharply and then seemed to recover, some months later. Ozone was first disappearing and then reappearing. The following year, the same thing happened. The decline was substantial—at first some 20% below the normal Antarctic springtime value of approximately 300 Dobson units, and much more severe in later years.

Farman was a cautious scientist, and he hesitated to publish his data. He wasn't sure of their significance, and he wanted to observe another year. He actually suspected that his trusty Dobson meter might have malfunctioned, and he installed a new one in 1982. The new one corroborated the low springtime ozone levels. Finally, in 1985, Farman and his colleagues published their results and conjectured that CFCs might be responsible for the loss of ozone.

Surprisingly, the depletion this time was not just a few percent, which might have been expected on the basis of Rowland and Molina's theory. It was almost 50%. Half of the ozone in the southern stratosphere over

Antarctica simply disappeared in the spring and then reappeared again. If this remarkable phenomenon was actually due to human intervention, then, for the first time in history, people had substantially changed the chemical composition of Earth's atmosphere.

Another actor enters the play at this point: NASA, the National Aeronautics and Space Administration. In late 1978, NASA had launched Nimbus 7, a satellite carrying instruments that measured many properties of the Earth, not only meteorological ones like cloud cover and reflectivity but also ozone. In particular, the Total Ozone Mapping Spectrometer, or TOMS, aboard Nimbus 7 represented a great advance in spaceborne ozone-measuring capability. TOMS measured ozone amounts over the entire globe while the satellite completed an orbit of the planet every hour and a half, passing over the North and South poles. The TOMS data from Nimbus 7 were radioed back to Earth and carefully archived on tapes.

NASA's record in ozone research is superb, and the TOMS data set is among NASA's greatest triumphs. The TOMS instrument on Nimbus 7 provided data from 1978 well into 1993, and these data are a primary source for research on the magnitude and severity of the ozone hole. Yet credit for the discovery of the ozone hole goes to Joseph Farman and his colleagues, using 1920s ground-based instrument technology. Why? Because of an easily understandable mistake in processing the TOMS measurements.

Before the NASA data were analyzed by scientists, they were processed by a computer program. You can't do satellite work without computers, because the data are so voluminous, made up of millions upon millions of numbers. Because the satellites are measuring all the time, and their radios are on all the time, the data come down to Earth continuously, and the numbers pile up. In fact, it's been said that trying to learn something from satellite data is like trying to drink from a fire hydrant.

So, before the data get analyzed by people, they get analyzed by computers. Part of the computer program is a "quality-control" check to make sure the data are good, that the instrument isn't malfunctioning and the data aren't being garbled in the radio transmissions. The quality control performed on the Nimbus 7 TOMS ozone data included comparing the readings with a range of numbers that was thought to be typical for ozone, such as might be measured under normal conditions.

NASA scientists had set maximum and minimum values of plausible ozone amounts. The numbers they chose were 650 and 180 Dobson units. Since nobody had dreamed that an ozone hole might exist, nobody told the computer that numbers lower than 180 might be real, rather than the result of defective instruments. In going from the outside of the ozone hole to the inside, Nimbus 7 measured values of ozone that were too low when compared to what the computer had been programmed to expect. As a result, the quality-control program invalidated perfectly valid data. Thus, the program designed to make sure the data were good actually delayed the discovery of the ozone hole.

After Farman's publication appeared in 1985, NASA went back to the data archive, where the raw data used as input to the quality-control program were still stored. It's just good scientific practice to archive raw data, however flawed they might seem, and NASA deserves credit for doing that in this instance. NASA reprocessed these data and found that the TOMS instrument aboard Nimbus 7 had indeed seen the ozone hole before Farman did, but NASA scientists, with misplaced faith in their computer program, had at first failed to realize what the satellite was trying to tell them. There's a lesson here.

Our understanding of the ozone hole today is that it's caused mainly by the catalytic effect of chlorine, which gets into the atmosphere in the form of CFCs. The CFCs are gradually mixed globally in the atmosphere and may take decades to reach the stratosphere. Once there, they're decomposed by ultraviolet sunlight, releasing the chlorine that eventually begins attacking the ozone. Initially, however, the released chlorine forms relatively stable compounds with hydrogen and nitrogen.

A key element in the process by which chlorine attacks ozone is a bizarre kind of cloud called the polar stratospheric cloud (PSC). Although the lower stratosphere is quite dry, with water vapor present in only a few parts per million, it can get so cold above Antarctica (78 degrees below zero Celsius or 108 degrees below zero Fahrenheit) that PSCs can form from nitrogen compounds and water. The tiny ice crystals in these PSCs provide the sites on which chlorine is liberated from its less reactive forms. The resulting molecular chlorine (Cl_2) is itself quickly decomposed by ultraviolet sunlight, freeing up atomic chlorine (Cl), which is the catalytic culprit in destroying ozone.

Thus, the surfaces of the little crystals in these very special clouds in the cold, dark Antarctic stratosphere are the sites on which chlorine from CFCs finally becomes reactive atomic chlorine. Although there are several ozone-destroying processes, this seems to be the main one.

But why Antarctica? After an armada of people descended on the South Pole in response to Farman's discovery—flying planes, running computer models, observing the continent from satellites, doing laboratory experiments—much was learned, and we think we've learned what's unique about the place. The first clue is that it gets cold enough there, probably colder than anywhere else on Earth, for these special clouds to form in the stratosphere. The second clue is a vortex of winds circling constantly around the South Pole every winter. This swirling mass of air keeps the Antarctic stratosphere isolated from neighboring air masses during the winter, which allows the destructive chemical reactions to act on a limited local stock of ozone that cannot be replenished by ozone from other latitudes.

As winter ends, the vortex breaks down, allowing relatively ozone-rich air from lower latitudes to reach the Antarctic. We don't know if this springtime recovery will always occur in the future. Each year observed so far has been different in some ways from other years. We don't know whether the depletion process will become more intense, because so many things are changing. But as the CFC concentrations continue to increase, the abundance of chlorine in the atmosphere will also increase. And if sufficient chlorine accumulates in the stratosphere, the winter depletions of Antarctic ozone could become so severe that ozone levels might not recover in spring.

Also, ozone affects temperature. Everything in the atmosphere, after all, is connected to everything else. The temperature in the stratosphere, in Antarctica and elsewhere, is largely determined by a radiative balance involving two gases: ozone and carbon dioxide. The essential notion of this balance is simple: warming occurs because ozone absorbs sunlight, and cooling occurs because carbon dioxide radiates heat away. Thus, the temperature of this region of the atmosphere will change if there's a change in the relative abundances of these two gases.

As carbon dioxide increases, which it's doing because we're putting more of it into the atmosphere, and as ozone decreases, which it's doing because we're helping to destroy it, the stratosphere theoretically should be cooling. There is some evidence—we can't be sure of it yet—that globally the lower stratosphere *is* cooling. If the stratosphere continues to cool, we may find that conditions in the Arctic come more and more to approximate those in the Antarctic. Conditions that favor the formation of polar stratospheric clouds, for example, may begin to occur in the Arctic.

But there's a fundamental difference between the North and South polar regions: the vortex. In Antarctica the polar vortex keeps stratospheric ozone isolated, but no such condition exists in the Arctic. And it's hard to imagine anything like the Antarctic vortex forming anywhere else. So, is this vortex essential to forming an ozone hole? We don't know with certainty, but we think it is. If clouds, however, rather than a vortex of winds, are the essential component of ozone loss, we may see an ozone hole in the Arctic after all. Some ozone loss over the North Pole, as well as over the entire Northern Hemisphere, *has* already been observed.

At the same time, Molina and Rowland's original idea that ozone destruction would be a gradual global process is not dead either. The global amount of ozone *has* apparently decreased. Thus, not only have we the dramatic phenomenon of the Antarctic ozone hole to ponder, but the ozone layer *everywhere* may be in danger of dying—by a slower, more insidious form of depletion.

Meanwhile, in the 1970s, a young scientist named Veerabhadran Ramanathan who had just finished his Ph.D. at the State University of New York at Stony Brook also became interested in chlorofluorocarbons. He's now at the University of California, San Diego, at Scripps Institution of Oceanography.

Ramanathan's interest in CFCs was focused not on their effect on ozone, but on their role in the greenhouse effect. This is the process by which water vapor, carbon dioxide, and other gases warm the atmosphere by absorbing some of the Earth's radiation that would otherwise escape to space. The greenhouse effect keeps the planet some 33 degrees Celsius, or 59 degrees Fahrenheit, warmer than it would otherwise be. Many people, including Ramanathan's Ph.D. thesis advisor, told him that this was not a good subject to be working on, that it was obvious that CFCs were unimportant to the greenhouse effect. Fortunately, he ignored them and persisted in working on the theory. As it turned out, he was right. Science is often like that, and creative scientists who follow their own hunches often discover important things. Joseph Farman, before he became famous for discovering the ozone hole, was sometimes chided for his dedication in returning each year to Halley Bay to carry on the boring task of measuring stratospheric ozone.

Ramanathan's research provides a connection between two of the topics that concern us: ozone depletion and an increase in the greenhouse effect. CFCs, the same gases implicated in the destruction of the ozone layer, also add to the greenhouse effect. According to Ramanathan's theoretical calculations, CFCs trap heat in the same way that gases such as water vapor, carbon dioxide, and methane do. Although we can't prove it, many scientists think the Earth today is a little bit warmer than it would have been if CFCs had never been invented and allowed to accumulate in the atmosphere. In general, the level of scientific uncertainty is greater in the case of climate change due to an enhanced greenhouse effect than it is in the case of ozone depletion. The science of the greenhouse effect and climate is inherently more complex, and as yet there's no climatic analog to the ozone hole, a dramatic and undeniable piece of evidence that the planet has changed because of human activity. But from a theoretical standpoint, Ramanathan's work is unassailable: CFCs are greenhouse gases.

Thus, even if we weren't worried about CFCs because of their role in destroying ozone, even if ozone in the stratosphere didn't matter to us and skin cancer weren't a problem, we'd still have to be concerned about CFCs today because they increase the greenhouse effect. In fact, molecule for molecule, they're much more powerful in this respect than carbon dioxide and some of the other gases that we'll learn about when we discuss the greenhouse effect in detail. Thus, banning CFCs for the purpose of preserving the ozone layer has the nice side effect of slowing the rate at which we're increasing the greenhouse effect.

The melancholy story of ozone depletion will have, I hope, a happy ending. We don't know that ending yet, but most of the recent developments are promising.

As the evidence piled up, it became harder and harder to deny that chlorofluorocarbons were responsible for ozone loss. Fortunately, there was the appealing prospect of a technological fix: it seemed possible to manufacture other chemicals that would be good refrigerants, solvents, and propellants without contributing to this undesirable effect on ozone. Thus, in a remarkable and dramatic diplomatic effort, an international agreement was reached to phase out the manufacture of CFCs, because they had been shown to be the "smoking gun" in the story of the Antarctic ozone hole.

An international conference was held in Montreal, Canada, in September 1987. The resulting agreement, the Montreal Protocol, ratified by 57 countries, put in place a global framework for phasing out the production of CFCs and halons on an agreed-upon schedule. It had become clear that although CFCs were the main culprit, other compounds also contributed to the destruction of ozone. Halons, used in fire extinguishers, for instance, introduce bromine into the stratosphere, and bromine has an even greater potential for the destruction of ozone than does chlorine. In fact, molecule for molecule, halons are ten times more powerful ozone destroyers than CFCs. Fortunately, there are fewer of them around.

In the years following the 1987 meeting, new scientific evidence came to light suggesting that ozone depletion might be worse than had been anticipated, and in June 1990, 120 countries met in London to strengthen the agreement for phasing out CFCs and related chemicals. The negotiators at Montreal had foreseen exactly this possibility, and a provision for subsequently subjecting the terms of the treaty to modification had been included in the Protocol. One new development was confirmation that the ozone loss over Antarctica was indeed due to CFCs. A second persuasive factor was the detection of ozone loss over heavily populated parts of the Northern Hemisphere.

One of the results of the London meeting was to accelerate the timetable for the phaseout. The Montreal Protocol, for example, called for a 50% reduction of CFC production by 1998. In London this timetable was accelerated: these chemicals were to be totally phased out by the year 2000, in some cases earlier.

The negotiators at the London meeting were environmental ministers, from agencies such as the Environmental Protection Agency (EPA) in the United States. The meeting of these ministers had been preceded by meetings of technical experts who were to advise the ministers on the feasibility of various timetables and on the costs that would attend the phaseouts. When the technical experts arrived, the draft documents were full of square brackets surrounding phrases that were contentious, or numbers that had to be decided upon—reductions of 50%, or 75%, or 100%, by 1995, or 2000, or 2010. There were, in fact, 190 sets of square brackets in the draft document.

One person at the conference was a 17-year-old Australian. Her name was Susannah ("Zanny") Begg, a member of the Australian Conservation Foundation Youth Delegation, a young woman with a flair for words. In her address to the conference she said to these ministers and technical experts, "Our fate lies in your square brackets." (We'll hear more from Ms. Begg shortly.)

Among the countries attending the London conference were some that hadn't ratified the Montreal Protocol. It became clear that, among other disputes, there was an issue of equity between developed countries and developing countries. China and India, for example, with large populations but relatively low degrees of economic development and standards of living, were reluctant to embrace a treaty that foreclosed many of their options for development. In effect, they said to the developed countries of the West, "You have already benefited from air conditioning and refrigeration that's free of corrosive and toxic chemicals, and from a semiconductor industry that uses CFCs as solvents. We haven't yet realized those benefits. Why does the industrialized West now dictate to the Third World that it must behave in a more environmentally responsible way than you yourselves have done? You caused the damage in the first place." These issues were negotiated, and a number of imaginative solutions were reached.

One of the major achievements of this 1990 meeting in London was to set up an international fund into which the developed countries would contribute. The United Nations has a set of rules for determining the proportion of total contributions for each country, dictating that large, rich countries pay more than small, poor countries. The United States and the United Kingdom were the major contributors. In addition to moneys pledged in Montreal in 1987, representatives at the London meeting reached agreement that there would be a three-year budget of $360 million over the period between 1991 and 1993. This figure would be increased by $40 million when China ratified the Montreal treaty, and by another $40 million when India joined the ozone-protection club. The London agreements were signed by 93 countries. India and China, which had not signed the Montreal Protocol, ultimately did sign the London agreement.

The purpose of the fund is to provide technical assistance to countries that need it to develop CFC substitutes and to implement them. For example, you can't just instantaneously trade in all your old refrigerators or air conditioners and get new ones. It's not a simple matter of taking one substance out and putting another substance in. Changes have to be made, and changes cost money. Developing a new technology is expensive, as is making it widely available. So, although the amounts of money may not seem very large, the pledges were a step in the right direction. Countries recognized the disparity between the effects that an agreement like this would have on the developed world and those it would have on the less-developed world.

There seems to be general agreement that more than one step is needed. First, we must phase out the harmful chemicals, the chlorofluorocarbons and related compounds. We must also design alternative chemicals and be as sure as we can that these new alternatives don't themselves have deleterious side effects. We need to make sure that present-day Thomas Midgleys aren't making breakthroughs that our grandchildren will discover are harmful. And we have to do a good job of monitoring changes in the ozone layer.

Despite the Montreal agreements, there are more CFCs in the atmosphere now than ever before, because they've been accumulating for so long and because they're still being produced. CFCs take many decades to decay naturally. So, although the rate of production has gone down following the Montreal and London agreements, the total amount in the atmosphere is still very large, and still growing.

The Montreal Protocol and its subsequent update in London are very hopeful steps. Certainly they bear watching and will have, we hope, analogs in other environmental problem areas where solutions aren't so clear-cut.

I mentioned that 17-year-old Zanny Begg has a flair for words. Here's some more of her address to the London conference:

We are speaking on behalf of the young people of Australia. We are here because we have a right to be involved in these decisions.

Over the past week of negotiations, we have been watching you. It has been at times fascinating, at times confusing, at times horrifying. We have had to keep reminding each other that what is actually being debated here is the future of the ozone layer. This debate has been largely guided by short-sighted commercial gains and national self-interest. There has been more concern for semantics than substance. . . .

The scientific imperatives are clear. Only an immediate end to the use of ozone-depleting chemicals will truly reflect the urgency of the situation. Even if we do this, it will be a further 60 years before the Antarctic ozone hole is repaired. We came to the conference with this knowledge, but it seems you did not. Your diplomatic compromises are compromising our future.

We have a right to demand a safe future for ourselves and all generations to come. . . . What is required is a fundamental change of attitudes, values, and lifestyles, particularly in the developed nations. We insist that over the next three days, you make decisions which reflect intergenerational equity and an active concern for the environment. Remember that we will inherit the consequences of your decisions. We cannot amend the Montreal Protocol. **You** can! You will not bear the brunt of ozone depletion. **We** will!

We demand that you think in the long term. Even the best proposals on the table now sanction an unacceptable increase in the chlorine loading of the stratosphere. Your rhetoric is not being matched by your action. Will you condemn us to a future fraught with skin cancer, eye cataracts, immune deficiency, depleted food sources, and a vanishing biodiversity?

At the moment we are afraid. Do not leave our generation without hope. Our fate lies in your square brackets. You are making history. Have the courage to save the ozone layer.

These are eloquent words, but not everybody agrees with them. There are those who have long felt that anything short of an immediate ban on ozone-depleting chemicals is an inadequate measure. There are others who think gradually weaning the world from CFCs and related chemicals is both preferable and adequate. These people believe that the consequences of reduced ozone are bearable and less burdensome than the economic costs of instantaneously eliminating these chemicals. Firing the debate is the fact that these issues are not black and white. You can't ask people to make radical changes in areas that have enormous economic and social implications without a great deal of debate and a broad spectrum of opinions. I've offered a couple of samples of opinion here, and you may certainly have your own.

The trend among governments recently has been to accelerate the timetable for banning the chemicals that destroy ozone. In November 1992, another conference was held in Copenhagen, attended this time by representatives of 87 countries. They agreed to move up the deadline for a total phaseout of these chemicals from the year 2000, which had been agreed to in London, to 1996. In the United States, the government established December 31, 1995, as the deadline for ending the production of virtually all chemicals that are known to destroy ozone.

You might ask whether there are other chemicals that we could make and intentionally release into the atmosphere to counteract the process that leads to the destruction of ozone. Not much research with that particular aim is going forward, but scientists would be sensitive to potential applications of this type if they turned up as by-products of other research. In any case, many scientists are skeptical of planetary engineering, of trying purposefully to alter the environment on a large scale, because of the risk of damage posed by unforeseen effects. We'll come across this problem again when we talk about the greenhouse effect.

There are many proposals for planetary engineering being thrown about, but I'm leery of notions like that. I liken them to taking a pill you've prescribed for yourself, one whose properties you don't fully understand, to cure a disease that hasn't been properly diagnosed or evaluated. I'm worried about piling error on top of error. We didn't know what chlorofluorocarbons would do for 46 years after Midgley invented them in 1928. It was in 1974 that Molina and Rowland pointed out, in the paper they published that year, that in the stratosphere, chlorine dissociated from CFCs might be trouble. Two decades later, we continue to learn more about how CFCs behave, and we continue to learn more about how the ozone hole is created. So I think it's dangerous to hunt for an easy out in the form of a "technological fix." It's a little bit, it seems to me, like saying, "Well, I eat too much fat, and I drink too much alcohol, so I think I'll try to find a pill that somehow keeps my arteries from clogging up and prevents my liver from being damaged, instead of modifying the way I live."

Incidentally, trying to pump gigatons of chemicals into the upper atmosphere intentionally would not be easy anyway. In fact, for me, one of the most comforting things about proposals for large-scale planetary engineering is that they're usually not feasible.

The Earth always changes, often for reasons we don't know. Ice ages just come and go, as a dramatic example. Their comings and goings aren't caused by people. In the same way, the amount of ozone in the atmosphere might change slowly over many years, due to natural changes in the processes that create and destroy the ozone.

It's true that ozone is created by photodissociation of ordinary oxygen by ultraviolet sunlight. It's also true that in the natural atmosphere, ozone is destroyed by the processes that we described, and by a few other processes as well. And it's true that on balance—at least in recent years—there are at any given time about 3 billion tons of ozone in the atmosphere. In a given year, about a third of it cycles through the processes of creation and destruction; that is, about 1 billion tons are created and 1 billion tons are destroyed, yielding an approximate equilibrium. But over very long periods of time that could change, owing to natural changes in the system, as well as to human activities such as the releasing of CFCs. For example, volcanoes can produce gases that could alter the chemical composition of the atmosphere, and this would happen naturally. But natural changes take place over a much greater time span than do the changes we've made to the ozone layer. Our changes, occurring in only a few years, were caused by adding certain chemicals to the atmosphere and thus producing the catalysts for the destruction reaction.

It's ironic, by the way, that some airplanes may actually have *added* to the ozone layer. There you have an example of inadvertent planetary engineering. An airplane, if you think about it, is a big engine burning fossil fuels (jet fuel is very like kerosene) and producing exhaust that goes out the tailpipe and makes smog. There's smog in the high troposphere and lower stratosphere where airplanes fly. You can see it when you fly. Just as the tailpipes of cars help to produce ozone in Los Angeles, so the tailpipes of airplanes help to produce ozone in the high troposphere and the low stratosphere, about 10 miles up. It may very well be that the net result of our inadvertent tampering with the atmosphere through the operation of aircraft is to increase slightly the amount of ozone. Of course, that's been more than outweighed by the inadvertent *decrease* produced by CFCs.

During the 1991 Northern Hemisphere fall, in October and November, which corresponds to the Southern Hemisphere spring, there was a relatively severe Antarctic ozone-loss episode. A year later, the ozone loss over Antarctica was greater still, and evidence of loss in the Arctic and in lower latitudes has also been found. So, we continue to learn as we go along. One characteristic of global-change problems is that they often seem to demand action before all the scientific results are in.

As the Montreal Protocol and subsequent international accords have demonstrated, the world has decided to act. The world has agreed to remove chlorofluorocarbons from industrial production and to find substitutes for them.

Because they last so long in the atmosphere, typically about a century, the CFCs in the atmosphere are still increasing. Indeed, even after production has been phased out altogether, we will have to wait many decades for most of the CFCs to disappear. They're out there in the atmosphere right now. The molecules we put out there in 1970 are mostly still there, and the ones put out there in 1950 are mostly still there, and even some of Thomas Midgley's original molecules from before 1930 are still there. They continue to accumulate. Thus, we now appear to be inexorably committed to substantial increases in ultraviolet radiation for decades to come, with ensuing health and ecological effects. The consequences of producing CFCs for over half a century cannot be evaded by agreeing not to produce any more. The atmosphere remembers our past behavior. There are limits to the compassion of the forgiving air.

3

THE GREENHOUSE EFFECT

We come now to a subject with even larger implications. In many countries today, governments are beginning to take actions that may well have far-reaching economic and social consequences for all of us, actions based on a chain of scientific reasoning and scientific evidence that may seem slender, uncertain, and to some people even arcane. This subject is the greenhouse effect.

The greenhouse effect seems to me to be the paradigm problem that defines what we mean by global-change research. It's a much more difficult problem than the ozone hole, and, like the ozone hole, it's been widely publicized. By now many people have at least a basic notion of what the greenhouse effect is all about. There are gases in the atmosphere—including water vapor, carbon dioxide, methane, nitrous oxide, ozone, and chlorofluorocarbons—that act a little like the glass of a greenhouse. They're partially transparent to sunlight. As sunlight comes through, some ultraviolet radiation gets absorbed by the ozone, and some sunlight gets absorbed by other constituents of the atmosphere, but the sunlight reaches the Earth's surface largely unimpeded by these gases in the atmosphere. This sunlight, or solar radiation, is largely absorbed at the surface of the Earth and re-emitted as infrared radiation, or heat. But these same gases are *not* transparent to the infrared radiation, or heat, that the Earth emits. They absorb some of it, and part of what they absorb is radiated back toward the surface of the Earth. The overall effect of these gases is to trap some of the heat, and thus, like a blanket, they make the Earth warmer than it would otherwise be.

Except for water vapor, these are trace gases, meaning that they are present in very small concentrations, typically just a few parts per million. Recall that the major gases in the atmosphere, nitrogen and oxygen, combine to make up 99% of the molecules in dry air. But nitrogen and oxygen contribute nothing to the greenhouse effect. It is water vapor and the trace gases that are responsible for the natural greenhouse effect. We shall refer to them as the "greenhouse gases." When the Earth radiates heat in the form of infrared radiation out toward space, heat that you can feel coming off a hot street or a hot desert, it's these greenhouse gases that trap some of it. Clouds, too, are big contributors to the greenhouse effect. There are everyday examples of the greenhouse effect due to clouds. When you're outdoors at night, clouds keep you warmer than you would be on a clear night, because they trap some of the heat. Clear nights are colder.

The greenhouse effect isn't mysterious. It has been keeping the planet habitable for billions of years. Without the greenhouse effect, the surface temperature of the Earth would be well below freezing.

Concern about the greenhouse effect does not involve whether or not it's *there*. It's as real as gravity, and we should be grateful for it. The worry is that we're *adding* to the greenhouse effect in a variety of ways by adding more of these trace gases to the atmosphere. When we refer to the greenhouse effect as a problem, we're being rather careless with our terminology. What we really mean is the problem of the *enhancement* of the greenhouse effect, the unnatural change we're forcing on the planet by changing the chemical composition of the atmosphere.

One of the things to think about as we examine this issue is the difference between the enhancement of the greenhouse effect, on the one hand, and the ozone hole, on the other. These two global problems, both serious, are very different in many ways.

We're adding carbon dioxide (CO_2), the main culprit in the greenhouse problem, by burning coal, oil, and natural gas. It comes out of our chimneys, and it comes out of our tailpipes.

We're adding methane in a variety of ways, too, some of which aren't particularly pleasing to contemplate. It comes out of both ends of cows, for example. It also comes from rice paddies, leaks in natural-gas pipelines, and swamps. Like carbon dioxide, methane is also one of the products of combustion, released into the atmosphere whenever wood or fossil fuels are burned.

In the main, the greenhouse gases we produce are by-products of the modern industrial world. One of the main reasons why the enhanced greenhouse effect is so much more difficult to grapple with than the ozone hole is that these gases are not like CFCs, which are manmade, have very specific applications, and for which we can invent ingenious substitutes. It's difficult to find a substitute for CO_2. To put it another way, there's no efficient engine that doesn't produce CO_2 when it burns gasoline. CO_2 is an inevitable by-product of combustion. It's in many ways an innocuous gas. It's what's in the bubbles in soft drinks, beer, and champagne. It's colorless, odorless, and tasteless. But it contributes to the greenhouse effect.

It's difficult to imagine today's governments signing an international treaty, one like the Montreal Protocol, calling for the elimination of most CO_2 emissions by phasing out fossil fuels. This would be a lot tougher problem to face than the problem of how to phase out CFCs. The problem is not that alternative sources of energy would necessarily require major lifestyle changes. Indeed, for many, perhaps most, of the Earth's people, little or no change would be necessary. Even for the people of the developed world, accustomed to energy-intensive living, alternative energy sources are at least conceivable. Airplanes and automobiles can run on alternative fuels. The major obstacles to such a massive change in the way humankind generates energy are not so much technical as they are economic and political. When we discuss how best to arrive at a sustainable future, we should distinguish carefully between what we do not know how to do and what we cannot bring ourselves to do.

Another difference between the story of the ozone hole and the story of the greenhouse effect is that in the example of the ozone hole we have a rather dramatic confirmation, so striking and so convincing that there's no longer any serious argument about whether CFCs cause ozone depletion. For a while there was skepticism that CFCs were the culprit, just as there used to be skepticism that cigarette smoking causes lung cancer. But the scientific case is now much more than a statistical connection. There's now a very persuasive chain of physical reasoning that links CFCs to ozone loss, and there are extensive corroborating observations that have convinced not only scientists but also the governments of the world, that CFCs really do deplete ozone.

With the greenhouse effect, we don't yet have that "smoking gun." We don't have a Joseph Farman, who has seen the environment change dramatically, and has measured the change. Although we've been putting increasing amounts of carbon dioxide into the atmosphere for over a century, we still don't have clear evidence of global climate change that we can point to and say, "This is something our production of CO_2 is responsible for." It's hard to get people excited, and it's hard to get governments to react, when you can't lay out that kind of convincing evidence.

Though we can't prove to everyone's satisfaction that the greenhouse effect will get stronger soon enough and fast enough to matter, *we think it will*. In fact, scientific consensus is that the greenhouse effect, during our lifetime—perhaps during this decade, perhaps during the next—will increase enough that *everyone* will notice the results. Then we won't have just a long list of questions like, "OK, it was warm this year and there were some warm years in the '80s, but is that a global effect? Couldn't these have been natural fluctuations? Wasn't this just Mother Nature tossing a coin?" Instead, there will be an unambiguous, incontrovertible, impossible-to-deny climate change. We'll see warmer temperatures; icecaps will begin to melt and sea level will rise; and we may see changes, too, in specific climatic phenomena, such as a greater frequency of drought. That's the consensus.

Unfortunately, it's the nature of the problem, as we understand it, that the longer we wait to react, the greater the problem we must cope with. Scientists use the word *committed* in this context to refer to future change that will occur because of past human actions. The scientific consensus is that we're *already* committed to a certain amount of climate change, because of the CO_2 we've already put in the atmosphere, even if today we suddenly stopped adding it, which we can't. Furthermore, people have not yet agreed on a practical and relatively simple technological fix analogous to the development of substitutes for chlorofluorocarbons. Instead, there are competing paths to attaining energy sufficiency while reducing dependence on fossil fuels. So we don't yet have a consensus on how best to go about reducing CO_2 emissions, even if we had a very strong consensus that it was worth doing. And that applies to many of the other greenhouse gases too.

Although there is a scientific consensus on the issue of climate change owing to an enhanced greenhouse effect, it's by no means a unanimous consensus. Some scientists dissent from it emphatically, and the scientists who generally subscribe to it typically disagree with one another on specific points, such as how fast climate will change. Even if everybody were to agree on all these issues, everybody might later be found wrong. What we shall try to do here is to examine the basis for this consensus, to understand which parts of the scientific evidence seem relatively firm, and which are more speculative and conjectural. We'll have the exciting experience of tracking a branch of scientific research while it proceeds, not one like plane geometry that is dead and fossilized and codified in textbooks.

With both the greenhouse effect and the ozone hole, we're talking about scientific predictions that appear to be generally consistent with actual observations, although in both instances the observations have been different from what the scientists who originally developed the theories envisioned.

In the case of ozone depletion, Rowland and Molina theorized in the early 1970s, purely from doing interesting basic science, that there might be a slow, gradual depletion in stratospheric ozone due to a growing accumulation of chlorofluorocarbons. They did not predict the catastrophic 50% loss of ozone in the Antarctic spring. They didn't predict either the existence or the magnitude of the hole, and they didn't anticipate that ozone loss would be most severe over Antarctica. The basic idea that CFCs could cause ozone loss turned out to be true, but the way in which the phenomenon first came to be observed was a surprise to the theorists.

In the same way, enhancement of the greenhouse effect started out, from the scientist's point of view, as an interesting abstract problem, an experiment. Roger Revelle and Hans Suess, two scientists at Scripps Institution of Oceanography of the University of California, San Diego, remarked in the 1950s that humankind was doing a onetime geophysical experiment by putting carbon (in the form of carbon dioxide) back into the atmosphere from its storehouse in fossil deposits like coal and oil. They didn't think of the process as anything catastrophic or calamitous, or even necessarily bad for humankind. It was just an interesting idea. In a way, it was rather nice that the Earth would conduct an experiment, so to speak, and let scientists observe it.

The person who originally contemplated the enhanced greenhouse effect, purely theoretically, was Svante Arrhenius. An eminent chemist who won a Nobel Prize in chemistry, he published in 1896 what is arguably the first theoretical paper on the enhanced greenhouse effect. Arrhenius was from Sweden, a cold place, and he looked at the idea of the planet warming up as something that, on the whole, might be a good thing. Arrhenius's final words on the greenhouse effect, from his 1906 book *Worlds in the Making,* are not at all gloomy: "By the influence of the increasing percentage of carbonic acid [carbon dioxide] in the atmosphere, we may hope to enjoy ages with more equable and better climates, especially as regards the colder regions of the Earth, ages when the Earth will bring forth much more abundant crops than at present, for the benefit of rapidly propagating humankind." Thus, the notion that the greenhouse effect—or, more accurately, its enhancement due to human causes—might have deleterious consequences for people is a realization that has dawned on us only slowly. A train of thought has evolved—in scientific circles, in the public mind, in the policy world—concerning what those consequences might be. That evolution continues.

The greenhouse effect is a complicated problem. It involves pure science, and, like the ozone problem, it also involves public perception and interaction between the scientific world and the world of policy-makers. But it's inherently a more difficult problem and one that's harder to comprehend than the issue of the ozone hole.

And it's a global problem. Everybody contributes to the greenhouse effect. Chlorofluorocarbons get produced mainly in industrialized countries, but carbon dioxide gets produced everywhere. Even China, which has a low per-capita consumption of resources compared to the United States, has so many people—four or five times the population of the United States—that it may well surpass the United States as the leading producer of carbon dioxide by about the year 2020. So Americans could all go back to eating nuts and twigs and living in caves and not producing any industrial gases at all, and we'd still have a problem. That's not to say that the United States need take no action. On the contrary, the United States can do more than any other single country to lead the world toward a sustainable future. American initiative is essential, but global problems require global solutions, and all countries will have to play a part.

Like so many other global problems, this one is inextricably linked to population. Thus, the question of sustainability of the Earth's environment is linked to how many people there are and how they behave. That's a theme that links all the global-change issues. We'll examine population and its relation to the sustainability of the planet in greater depth later. For now, let's delve into the science of the greenhouse effect.

Most sunlight passes through the atmosphere unimpeded. The Earth is warmed mainly by the sunlight that's absorbed at the surface, by both the land and the sea. Some sunlight, about 30%, is reflected back to space, mainly by clouds, and thus doesn't interact with the climate system at all. This fraction of reflected radiation is called the albedo of the Earth.

The Earth radiates heat in the form of infrared energy. It doesn't radiate visible light as the sun does. We'll analyze why in detail later, but the short answer is that the sun is much hotter than the Earth. Instead, the energy that goes out from the Earth is in the form of heat. It's this infrared energy that's partially trapped by the greenhouse gases in the atmosphere.

Real greenhouses, by the way, don't work entirely by the greenhouse effect. One of the ways the greenhouse in the nursery keeps plants warm is simply by keeping wind out. When wind blows across plants, it carries heat away. The glass in the greenhouse, aside from whatever it does to the radiation, helps keep plants warm just by preventing air circulation around the little leaves and shoots.

There are many convincing demonstrations of the greenhouse effect in the atmosphere. A clear example of the impact it can have on climate is seen when comparing the Earth and the Moon. Both are about the same distance from the Sun, both get their energy from the Sun, and in fact the Moon's albedo or reflectivity is lower than the Earth's, so you might expect that the climate of the Moon would be warmer than that of the Earth. Instead, the Moon is much colder than the Earth. The average temperature difference between them is about 35° Celsius, or 63° Fahrenheit. This difference is due almost entirely to the presence or absence of a greenhouse effect. You wouldn't want to live on the Moon, quite apart from the fact that there's no cable television. The Moon has a brutal day/night temperature difference, with scorching hot days and bitter cold nights, because there's no atmosphere to mediate the temperature change and make sunrise and sunset less jolting.

The Earth has an atmosphere that traps heat, but the Moon has no atmosphere; it's so small, its gravity so weak, that any atmosphere it once had long ago escaped to space. What surrounds it, right down to its surface, *is* space. The early Moon may have had an atmosphere, but small planets and small satellites of planets—small moons—no longer have atmospheres, because they're not gravitationally strong enough to hold them. For the same reason the astronauts frolicking on the Moon could make gigantic leaps almost effortlessly. Earth has sufficient gravity to have retained an atmosphere, and the giant planets like Jupiter and Saturn, with their massive gravitational fields, have very heavy, very dense atmospheres.

The greenhouse effect can also be seen on other planets. Compare the climates of Mars and Venus. Both have mostly carbon dioxide in their atmospheres, but Venus has a very dense atmosphere, about 100 times denser than Earth's. The Martian atmosphere is about one hundredth as dense as Earth's. So the greenhouse effect is very small on Mars and very powerful on Venus. Venus is very hot; Mars is very cold. You need radar and a satellite to look at Venus, for two reasons. One is that it's completely covered by clouds, so you can't "see" the surface unless you use the special capability of radar to penetrate the cloud cover. The other is that you wouldn't want to put an instrument on the surface of Venus. It's been done, but the instrument doesn't last very long, because the surface of Venus is hot enough to melt metal.

The graph on the facing page is in some ways the most famous in all of Earth science. It is the Keeling curve, the result of the persistence, vision, and skill of Charles David Keeling, who has spent his entire career at Scripps Institution of Oceanography at the University of California, San Diego.

This wiggly curve (scientists call every graphed line a curve, no matter what its shape—nobody knows why) shows the results of measuring atmospheric carbon-dioxide concentrations since 1958. This curve is now the result of measurements made by many people. But originally, and for many years, the work was carried on entirely by Keeling himself. He realized it needed to be done. He created the technology. There was no instrument to measure CO_2 accurately until he invented one. There are nearly six billion people on this Earth, and one of them has measured CO_2 and shown the rest of us that it can be done, that CO_2 is rising, and that it's rising due to human causes. Keeling has received many awards for his research, and his fellow scientists regard him and his work with great respect. His attention to detail and his passion for accuracy are legendary. His measurements of atmospheric CO_2 are unanimously acknowledged to be rock-solid. Scientists like to argue, and they do argue about many aspects of the greenhouse effect and climate change, but nobody argues about Keeling's data. (Incidentally, there are two prominent Keelings in atmospheric chemistry. Charles David Keeling's son Ralph is also a faculty member at Scripps, but he has not been measuring carbon dioxide. Among other things, he has been measuring the concentration of oxygen in the atmosphere.)

The annual average concentration of CO_2 in 1995 is almost 360 parts per million, which reflects a rise of more than 10% since Keeling first

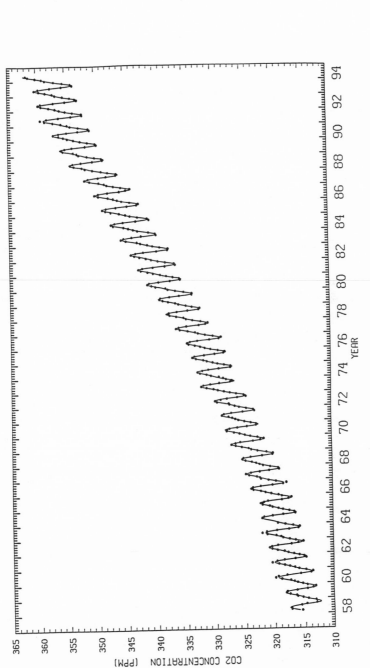

Keeling curve, showing rise of atmospheric carbon dioxide concentration, in parts per million by volume (ppmv), since 1958. (Source: C. D. Keeling, Scripps Institution of Oceanography, UCSD)

measured it at 315 in 1958. From analysis of ice cores, we know that the concentration was about 280 parts per million in the late 1800s. So, it has gone up about 25% since preindustrial times, and we know it was lower still during the ice ages. Thus, we have a very convincing record. CO_2 is now rising at a little less than 0.5% per year.

In Keeling's data, incidentally, you can see the temporary slowing in the rate of rise of CO_2 due to the 1973 oil crisis, as well as the effects of natural changes. The recurring wiggles in Keeling's CO_2 curve are evidence of the natural annual cycle of carbon in the biosphere, the world of living things. Plants, mainly the trees on land, grow during spring in the Northern Hemisphere—since there is far more land in the northern half of the globe than in the south, most of the trees are found there. During the spring they take in carbon in the form of CO_2 from the atmosphere, producing the low points on Keeling's curve. In the fall, when these plants shed their leaves, they give off carbon and the curve goes back up again. The rhythmic, seasonal rising and falling of the curve that results is the signature of the biosphere breathing, the trees taking in and subsequently giving out carbon in a yearly cycle. It's a clear example of how living things influence the global environment.

The feature of the Keeling curve that's significant to the greenhouse effect, however, is its steady upward climb, due primarily to the release of CO_2 every time we burn coal, oil, gasoline, or natural gas. Today, fossil-fuel combustion is the main source of CO_2. Deforestation—the ravaging and incineration of rainforests and other wooded areas—is the secondary source. Not long ago, when we didn't burn so much fossil fuel and when there were more forests, deforestation was the primary source.

The fuel that we're burning today was formed in the distant geological past from the carbon-rich remains of plants and animals (hence the term "fossil fuel"). It's in this sense that Revelle and Suess spoke of our doing a onetime geophysical experiment. We can do it only once, for once we've taken the fuel that's stored up as coal, oil, and natural gas and burned it, thus putting the carbon back into circulation, we can't do it again. It will be used up. It took millions of years to form, and we can use up essentially all of it in a few centuries, which is but the twinkling of an eye on the geological time scale. Thus, fossil fuels are truly nonrenewable resources.

A central, evolving issue in global change is people: how many there are, where they live, and how they use energy. The places with big potential differences between current and future use are not North America or Western Europe or Japan, but rather the Third World and the former communist world, or Second World. The developing countries are the countries that are expected to increase their energy consumption the most.

The annual global production of CO_2 is something we know, approximately. We don't have accurate estimates of the amount of CO_2 added from deforestation and other land-use changes, but we do know how much coal, oil, and gas is extracted from the ground. From fossil fuels, we're currently putting 5 to 6 billion tons of carbon in the form of CO_2 into the atmosphere every year—about 1 ton for every person on Earth. Only about half of the carbon produced by the burning of fossil fuels appears in the form of an increase in the measured atmospheric concentration of carbon dioxide. The other half apparently is absorbed by the ocean and by the terrestrial biosphere, that is, the world of living things on land, such as trees. Carbon is transferred continuously between the atmosphere, the oceans, and the land, and many aspects of this "carbon cycle" are imperfectly understood.

Let's look again at the composition of the atmosphere. It's important to keep these facts in perspective. Dry air is a mechanical (not chemical) mixture of gases, of which the most abundant by far is nitrogen (78%). The second most abundant is oxygen (21%). Thus, together they make up about 99% of the dry atmosphere. Argon (chemical symbol Ar), an inert gas, accounts for most of the remaining 1%. The greenhouse gases *altogether* are thus very rare relative to those three gases.

Real air contains not just dry air, of course, but also water vapor, which is present in all natural air in highly variable concentrations. There's hardly any of it over the desert, for example, and there's a great deal of it in tropical rainforests. It's also much more abundant near the Equator than near the poles. In the tropics, water vapor may be as much as 4% of the atmosphere, by volume. Near the poles, it may be much less than 1%. In any one place, the abundance of water vapor in the air also varies a great deal from day to day. Its abundance, as measured by relative humidity, is reported as a standard meteorological observation. (Relative humidity is a measure of how saturated the air is, expressed as a percentage. It's the ratio of the amount of water vapor in the air at some spot compared to the maximum amount that the air *could* "hold" at the particular temperature and pressure at that spot.)

Water vapor is a powerful greenhouse gas, whereas nitrogen, oxygen, and argon don't contribute at all to the greenhouse effect. The reason for this difference lies in the fundamental physics of how gas molecules interact with radiation. To absorb infrared radiation significantly under the pressure and temperature conditions of the Earth's atmosphere, a gas molecule has to have at least three atoms. Both nitrogen (N_2) and oxygen (O_2) have just two atoms and therefore don't absorb infrared radiation. Water (H_2O) has the necessary three atoms to produce a greenhouse effect. The water molecule is thus able to absorb radiation, but only at certain wavelengths. Other substances, too, have the ability to absorb radiation, but at different wavelengths, so that each absorbing substance has its own unique radiative signature. Other molecules with three atoms or more include carbon dioxide (CO_2, one carbon and two oxygen atoms) and methane (CH_4, one carbon and four hydrogen atoms). Both of these molecules absorb radiation. In the atmosphere they're present in relatively small concentrations.

At almost 360 parts per million, CO_2 comprises 0.036% of the atmosphere. That's 36 thousandths of 1%. It's a very rare gas. And the concentrations of the greenhouse gases other than water vapor are even smaller. Intuitively, it may seem unlikely that a gas that makes up so little of the atmosphere should have such a large effect on radiation, but nature is sometimes surprising.

Chlorofluorocarbons (CFCs) are present in even tinier concentrations, but molecule for molecule they are incredibly effective at trapping heat in the form of infrared radiation, as we've seen. One of the many intricate linkages between the greenhouse problem and the ozone depletion problem is that the CFC substitutes being developed as a result of the Montreal Protocol, designed to be less harmful to the ozone layer, nonetheless have serious greenhouse consequences. The substitutes are themselves greenhouse gases, absorbing infrared radiation just like the CFCs they will replace. In addition, they have long lifetimes in the atmosphere. In calculating how much the greenhouse effect is changed by adding a gas, it's important to know not only what an individual molecule can do in terms of absorbing heat but also how long that molecule will stay in the atmosphere. CFCs typically have a lifetime of about a century. CO_2 lingers about that long too. Methane is cycled through the atmosphere relatively quickly, in about 11 years.

In units of parts per million by volume (ppmv), the present-day (1995) CO_2 concentration is almost 360. Remember, that figure varies from spring to fall as trees take in and give off CO_2. But it was 315 when Keeling started his measurements. These are well-established numbers and are not at all controversial.

The number 280, for the nineteenth-century CO_2 value, is a little less certain, since it's measured from air trapped in ice. The process used to arrive at that figure involves actually drilling into glaciers in Antarctica and Greenland and the Alps and bringing up an ice core, a slender cylinder often many meters long. The core is kept frozen before being crushed and analyzed in the laboratory. The air thus released from the ice is trapped, and its CO_2 content is determined by shining an infrared laser through the air to determine its ability to absorb infrared radiation.

That process allows us to determine the CO_2 concentration in the late nineteenth century and in earlier times as well. Since the ice can be dated, we also know what the concentration was thousands of years ago, so there's essentially an unbroken record of CO_2 measurements, from the geological past through the preindustrial period and into the twentieth century—right up to 1958, when the amount of CO_2 in recently formed ice matches the concentration Keeling found when he first started measuring it in the air. Thus, Keeling's curve, the record of the last 35 years or so, is tied to and extended backward in time through this ancient record.

The present rate of increase of CO_2 is about 0.5% per year. That figure depends not only on the amount of CO_2 we put into the atmosphere but also on the carbon cycle, which determines how carbon is transferred between the ocean, land, and atmosphere. One of the uncertainties, yielding an area of major active research, is the nature of the carbon cycle. We know that carbon is transferred from fossil fuels into the atmosphere in the form of CO_2. From there, some of it is absorbed by plants in the process of photosynthesis. And plants, when they decompose, return carbon to the soil. This is one of the ways in which carbon is cycled from the Earth to the atmosphere through living things. Carbon is also continually exchanged between the oceans and the atmosphere. Thus, carbon is constantly cycling through the land-sea-air system, including the biosphere—the world of living things both in the sea and on land. The rates at which this happens—the rates of "flux" or exchange of carbon between oceans, land, and air—are still imperfectly understood. Right now, about half of the CO_2 put into the atmosphere appears in the measured record of increasing atmospheric CO_2 abundance.

In recent years, about 6.5 to 8.5 billion metric tons of carbon have been added each year to the atmosphere by human activities, but only about 3 billion of these metric tons of carbon have appeared in the atmosphere in the form of an increased amount of CO_2. What became of the other 3.5 to 5.5 billion metric tons? We're not sure. Presumably, they've somehow been taken up by the land, including the plants, and the sea. This area of research is complicated by the difficulty of measuring the rates of exchange of carbon on a global basis. Yet it's vital that we understand more about the carbon cycle if we're to forecast its behavior and its role in climate change. For example, will the fraction of carbon added to the atmosphere that appears in the form of additional CO_2 remain at 50%, or will it change? We're not yet able to say.

We've been focusing on carbon dioxide, but remember that *CO_2 is only half of the man-made problem*. The other half of the enhanced greenhouse effect is due to methane, nitrous oxide, ozone, and chlorofluorocarbons. The growth rates of some of those gases, the rates of increase of their concentrations, are higher than the rate of increase of CO_2, but may be more changeable. For example, if we're successful in phasing out the manufacture of chlorofluorocarbons, their growth rate in the atmosphere will fall to zero. (Production of the major CFCs decreased 40% from 1986 to 1991.)

When we speak of CO_2 increasing the greenhouse effect, then, *we're using it as shorthand for a whole suite of gases*, of which CO_2 is the most important, because it's the most abundant. Like every other aspect of this problem, the mix of these gases will change as time goes on.

With an understanding of how the atmosphere's chemical makeup has changed to date, we can now move on to the central questions: Is the Earth warming, and if so, why?

Scientists have been able to compile a record of how the global average temperature has changed over the last century or so. This record is an estimate—it's not free of errors and uncertainties. How does one estimate the global average temperature? By carefully piecing together records from many thermometers, including measurements made both on land and from ships at sea, correcting them for known errors, and judiciously interpreting them. The record shows that temperatures in recent years are about half a degree Celsius (about one degree Fahrenheit) higher than the average temperatures of a century ago. *But we don't know why*. We can't unambiguously claim, thereby convincing ourselves or anyone else, that this observed warming of the surface of the Earth is due to the enhanced greenhouse effect, either entirely or in part. Although the temperature rise is *consistent with* the greenhouse theory, it's not convincing evidence *in support* of it.

Measuring the temperature of the Earth is neither easy nor straightforward, though there are fewer difficulties today than there were in the past. I want to mention a few of the difficulties to help you start thinking about how to interpret this kind of scientific data.

One of the things to keep in mind is judging how much we should trust the results of a certain kind of science. We shall see that neither observational data, like the temperature measurements, nor theoretical results, like climate predictions, are perfectly reliable. The models that we'll look at later, the computer programs on which our projections of the climates of the twenty-first century are based, are subject to considerable interpretation and uncertainty.

Models are uncertain because the equations we feed into the computers aren't perfect representations of the way the real world works. Science is not yet at the point where we understand the climate system well enough, or have the resources to collect sufficient data, to make the equations accurate enough. So the models give us a prediction, and then we have to make a judgment about how far to trust it.

Data, as contrasted with models and equations, do have a certain reassuring solidity to them. You make a measurement, you get a number. And isn't that a scientific fact, and shouldn't you believe it? Shouldn't we take such a number for what it purports to be?

No. Measurements, just like theories, models, and equations, are subject to uncertainties, for lots of different reasons. Maybe a thermometer was inaccurate. And there are many, more subtle reasons than that.

The measurements on which we base our estimates of the Earth's global average surface temperature are contaminated by several serious sources of error. One of them is sampling error: we haven't made measurements uniformly in space and time with identical instruments at identical locations over the whole 100-plus years of record. About 70% of the Earth is covered with ocean, and the Southern Hemisphere is nearly all ocean. Few measurements are made at sea because people don't live there. And even within the remaining 30% that is land, there are vast areas (imagine the great wastes of Antarctica and Greenland) where very few people live and very few measurements are made.

The climate record includes measurements not only of air temperature but also of ocean temperature. The early part of the record of sea-surface temperature comes from very sparse measurements made from ships, originally sailing ships, and, later, motor-driven ships. Those data are also contaminated by changes in the way measurements were made as time went on. The earliest measurements were made by hoisting a bucket of water up on the deck and sticking a thermometer in it. Later, people measured the incoming temperature of the sea water used to cool the ship's engine, using instruments placed under the water line at the cool-water intake. But as ships got bigger, this intake was located lower in the water. Measurements were made at gradually lower depths, on the average, as bigger ships gradually replaced smaller ships. The temperature of the upper ocean changes rapidly with depth. It gets colder quite quickly as you descend in the ocean, as you may know from swimming. Hence, a cold bias was introduced into the data as ships got bigger and measurements were taken deeper in the sea. Moreover, ships don't travel everywhere on the ocean, but remain confined mainly to well-established areas. As shipping lanes changed over the years, these geographical sampling errors changed for that reason, as well.

Air-temperature measurements, too, are not immune to error. Measurements on land are made largely from the network that's in place to take daily records for weather-prediction purposes. A lot of those measurements are made at airports, but temperatures at many airports have increased artificially as the cities around the airports have grown. This phenomenon is known as the urban heat-island effect, and it arises because city streets and buildings absorb sunlight more effectively than does bare or vegetated land. The airport that was built outside of town is often now well within the city's developed periphery, resulting in higher temperature readings.

There are many other ways in which these measurements have been dirtied up—by instrument errors, by sampling errors, by plain old mistakes. Some of those ways occur despite great technological sophistication. In the modern record, the weather-forecasting people, before they use data, run them through a complicated series of quality checks. But remember the story of the ozone hole. The quality check on the satellite measurements of ozone levels threw out the first satellite evidence of decreasing ozone because the readings were "too low," lower than what some computer programmer had set—with all good intentions—as the threshold. Because of someone's preconceptions, a great body of accurate measurements was discarded as being unbelievable.

In the same way, processing the data used by weather services as a basis for the daily forecast involves passing the measurements through several "filters"—running them through a model like the weather-forecasting model, checking them for internal consistency. As time has evolved, models have changed, quality checks have changed, filters have changed. In fact, a very large and expensive re-analysis of the raw data of about the last 30 years is now under way to try to reprocess at least the most recent data—presumably the best measurements—with one consistent procedure.

These comments apply in general to climate measurements other than those of temperature, as well. Measurements themselves are like results from theories and models. They need to be questioned. They need to be interpreted. They need to be treated intelligently by people who know how they were created. If you don't understand where the numbers came from, you're likely to make errors in drawing conclusions from them.

So it remains a matter of debate today not only *whether* the Earth is warming but also how rapidly. The average consensus figure is that the planet is about one-half degree Celsius, close to one degree Fahrenheit, warmer now than it was about a century ago.

The warming hasn't been the same in the two hemispheres. If we had broken the data down into smaller regions, it would be clear that the warming has been different even from region to region. And it's clear that the warming hasn't occurred uniformly through time, either. Although the atmospheric concentrations of carbon dioxide and the other major greenhouse gases have always been increasing over this period and have never diminished, the average global temperature has nonetheless sometimes declined. There was apparently a warming trend for about the first 40 years of the twentieth century and then a prolonged decrease, from about 1940 to about 1970, that we don't really understand. That decrease appears to be mainly a Northern Hemisphere phenomenon (again, the Southern Hemisphere is much less well observed). Some scientists attribute the decrease to a change in the circulation pattern of the North Atlantic Ocean, rather than to any global phenomenon. These uncertainties of fact and tentative interpretations are typical of all kinds of weather and climate records.

One of the most useful things you can do with climate records is to get an idea of how variable climate can be. Sometimes the best way to think about what the climate of the future might be is to look at how the climate has varied over the past. Even if you don't understand what caused the variations—and we surely don't—you at least gain insight into how variable Mother Nature herself can be. There's more to be learned from the global average surface-temperature record than just the fact that an irregular warming has occurred over the last century.

There are imaginative ideas afloat in the scientific community about alternative ways to measure changes in the Earth's temperature. One is by using sound in the sea. Walter Munk is a renowned physical ocean-ographer who has spent his whole career, more than 50 years, at Scripps Institution of Oceanography at the University of California, San Diego. He and other scientists have recently carried out an experiment at Heard Island, which is near Australia. The experiment consists of creating sound waves in the ocean off Heard Island and listening for them all over the world.

The reason Heard Island was picked is that it just so happens, as an accident of geography, that there are sound paths from the island to the other side of the world over all the ocean basins. One set of sound waves comes up around the bottom of South Africa, up the South Atlantic, and into the North Atlantic. Another set goes through the New Zealand region and the archipelago there, past Hawaii, and up into the North Pacific Ocean. Thus, you can sit in many places in the world, put an earphone, so to speak, into the ocean, and hear the noises made at Heard Island. It's an extraordinary location for that purpose. Other-wise, it's a ghastly, barren place, with miserable weather and huge seas.

As the ocean warms up, the speed of a sound passed through it changes. Sound waves travel faster in warmer water and thus arrive sooner. Though the ocean is warming up, if it's warming up at all, by only small fractions of a degree over several years, these sound travel-time measurements are very accurate. You can measure the time be-tween the moment Munk makes the noise at Heard Island and the moment when somebody off the west coast of North America hears it. You can measure that to the one-thousandth of a second. The idea is that by making these measurements intermittently over a period of a decade or so, you can tell whether the ocean is warming. It's a method that has tremendous natural advantages.

One is that it naturally averages over the whole Earth. In fact, Munk has confessed that to him one of the aesthetic appeals of the experiment is the global scale of it all. He isn't just sitting somewhere measuring a local change; the whole Earth is his laboratory. That's what's needed anyway. We'd like to have a globally averaged measurement that avoids some of the problems of sampling errors.

The ocean *ought* to be warming, if the theory of global climate change due to an enhanced greenhouse effect is valid. These high-accuracy, large-scale geographical measurements, taken over a long time span, should be able to establish whether such an ocean warming is detectable. The method is feasible, too, in contrast to the impossible problem of sending out lots of ships to cover the whole ocean. But it has its disadvantages as well. One is that the measurements follow a part of the ocean called the sound channel, where sound waves are trapped. In parts of the oceans, that channel is near the surface; in other parts, it's deeper down, and the method is therefore not measuring the same slab of ocean, so to speak, everywhere.

One interesting aspect of this novel technique is that the speed of sound in the sea is affected by the oceanic equivalent of storms. There are eddies in the ocean, big, swirling things that last for months and are hundreds of kilometers across. If a sound wave passes through an eddy, both the signal and its travel time are distorted, but because the sound travels across an entire ocean basin, the measured speed, which is converted to temperature, is an average over *many* such eddies. The averaging process greatly reduces the error that might occur if the measurement were made in a geographically limited region.

Incidentally, much of the equipment used in this experiment was made available by the U.S. Navy. It was originally designed for detecting submarines, and its conversion to peaceful civilian research use is a triumph of both politics and technology. The sound waves that this equipment produces are readily distinguishable from all the other noise in the ocean because what is being sent is essentially a code. Munk and his colleagues can listen specifically for that code. Think of it as Morse code, if you want. But it's not just somebody clapping hands under water. It's a special signal, and the very sensitive receivers used in this experiment are tuned to recognize it, dependably.

As you can imagine, it takes very large gadgets to make enough noise to be heard around the world. One of the worries was whether that sound would bother animals who live in the sea. Suppose you were a whale and someone set off the equivalent of a blaring horn next to you. That might bother you. This was a very serious concern for a lot of the countries involved, including particularly the countries through whose waters the sound had to pass. Several of these countries had to decide whether to issue permits allowing the experiment to take place, and so they were especially sensitive to this concern.

So were Munk and his fellow oceanographers. A Scripps expedition to Heard Island in 1990 included biologists and environmental officials from various countries, who would study the effect of the first test pulses on sea animals. Apparently there was no ill effect, and some big marine mammals even seemed attracted to the sound. Perhaps they were curious about what the small oceanographer animals were up to.

The team is continuing its research on the effects of sound on marine mammals, including whales. In fact, the effort to measure ocean temperature by acoustic techniques is now the largest single source of research funding on the little-understood subject of how animals in the sea react to sound. We're now confident that the sound signals do no physiological damage to marine animals. There is no basis whatever for fears that animals might be deafened or otherwise injured. The intensity of the sound is comparable to the noise made by a large ship, such as a tanker, and, of course, there are many tankers at sea. Thus, the experiment simply adds a little more noise to an already noisy environment. And in any case, the sound sources are at low frequencies and are run in pulses, not continuously. Because the intensity is increased gradually during each pulse, an animal that's nearby has time to move a comfortable distance away. An area of research that's still under way is that of possible effects of sound on the social behavior of animals such as whales. Very little is now understood about that aspect of the effects of sound on marine life, and much may be learned from the current research.

The Heard Island expedition actually got the experiment off to a premature start. The sound pulses first put in the water as a test of the system and as a preliminary test of the effect on animals were actually heard by the people that were setting up their receivers around the world. Before the experiment had even begun, the first results were in. The scientists had heard Heard before they had planned to.

Plans are well along for a larger-scale experiment, known as ATOC, an acronym for acoustic thermometry of ocean climate. I think we can say with certainty that if we do that experiment for ten years, we'll learn a good deal about the ocean that we didn't anticipate. We may have the first clear, unambiguous evidence of a systematic change in ocean temperature. It's a nice experiment, essentially an upgrading of the Heard Island project. The hope is to have a decade-long experiment under way pretty soon. It's expensive, but the U.S. government has agreed that it's worthwhile and will pay for it.

"It is a test of true theories not only to account for but to predict phenomena," wrote William Whewell in 1840. After all this analysis of the past and present, what can we say of the future?

As far as carbon-dioxide levels are concerned, we don't know what will happen in the decades to come. The farther ahead we look, the more uncertain we are about how much energy we'll be using and what sources it will come from, and therefore the more uncertain we are about how much higher the CO_2 concentrations will go. We can predict how much of each energy source we'll use next year and the year after that. But ten years from now, who knows? Fifty years from now, who would dare guess? Who can predict whether nuclear fusion will become an energy source that's reliable and cheap in 50 years? I don't think anybody can. Neither can we predict whether political attitudes will change so that in 50 years the United States, like France today, will make most of its electricity from nuclear power. Nobody knows.

And who can deal with the most important question of all when trying to forecast global production of CO_2: What will the developing world do? Can anyone predict what China and India will do—especially China, with its enormous population and, relatively speaking, almost inexhaustible reserves of coal, enough for the next century or so?

The farther ahead we look, the more difficult it is to predict what the CO_2 burden on the environment will be, because we're forecasting human behavior, something even harder to predict than the weather.

It seems likely, however, that sometime in the mid-twenty-first century—2030, 2040, 2050, nobody knows just when—CO_2 will have doubled its preindustrial concentration. A CO_2 level that was 280 parts per million in the nineteenth century and is almost 360 in 1995 will be twice 280, or 560.

This particular benchmark, the doubling of CO_2, predominates in the scientific analysis of this problem, because it's easy for a climate modeler, someone who is carrying on research with one of the big computer programs we will look at later, just to turn the CO_2 value up to twice its present-day value. Doing so provides a measure of the sensitivity of the climate system to CO_2. Settling on "doubling" also simplifies efforts to educate governments, the press, and the public.

But there's nothing magical about this doubling. It's just a benchmark. If your son is 2 feet tall and on his way to adulthood, he'll grow to 4 feet tall, too. He'll double his size. Later he may triple his earlier 2-foot stature. Those are just benchmarks. Similarly, CO_2, which has already grown considerably, will indeed double and later may well triple its preindustrial concentration.

But remember that the greenhouse gases that matter most—methane, nitrous oxide, chlorofluorocarbons, and ozone—are generally growing at faster rates than CO_2, and the rule of thumb is that carbon dioxide right now is only about half the problem, while the other greenhouse gases account for the other half. Although we'll use the doubling of atmospheric CO_2 as our benchmark, keep these other gases in mind as well.

So how will the addition of these greenhouse gases affect the climate? If answering this question is not absolutely impossible, it's at least frighteningly difficult.

When we try to foresee the future global climate, we're not simply extrapolating past behavior. We're not projecting into the future the changes we've observed in the past. You can't look at the child who is 4 feet tall today and predict that he'll be 6 feet tall later just because he used to be 2 feet tall. But you can use your knowledge of the growth of children and of parents' heights to predict what his height is going to be. In the same sense, we're not simply extrapolating a past trend into the future when we make a climate prediction. We're using our understanding—rudimentary, fallible, and incomplete as it is—of how that system works.

Keeping that distinction in mind, then, 2.5°C (Celsius), or 4°F (Fahrenheit), is the typical benchmark figure by which many scientists predict the climate will warm in response to a doubling of CO_2. Later we will consider in detail where that figure comes from.

It's interesting to note that this number of 2.5°C is not so far from the prediction made in the first paper published on this topic, by Svante Arrhenius—in 1896. He predicted an average temperature increase of 5° to 6°C (9 to 11°F) due to the anticipated doubling of CO_2.

Now is a good time to mention one of the special consequences of characterizing climate only by global temperature. It's misleading in many ways to talk about climate change in terms of temperature change, as misleading as it would be to talk about health in terms of body temperature alone. If you say you have a fever of a degree or two, you've made it clear that you're not entirely healthy, but you haven't said what's bothering you. We don't know whether you have a mild cold or a serious disease. In the same sense, when we talk about a climate change of 3 degrees Celsius, we can judge that it's more serious than a change of 1 degree, but we haven't addressed the full nature of the climate change reflected by that single number. We haven't said anything about other aspects of climate that really matter. We haven't talked about whether droughts will be more frequent. We haven't talked about whether the strongest hurricanes will be still more intense. We haven't talked about whether sea level is going to rise, what the pattern of rainfall will be, what the effects on agriculture are likely to be. We haven't talked about the aspects of climate that matter to human beings and other living things, or the aspects of the economy that are sensitive to climate, especially agriculture. So it's rather artificial and abstract to talk of climate change simply in terms of temperature.

The idea of using carbon-dioxide doubling as an index of climate change on which to base the discussion is likewise a bit misleading. In the real world, we're not instantaneously doubling CO_2—making it twice as much tomorrow as it is today—and then waiting for the climate to come into equilibrium with that new chemical composition of the atmosphere. Instead, we're gradually adding CO_2, and while we're adding it, we're also adding the other gases. We're doing all this over a period of many decades. And while that's happening, we're also making other changes on the planet. We're changing the land surface by deforestation and by urbanization and by agriculture, for example. Other global factors may be changing as well. Over a century, the Sun can change intensity, for instance, or volcanoes and people can add aerosols—small particles—to the atmosphere. Climate researchers have only recently realized that aerosols can have globally large effects.

A lot of things are happening at the same time. The experiment we're all conducting on the Earth isn't an instantaneous one in which we hold everything else constant and change only the greenhouse gases. Instead, it's an experiment in which we're modifying the evolution of a planet, one that would have been evolving into something different anyway, without our help. We know from the temperature record of the distant past that climate is always changing. It shifts on time scales of hundreds of thousands of years between ice ages and interglacial periods like the one we're in now. On shorter time scales, we see climate variations that we can't explain and can't predict. We think such variations, such as the Dust Bowl of the 1930s in the U.S. Midwest or the more recent drought in sub-Saharan Africa, are due to the natural variability of the climate.

Hence, in addition to all this natural evolution—on top of what an engineer would call "noise"—we're adding something else to the climate. We're stirring one more potent ingredient into what is already a very complicated soup. What we're doing is very different from, and vastly more complex than, the clear, simple, idealized computer experiment of instantaneously doubling CO_2.

In short, using the doubling of carbon dioxide as a prime indicator is partially misleading, and measuring climate by globally averaged temperature is also partially misleading.

Keep in mind that the difference between one climate and another can be due to a subtle change somewhere. The difference between a desert and a neighboring rainforest can be due to nothing more than a mountain range or a difference in the pattern of storms. Climate is subtle, and big changes in climate can arise from small causative effects. Just as a finger on a trigger can set off an explosion, so a very subtle change in a climate input can have a massive change in a climate output. There are also processes in the climate system that have an amplifying effect. We'll see that again and again as we look at the climate conse-quences of a change in the greenhouse effect, as simulated by the climate models we'll examine next.

4

COMPUTING WEATHER
AND CLIMATE

One of the purposes of this book is to offer insights into how scientists do research. We'll turn now to subjects that are a little more technical and a little more uncertain than those we've looked at up to now. The aim is to depict science in the process of happening. This current research is work at the frontier, the search for knowledge at the boundary between what we think we know and what we don't know yet.

Frontier research illustrates one of the fascinating things about science. Asking questions at the frontier provides some answers but also brings to light more new questions. Scientific knowledge is ever-expanding. We never reach the end. We never run out of questions to ask. And we never assume that what we think we know could not be overturned by new knowledge.

As we consider how climate models work and how greenhouse research works, we're finding new questions that we now think are important, but that we didn't suspect were important only a few years ago. One of the results of hunting for new knowledge is to uncover areas of new ignorance. That's progress.

Albert Einstein was fond of talking about *gedanken* experiments, or thought experiments, experiments you can't actually perform but that are instructive to contemplate. He used them all the time in thinking about relativity.

The global effect of carbon dioxide in the Earth's atmosphere is often considered by means of a thought experiment. One thinks about the problem and devises a way to find the answer to it, or an approximate answer to it, through a computer simulation. The computer—which wasn't available to Einstein—serves as a tool to help us carry out our thought experiments.

Earlier, we introduced the pivotal question of what would happen if we doubled atmospheric CO_2. This sort of experiment is contemplated often. Never mind how it would happen. We just buy CO_2—go down to the CO_2 store in the shopping center, buy another 360 parts per million, several hundred gigatons of carbon in the form of CO_2—and dump it into the atmosphere. Then we sit around and wait a few decades. We know that the ocean takes a long time to heat up. So we wait until the climate changes, until it reaches equilibrium with its new chemical composition. And then we see what the doubling did. That's the sort of experiment we do.

We'll be discussing this thought experiment of climate in a doubled-CO_2 world again and again. Keep in mind that this is different from the climate change that we *expect* to experience. We're putting the models to an artificial test. The experiment is a benchmark. It's not one designed to mimic the real climate. It will only give us clues to what the real climate might do.

That's an important distinction to make. When we instantaneously double CO_2 and then wait for equilibrium, we're doing something that's not intended to be a forecast of the real world. The equilibrium and the doubling are the key words there. Why? Because that's not what people are doing to the real world. We're not instantaneously doubling CO_2. In the real world, CO_2 is gradually increasing. It's expected to arrive at double its preindustrial concentration sometime in the twenty-first century—but gradually, not instantaneously.

Moreover, the real climate never comes into equilibrium with the CO_2 that's there, because it's a moving target. That is, while the climate is catching up with one CO_2 concentration, while the ocean is gradually warming, the CO_2 concentration is meanwhile changing too. It's a transient experiment, rather than an equilibrium experiment, that we're conducting in the real world.

Furthermore, we're doing other things to the climate system. We're cutting down rainforests. We're cultivating new lands. We're paving more roads. We're changing the climate system in lots of different ways.

Mother Nature is doing unpredictable things as well. Mt. Pinatubo, the large volcano in the Philippines that erupted in June 1991, is a good example.

If we wanted to design a thought experiment that really did attempt to simulate the evolution of the actual climate, we'd need to take into account many of these additional factors. Such an experiment might be difficult to interpret. We'd be hard-pressed to say which of all the factors we put in were responsible for the resulting changes. Instead, we first try an experiment that may be less realistic but may give us more insight into how the climate system works. We simply ask how sensitive the system is to doubled CO_2. The difference between such a simple, idealized sensitivity test and a more realistic simulation is an extremely critical distinction to keep in mind. It's typical of thought experiments that go on not only in climate modeling, but in all kinds of science. For if you try to throw in everything at once, you can't figure out what's causing what.

Because our thought experiment involves the science of prediction, it's only fitting at this point to introduce a pioneer in this field. Lewis Fry Richardson was a profoundly original English scientist who lived from 1881 to 1953. He did the work for which he is most famous in meteorology around the time of World War I. Richardson was much more than a meteorologist, although his achievements in meteorology were certainly influential and important. He was above all a mathematician and physicist.

Richardson became interested in what we now call computational mathematics while that subject was still in its infancy. He was a pioneer in numerical analysis, which for our purposes means using arithmetic intelligently to find approximate solutions to mathematical problems that are too complicated to solve exactly. Many problems involving calculus are of this type. The reason why numerical analysis is practical today is that we now have computers, which are simply machines that can do arithmetic very fast without making mistakes. Thus, if you can cleverly convert a complicated calculus problem into a job requiring only a lot of arithmetic, then these machines can solve your problem.

Richardson, however, worked long before the digital electronic computer was invented. All his arithmetic was done the old-fashioned way, with pencil and paper. He was attracted by the idea of using the newly developed mathematical methods to forecast the evolution of the atmosphere—in other words, to predict the weather by solving equations. He thought that this was the way to make the imperfect art of producing weather forecasts into an exact science. His goal was to make accurate weather predictions in much the same way that we make accurate forecasts of phenomena like eclipses.

Today we don't even seem to think it's remarkable that eclipses are predicted with great accuracy far in advance. People take it for granted. We read in the paper that there will be a solar eclipse next Tuesday at 10:51 A.M., so we go outside at that time and look, and there it is. That's really astounding, if you stop to think about it. Somebody has figured out how eclipses work and calculated the orbits of the Moon around the Earth and the Earth around the Sun. What's even more amazing is that the forecasts of eclipses are always exactly right.

Why shouldn't we be able to predict the weather like that? After all, there's nothing occult about the atmosphere. The wind ought to change according to physical laws, just as the relative positions of the Earth and the Moon change within their orbits.

So Richardson tried to work out a mathematical system for predicting the weather. He started by doing theoretical meteorology, deriving equations representing the physical laws that describe the evolution of the familiar meteorological properties, such as wind, temperature, pressure, and humidity. These equations involve calculus. Then he applied numerical-analysis techniques to his equations, converting them in such a way that all that was needed to make a forecast was to do a lot of arithmetic.

Richardson worked alone on this task while holding down a series of jobs in government, teaching, and industry. In many ways, this part of his story is very much like that of Einstein, who invented relativity theory in his spare time while earning his living in a routine job in the Swiss patent office.

Then World War I came along. A devout Quaker and a pacifist, Richardson was torn between his religious convictions and an intense curiosity to see war close up.

Now the story becomes more interesting as a human drama, as well as a scientific adventure. Richardson found a way to participate in the war as a noncombatant, by driving an ambulance in France. For two years, as he later said, he was "not paid to think." But he did think. Between trips to the front to evacuate the wounded, he did the arithmetic to make the world's first scientific weather forecast. The job took six weeks. Remember, the arithmetic, many individual calculations, was all done by hand. Richardson's "office" was a series of temporary rest camps near the front lines of World War I. His story would make a great movie.

To see how the procedure works, imagine a map of the world with a gigantic grid or chessboard pattern superimposed on it. The squares on the chessboard might be a few hundred kilometers or miles on a side. We'll regard the chessboard as a way to describe how meteorological quantities, such as temperature, vary from place to place on the map. The procedure is to use the values at the center of each square to represent conditions everywhere in that square. This procedure is appropriate, recognizing that we will never have enough measurements to know the temperature everywhere. For example, thermometers might be located only at observing stations near major cities.

The starting point of a forecast is a depiction of the meteorological conditions at one specific time, say noon today, Greenwich time. More exactly, what's needed is the temperature, wind speed and direction, air pressure, humidity, and so on at the center of each of the squares of the chessboard. These quantities, determined all at one time for every square, describe the starting point for the forecast. The mathematical term for that starting point is "initial conditions."

Then the arithmetic comes into play. The equations require knowledge of how much temperature and the other quantities change from one square to the next—from east to west and from south to north at all of the squares on the chessboard. These changes, called gradients, are calculated from the initial conditions. From a physical point of view, without doing any mathematics, we can easily appreciate why the gradients are important. For example, one way that the temperature at a given point, say Munich, Germany, can change is if the wind blows colder air into the Munich region. The jargon term for that process is temperature advection. On the chessboard, as in the real world, if we know that it's colder to the north of Munich, and the wind is blowing *from* the north, then we can expect that the temperature in Munich will drop, because of temperature advection.

Of course, at the same time, something else might be happening to make it warmer instead of colder, such as the sun shining down brightly on Munich all day long. To calculate whether the day will be sunny, we need to know whether clouds will form over Munich. To solve that problem, we need to know many other things, like humidity. And just as knowing that the temperature gradient is important in predicting temperature advection, we need to know the humidity gradient to calculate humidity advection to predict humidity to predict clouds to predict sunshine to predict temperature changes.

This example is typical in the sense that all of the quantities that affect weather are connected to one another in complicated ways. You can easily see that it takes a lot of data and a lot of arithmetic to make a single weather forecast.

Richardson's first numerical weather forecast, obtained after a great deal of tedious calculating, was not very accurate. In fact, it was wildly inaccurate. The changes that he predicted would occur in six hours at a point near Munich did not occur. In fact, these changes were impossibly large and could never have occurred. Richardson suspected that the error was due to poor observations, so that the initial conditions of the forecast were not known accurately, and in hindsight we know that he was right. The observing stations were neither numerous enough nor sufficiently close to one another to provide representative values at the centers of all the squares. In addition, the atmosphere is three-dimensional, and conditions at higher altitudes are just as important to the forecast as conditions at the Earth's surface. In Richardson's day, there was no accurate way to know what was happening just above the surface, let alone *far* aloft.

These observational problems alone would have been sufficient to doom the forecast. In addition, we now know—although Richardson did not—that the mathematical techniques he used were seriously flawed, so that even if the initial conditions had been adequately observed, the arithmetic calculations would have led to catastrophic errors in the forecast.

There was yet one more embarrassing circumstance. A weather forecast for six hours hence, even if accurate, is not particularly useful if it takes several weeks to produce. One feature of a practical weather forecast is that it be made in advance of the actual weather.

A less determined scientist than Richardson might have become discouraged and given up. In fact, Richardson did move on to different fields of science, and he has achieved lasting fame for his research in mathematics, in the physics of fluids, and in what today would be called arms control and other aspects of the psychology of peace and war, as well as in meteorology. In all of these fields, his work displays great innovation and creativity.

Fortunately for us, Richardson did one other thing in the area of meteorology. He courageously published his failed forecast. In fact, before he could publish his work, he had to find it; it had become lost during the war before turning up under a pile of coal. (Filmmakers will love that, too, I'm sure.)

When Richardson did publish his work, he did not confine it to a short article in a scientific journal. He wrote a book, called *Weather Prediction by Numerical Process*. It appeared in 1922 and is arguably the first modern treatise in my field, which is called dynamic meteorology. The book is densely mathematical and not easy going, but it's still well worth reading today. In it, Richardson describes his method in excruciating detail and reproduces the arithmetic calculations, warts and all.

Despite the dismal result of his forecast, Richardson was optimistic about the future prospects for his approach to weather prediction. He knew he was on to something, and he was confident that the observational requirements could eventually be met and that the difficulties that had plagued him could be overcome. He even had a remedy for the problem of producing forecasts faster than the actual weather evolved: near the end of his book, Richardson describes a vision of a theater-like room holding thousands of people, each doing the arithmetic for one part of the calculation, with a system for transmitting results as needed from one part of the room to another. In modern terminology, this approach to getting arithmetic done quickly is called massively parallel computation, and it underlies the design of some of the most advanced supercomputers of today. Richardson was ahead of his time in many ways.

Over the next 70 years of research, developments unfolded along the lines foreseen by Richardson. Observations improved, as did the theories of both meteorology and numerical analysis. The invention of the digital electronic computer rendered Richardson's theater full of people unnecessary. In the late 1940s, at the Institute for Advanced Study in Princeton, New Jersey, a team of meteorologists and mathematicians, using one of the earliest computers, produced the first successful numerical weather prediction. By the 1950s, routine weather forecasts were being produced by techniques based closely on Richardson's method. Subsequently, the same approach was extended to produce computer simulations of climate. Modern computer climate models are based largely on weather-prediction models. Climate models are allowed to run for a longer simulated time, say a few months or years, instead of the few days needed to produce a weather forecast. This difference in time scales is part of the fundamental difference between weather and climate.

Today's global models of climate change due to the enhanced greenhouse effect are the direct intellectual descendants of the hand calculations carried out during World War I by Lewis Fry Richardson. True, his first numerical weather forecast was ludicrously wrong, and in that narrow sense was a failure. But he had the right idea, and history has vindicated him. He was a pioneer and a visionary.

There is an interesting footnote to Richardson's chessboard concept. What do you think is the right size for the squares, which mathematicians call grid elements? As you might imagine, the smaller the squares, the more accurate the simulations of weather or climate. In the jargon, that is called "increasing the horizontal resolution." But having smaller grid elements, or finer horizontal resolution, requires more arithmetic, so that in practice the affordable horizontal resolution depends on the speed of the computer. One reason why weather forecasts today are more accurate than those of 10 or 20 years ago is that the fastest computers have gotten faster. The weather services of the richer nations have been steady customers for the makers of supercomputers. When a weather service buys a faster computer, it often upgrades its forecasting program to finer horizontal resolution, and the predictions get a little better, just as a more powerful engine improves the performance of a race car. It just so happens that with today's fastest computers, the affordable resolution of global models is only a little better than that of the chessboard that Richardson intuitively thought would be about right. Typical resolution for today's global weather-prediction models is about 100 kilometers, or 60 miles, across each square.

Let's introduce two computer terms here. "Numerical weather prediction," the product of Richardson's vision, is the use of a computer model to solve equations by doing a lot of arithmetic to predict the future state of the weather, given the present state.

"General circulation modeling" employs the same sort of models, but to simulate *climate*. In weather prediction, we start the model at an initial state and run it a few days or weeks into the future. We're interested in how the details of the model simulation at some future date correspond to reality on that date. That's a measure of the skill of the forecast.

General circulation modeling, by contrast, means taking a model, perhaps the very same model as the numerical weather-prediction model, and running it to simulate not two or three days, but two or three months, or two or three years, or two or three decades or centuries. This allows us to simulate each of the weather events in the whole period and look at the averages, extremes, and other statistics that characterize climate. It means simulating the climate by long runs of the model—simulating many days or months or years of weather events, rather than looking at the short-term evolution.

General circulation models, or GCMs, are sometimes referred to as global climate models—the same thing. These are the computer programs we're going to talk about.

I confess that there's something fascinating about climate modeling. It's computer simulation of a high order. You can turn a knob and make the Earth spin faster or spin backwards, you can turn the Sun off, you can make the seasons disappear, or you can change atmospheric carbon dioxide. Of course, you're doing all this with a make-believe Earth, not the real one. Some people, unfortunately, tend to believe literally everything that emerges from the model. Many things in the real climate system aren't included in climate models. Planet modeling by computer simulation is an exciting area of research that's fun to learn about. But the results are broad-brush overviews of the climate problem, not precise depictions.

As an example, phenomenal thunderstorms and even hurricanes are too small to be well resolved by the models' grids. Such storms thus cannot be taken into account in these models. They pass through the computed grid the way a small bug can pass through a coarse window screen. So it's important to keep in mind, when we're discussing climate, that we're talking about only large-scale features—things big enough to stand out if we looked down on the Earth from a spaceship. We're seeing only the big picture. What are small details to a climate modeler are real aspects of climate to human beings. To the climate models, our human ground-level perception of the climate is a sub-grid-scale phenomenon. Much of what we understand about climate is not in these models at all.

Regional and transient effects (in the jargon of climate modelers) are things that happen in limited regions of space and for limited periods of time. They are to be distinguished from the global, equilibrium effects. From people's point of view, plants' point of view, the ecosystem's point of view, the regional and transient effects are what's important. From the modeler's point of view, they are the details, and are largely left out of these models altogether. Models that are used to simulate climate change are too broad-scaled, too coarse-grained, to represent something as small as a hurricane. Models are not yet realistic enough to reproduce droughts or monsoons well. Yet, these aspects of climate, which can be dominant in large parts of the world for long periods of time, may themselves respond to climate change.

A little later we'll look into the specifics of how these models work. For now, let's consider some of the challenges the models must contend with. We're going to spend a lot of time talking about feedbacks. If there weren't any feedbacks, climate modeling would be a lot simpler, and so would real life.

Feedback is what happens in response to a prior cause, which then itself makes a change in what caused it. There is a story about a quint-essentially absent-minded and clumsy professor. He used to illustrate feedback processes for his students by picking up a pencil and saying, "Suppose I'm trying to bring this pencil to my nose, and I notice that it's going off to the left. I make the correction, bring it back so I can bring it more directly to my nose. When I do this, I'm feeding back. I see it's going off to the left, my eyes tell my brain to tell my hand to move back here." Then, according to legend, he dropped the pencil.

The feedbacks that we're talking about are ways in which the climate system, as it changes, generates processes that in turn affect the nature of the change. As we change CO_2, for example—that's our initial input into the climate system—the climate begins to change, and other things happen as a result. Some of these other things then affect the climate change. These feedbacks are many, and their aggregate effects are complicated. I'm going to mention a few of them. We'll talk more about them as we go along.

In a way, understanding what will happen when we add CO_2 to the atmosphere is equivalent to understanding the whole climate system and all of its ever-changing feedbacks. I think that when we're able to say confidently what the climate will be like in the middle of the twenty-first century—when we'll have more CO_2, methane, and perhaps chlorofluorocarbons than we have today—we'll be at the point where we'll have an explanation for the ice ages. We'll be good at predicting seasonal trends in climate. We'll essentially have a complete understanding of the climate system—atmosphere, oceans, ice, land surfaces, plant life, sunlight, all of the interactions that cause climate to change naturally. But until you understand that system and its many feedbacks, you're not going to be able to predict confidently what the climate's going to do.

The challenge in making climate models realistic is largely that of understanding these feedback processes and incorporating them. As the air warms, does water vapor increase? To what extent? How much does that change the warming? Do ice and snow melt? How rapidly? Does that change the reflectivity of the Earth's surface and change the warming? Does the ocean circulation change? In what ways? How does that affect climate? Do the clouds change? Are they more plentiful? Less plentiful? Higher? Lower? Darker? Lighter? How do they feed back to the climate? Getting all those things right is the hard part.

If all of those things stayed constant, if as we changed the CO_2 level nothing else changed, our task would be a lot simpler. But scarcely anything stays constant.

Among the most important of these global processes, the feedback involving water vapor may seem to be one of the clearest. The underlying concept is simple. Warm air holds more water than cold air. Air in the tropics is therefore more humid than that at higher latitudes. A warmer ocean will evaporate more water into the atmosphere. This is all very straightforward; it's understood theoretically, and it's observed experimentally. Warmer parts of the Earth are more humid; in absolute terms, there's more water vapor in the air there. So, as the climate system warms up, we confidently expect that more water will be evaporated into the atmosphere. Water vapor is itself a powerful greenhouse gas, more powerful than CO_2 in terms of its importance in contributing to the greenhouse effect.

In some ways, CO_2 appears to be simply the trigger for the humidifying of the atmosphere, and models predict that the resultant extra water vapor will powerfully amplify the warming caused by the CO_2. Once the CO_2 has warmed the air and the oceans, then the warmer oceans will evaporate more water into the air, since the warmer air has greater capacity for holding water vapor. The presence of more water vapor in the atmosphere in turn strengthens the greenhouse effect, warming up the oceans, adding still more water vapor to the atmosphere. The result is positive feedback: an amplifier. The additional water vapor may also alter clouds, giving rise to other feedbacks, which we'll discuss shortly. The water-vapor feedback itself, however, is not fully understood or universally agreed on by scientists, and our models necessarily treat it in an idealized way. Furthermore, measurements of water vapor, especially high above the surface, are sparse and not very accurate. Scientists do agree that more research is needed.

A feedback loop involving ice and snow is the main reason why it's thought that there may be more warming at high latitudes of the

Northern Hemisphere, and indeed why the warming of the Arctic may be stronger than that anywhere else on Earth. As the planet warms, ice and snow melt. The snow line in Canada, Northern Europe, and Asia recedes northward toward the Pole. Some sea ice in the Arctic melts. In place of that ice and snow is now either land or ocean, which in either case is darker than the ice or snow. Anyone walking to the beach knows that a dark asphalt street gets hotter than a white sidewalk on a summer afternoon, because the white surface reflects away some of the radiation from the Sun that a dark surface would absorb. Similarly, where ice and snow might have reflected sunlight away, the dark land or dark ocean exposed when the snow or ice melts is more effective in absorbing sunlight. So the poleward retreat of the ice and snow line darkens the surface of the Earth, leading to an increase in the absorption of sunlight, leading to warmer land and ocean, leading to greater melting of ice and snow. This is an example of a positive feedback, where a particular change affects the environment in such a way as to amplify the change itself.

Recall that characterizing climate change by global average temperature is as misleading as characterizing illness simply by the figure for your fever. You might be running a temperature without knowing whether you've got a serious illness or not. In the same sense, whether the planet warms by 1 degree or 5 may be less serious than what happens to some other aspects of the planet—sea level, for instance.

Sea-level rise is a serious problem. A consensus scientific estimate is that if the nations of the world do not alter their emissions of greenhouse gases significantly, then by the year 2030 sea level will have risen 15 centimeters (6 inches) higher than it is today. And by the year 2100 it will be 50 centimeters (20 inches) higher than it is today. This will affect the Netherlands, for example. Dikes and sand dunes will have to be raised and other measures taken. A cost estimate for protecting that country against a sea-level rise of 1 meter (about 3 feet) is 10 billion dollars. Sea-level rise will certainly affect other vulnerable areas as well, including low-lying island nations of the Pacific, Bangladesh, Florida, Venice, and the Nile Delta region of Egypt. And because of feedbacks sea-level rise is a complicated problem.

One area of intensive research involves examining sea-level rise as a result of feedback processes. Sea level rises basically for two reasons. First, the ocean expands thermally: warm water takes up more volume than cold water. That's straightforward: it's an experiment we can perform in the lab. Second, ice that's currently on land melts and flows as water into the oceans, increasing sea level. In fact, we know that during the ice ages, when more of the water was stored up in glaciers, sea level was many meters lower. Alaska and Siberia were connected by a land bridge many miles across. So you might expect that in a warmer climate, water that's now locked up in glaciers, say on Antarctica or Greenland, will end up in the oceans, and sea level will rise. And it surely will if you wait long enough, because if you warm the Earth enough and you wait long enough, some of the water that is now ice melts, and most of the meltwater finds its way into the ocean. That's pretty straightforward.

But now the story twists and turns. One thing that happens as the climate warms is that part of the increased evaporation from the warmer ocean serves to increase the amount of water vapor in the atmosphere. And that same water vapor will cycle through and fall out as precipitation. Rainfall thus increases as water vapor cycles through the atmosphere more rapidly. There's more snowfall and rainfall in a warmer world than there is in today's world, just as rainfall is more abundant in the tropics today than it is in the higher latitudes. Warmer places have an accelerated hydrological cycle. The whole process intensifies: more water evaporates from the sea, rises into the atmosphere, condenses into clouds, precipitates out, and flows down through streams and rivers into the ocean once again.

As a result, the glaciers in Antarctica and Greenland, while *losing* mass to the ocean by melting and by creating icebergs, *gain* mass because the snowfall is greater than before. So in a steadily warming world there may be a temporary situation where sea level rises less dramatically, or even *falls*, because glaciers gain more mass from extra snowfall than they lose from warming.

See how complicated this can get? It's not just a matter of saying, "Simple story: warmer world, more water in the sea, the sea takes up more volume." It's complicated, because of the feedback processes.

In addition to this hydrologic-cycle feedback and the ice-and-snow feedback, perhaps the most crucial feedback process involves clouds. Getting a sense of this feedback requires an understanding of how clouds affect the planet's thermostat, that is, its ability to regulate its temperature.

Like every other body in the universe that's not at a temperature of absolute zero, both the Earth and the Sun emit electromagnetic radiation. But they do so at different wavelengths. The competing effects of clouds—reflecting sunlight and retaining Earth's radiation—can be linked to how they react to these two different kinds of radiation. We'll return to this shortly.

One of the physical laws involved is that, for certain idealized, theoretical entities called "black bodies," of which the Sun and the Earth are good approximations, hotter bodies put out more energy than colder bodies, and they put it out at shorter wavelengths. Conversely, colder bodies emit less radiation than hotter bodies, and at longer wavelengths. On the Kelvin or absolute scale, the Sun is about 6,000° on its surface, and the Earth is roughly 300°. (To convert from Kelvin to Celsius, subtract 273; the Earth's average surface temperature is 288°K, or 15°C.) The Sun has a temperature of several thousand degrees, so its radiation is of much shorter wavelength than the radiation that comes out of the Earth.

We use several different names for the Sun's radiation. We call it sunlight, or visible light. Most of it is in the part of the electromagnetic spectrum that our eyes are sensitive to; it's "peaked in the visible," as a physicist would say. Solar radiation is another term for sunlight, and it's also called short-wave radiation. It's what you feel when you go outside and the sun shines down on you. You absorb some of that light, and your skin temperature increases.

Most of the radiation that the Earth emits is what we call radiant heat. You can't see it because your eyes aren't sensitive to it, although certain instruments are. It's also called infrared radiation, which is just a name for a different part of the spectrum of electromagnetic radiation. Within visible light, red has the longest wavelength and blue the shortest. What's longer than red, or infrared, you can't see, but it's there. It's also called terrestrial radiation, or long-wave radiation, because its wavelength is much longer than that of solar radiation. The Earth also emits a little radiation at other wavelengths, notably in the microwave part of the spectrum, but just as the Sun is peaked in the visible, the Earth is peaked in the infrared.

In addition, as noted, hotter bodies put out more radiation. Black bodies emit an amount of energy proportional to the fourth power of their absolute, or Kelvin, temperature. The fourth power of something is the number multiplied by itself three times. Thus, 2 to the fourth is 16; 3 to the fourth is 3 times 3, or 9, times 3, or 27, times 3, or 81. So, if you double something's temperature, you raise the amount of energy it puts out by a factor of 16, but if you triple its temperature, you get 81 times the energy.

Thus, the amount of energy emitted, whether it's heat or light or some other form of energy, depends on the temperature of what's producing it. It's approximately proportional to the fourth power of the temperature. (For the special, idealized objects called black bodies, energy radiation is *exactly* proportional to the fourth power of temperature. As soon as we hear "radiation," scientists think in terms of some temperature to the fourth power.)

Now it's time to consider the dual role of clouds. First, clouds affect the interaction between solar radiation and the Earth. Sunlight is reflected off clouds, and part of what gets through the atmosphere is reflected off the surface. We'll address reflectivity in greater depth shortly, but in round numbers, about 20% of the sunlight that hits the Earth is reflected outward by the clouds. An additional 10% is reflected by the Earth's surface and by particles in the atmosphere. Thus a total of about 30% of incoming sunlight is reflected by the total Earth system and escapes out into space. So, clouds reflect sunlight, cooling the planet by contributing to its reflectivity. Obviously, if less sunlight is absorbed by the Earth, the planet won't be as warm as it would be if more sunlight were absorbed. Thus, through *these* effects, clouds *cool* the Earth.

Second, clouds affect terrestrial radiation. They absorb some of the heat put out by the Earth, re-emitting it both upward and downward. Some of the radiation they emit upward is absorbed and re-emitted; some escapes into space. The radiation that clouds emit downward is partly absorbed by the atmosphere and the Earth below. That increases the greenhouse effect. Moreover, molecules of ozone, carbon dioxide, and water vapor (not all water vapor is in the clouds) do just what clouds do. By being partly opaque, by not being transparent to heat, they absorb some of the radiation that would otherwise escape to space, re-emitting part of it downward. That's what we mean by the greenhouse effect. Through *these* effects, clouds and greenhouse gases *warm* the Earth.

Clouds thus affect solar radiation in a way that cools the Earth. At the same time, they affect the Earth's infrared radiation in a way that warms the Earth. The same clouds do both of these things.

So, which effect dominates? Let's pose that question in terms of another *gedanken* experiment, a thought experiment. Suppose you have another planet just like the Earth, but one that lacks clouds. A naked, cloud-free Earth. Same sunlight, same oceans. As seen from space, this planet reveals blue ocean, land, ice, snow, and trees, but no clouds. Everything else on that imaginary planet is just like the Earth. Will that planet be warmer or cooler than Earth? The absence of clouds would mean that it's less reflective, so more sunlight would heat it up. That would help to warm it. But the absence of clouds would also mean a less powerful greenhouse effect. That would cool it off. Which effect dominates?

That's a nice question to pose to illustrate the importance of numbers to science, to demonstrate that science is inherently a quantitative subject. Lord Kelvin, the distinguished nineteenth-century physicist for whom the Kelvin temperature scale was named, said this about numbers: "When you can measure what you are speaking about, and express it in numbers, you know something about it; but when you cannot measure it, when you cannot express it in numbers, your knowledge is of a meager and unsatisfactory kind: it may be the beginning of knowledge, but you have scarcely, in your thoughts, advanced to the stage of *science.*"

In this case, we're not asking the fuzzy question—do clouds warm us up or cool us off?—to which the answer is that they do both. Rather, we're asking the hard, quantitative question—which of those events is dominant, the cloud's contribution to the greenhouse effect or the cloud's contribution to making the planet bright and reflecting away sunlight?

If our clouds do more cooling than they do warming, then the imaginary planet without clouds would be warmer. If our clouds do more warming than cooling, that planet would be cooler.

Satellites have been deployed to determine the contribution that clouds make both to the Earth's reflectivity and to its greenhouse effect. We can now quantify those two aspects of clouds, from space. The analysis was done by a team of scientists that included Ramanathan, now at Scripps, the same man who discovered that chlorofluorocarbons are greenhouse gases.

The answer is: on average, clouds cool the planet; the sunlight-reflecting aspect dominates over the greenhouse heat-trapping aspect.

Kelvin says that if we have numbers, we understand something. We have numbers. They're expressed in units of power per area, specifically watts per square meter (W/m^2). These are understandable numbers; ordinary, incandescent light bulbs typically use 25 to 100 watts of power.

The effect of the clouds on average over the whole planet, in heating the Earth by contributing to the greenhouse effect, adds about 30 watts of power to every square meter of the Earth's surface. The cooling effect of those same clouds, by contrast, on average reflects away sunlight equivalent to about 45 watts per square meter. Thus their contribution in reducing the amount of sunlight that reaches the surface substantially exceeds their contribution in trapping radiation that the Earth emits. (The figures of 30 and 45 watts are approximate, but typical.)

On the present-day Earth, then, on average, clouds cool the climate. So the imaginary cloud-free planet would be warmer than our Earth, but its temperature *variability* would also be greater. The days and nights would differ more from each other. At night, clouds obviously don't have an effect on sunlight, but they do have an effect on keeping nighttime temperatures higher. For example, the Moon has a far greater day-night temperature difference than does the Earth. The Moon not only has no clouds, it has no atmosphere, and thus has no greenhouse effect at all.

The Earth has a reflectivity, or "albedo," of about 30%. That means that 30% of the energy that strikes the Earth is reflected away. We know that, from instruments on satellites. We can calculate what the Earth's temperature would be if it had that same albedo but behaved like a black body—that is, if it had no greenhouse effect, if its temperature were determined only by receiving a certain amount of sunlight and reflecting 30% of it away. That number turns out to be about 255°K (273°K is 0°C). Each Kelvin degree is the same as a Celsius degree, and a Celsius degree is a little less than twice a Fahrenheit degree (1.8°F, to be exact). So 255°K is 18 degrees less than zero Celsius, or −18°C, roughly 0°F. A very low temperature.

As noted earlier, the actual temperature of the Earth, averaged over the globe, which we can also measure from satellites, is 288°K (15°C, or 59°F). That's a more reasonable temperature for people. The difference between the actual temperature of our climate (288°K) and the temperature it would have in the absence of the greenhouse effect (255°K) is quite substantial. In fact, it's 33°K (33°C, or nearly 60°F), a measure of the heat retention of the natural greenhouse effect.

We can also calculate how sensitive a black body's average temperature is to albedo. If the albedo were 1% different—if it were 31% or 29% instead of 30%—the temperature would change by about 1°C. So, if the albedo went up to 31%, less sunlight would be absorbed by the black body, and we can compute that the temperature would go down to about 254°K. If the albedo dropped to 29%, the temperature would rise to about 256°K. So we can say that a planet is sensitive to changes in albedo.

Earth's albedo is due mainly to clouds. Year in and year out, cloud cover on Earth is around 50%—though you will see different estimates. It's actually tricky to determine this percentage, because it's not a simple matter to say whether a cloud is present over a given area or not. You can go outside and see whether the sky is crystal-clear blue or completely overcast. But if you're looking down at the Earth from a satellite, which is where these estimates are made from, if it's very slightly hazy and there seems to be some thin, wispy stuff over a region of the Earth, is that a cloud or not? That's a delicate yes-or-no call. There are different ways of making that determination. The latest satellite estimates of cloud cover are closer to 60%, by the way, because newer instruments are more sensitive to the thin, almost transparent clouds that we can't see very well either from the surface or from the earlier satellites. Scientists differ about how to interpret these data on cloud cover, but for now, let's call it 50%.

That 50% cloud cover is responsible for two-thirds of the albedo— 20% out of the 30% albedo of Earth. Most of the other 10% or so is due to sunlight bouncing off ice and snow and the bright surfaces of desert regions. What you have here is a reason for thinking the climate would be sensitive to clouds. Just a small change in the cloud cover could result in a change in albedo of 1%, fairly easily. Thus a modest change in long-term average cloud cover could produce a substantial change in the albedo and, hence, in the Earth's temperature. On the basis of this simple reasoning, we think that the climate would be sensitive to cloudiness.

Those are the numbers, and they raise some interesting questions: Why in the world are these numbers what they are? Why is the global cloud cover 50%? There's no universal law of nature that says every planet you stumble upon should have 50% cloud cover. Venus has 100%. Mars has roughly zero. And why should Earth's albedo be 30%? Albedo isn't the same on every planet either.

But as the climate changes, do the clouds change? Are clouds what a mathematician would call robust, so that their present structure is immune somehow to climate change? Were clouds different in the last ice age than they are today? We don't know.

This may be the most important feedback question of all: How will clouds change as the climate changes? As the climate warms up, will clouds become more plentiful, lighter and fluffier, grayer and darker, higher, lower, more prevalent in the tropics? How will changes in the clouds affect their contribution to reflectivity and to the greenhouse effect? How will that feed back into the climate?

The biggest single uncertainty in predicting climate is thought to be our ignorance of how clouds will change and what their feedback on climate will be. That's important to keep in mind as we turn to the subjects of weather and climate predictability.

How far into the future is it possible to predict the weather? How long are current weather forecasts skillful? To the second question, from three days up to about a week is a reasonable answer. Of course, the morning weather forecast is sometimes wrong by the afternoon. Maybe on average, when you read in the paper or hear on television that it's going to be sunny today and warmer tomorrow and cloud up and cool off the day after, that's right more often than not. There's skill at three days, and sometimes for a few more.

That's a statement about how successful people are at forecasting the weather. Part of what causes errors in forecasting the weather is that we don't know *today*'s weather perfectly. We're unable to assemble a complete picture of where all the storms in the world are at any given moment. We don't know where the little baby storm is out in the Eastern Atlantic today that might be a hurricane two weeks from now. We're partly ignorant of the initial conditions, every day.

Parts of the world aren't well observed, and the parts that *are* observed aren't observed in minute detail. If you ask what it takes to make a weather forecast—the regular weather forecast for tomorrow or the next day or the day after that—it's two things. One is knowledge of the weather now. The other is a means for telling the future if you know the present—a computer program or model or rule for predicting the future, given your knowledge of the present.

We make mistakes in both parts of the problem. We make mistakes in the beginning by not knowing today's weather perfectly, and we make mistakes in the process by which we look forward in time. If you ask why the forecast is good for only about three days (if that's the right number), the answer is that both of these sources of error contribute.

Consider an analogy with the stock market. If you want to predict the stock market, you're spared the first problem, because you know exactly what the stocks are today. Look it up in the paper, get it off the computer. Unless you're more clever than anybody else, however, you don't know the rules by which stock markets change from day to day, or year to year. Or, if you think that the price of stocks in the future is determined by things you can't possibly know today, like what the president of the German National Bank is thinking, then that is a source of error in your stock forecast also.

Weather forecasts today are better than they used to be. They may not seem to be, especially to people who treat them casually. People to whose economic lives weather forecasts are critical—people like farmers or sea captains or air-traffic controllers—can tell you that weather forecasts today are much better than they were 30 years ago. Gross errors made routinely in the '50s and '60s rarely occur today. And the useful range of everyday forecasts is much longer today than it used to be. If it's three days today, it was one day then. We can document that in great detail.

Weather forecasts have gotten better, and they've gotten better as *both* sources of error have been decreased. We have better instruments, more satellites, more buoys, more balloons, and so on for measuring today's weather. And we have better computer programs, faster computers, and more technology for improving the predicting technique.

That's a measure of forecast skill or prediction. It's distinct from what I mean by predictability. How good the weather forecast is today, is a question of how well *we* do something. Predictability is a question about the natural system itself.

The way to pose the predictability question in these terms is to say: if we had perfect knowledge of the initial state, if we knew the weather everywhere on Earth today, down to every cubic meter, if we had as fast a computer as one could imagine, if we were so smart that we had completely realistic equations in that computer, if we had models of every last detail of how every cloud process works—if all the little nuts and bolts were just right and we were using the same equations that Mother Nature uses—how good would the prediction be? Three days? Thirty days? Three hundred days? Or would it be forever?

This is a question of what the intrinsic predictability of the atmosphere might be. How well does Mother Nature *herself* know what the future's going to be?

This is a subject that may seem arcane, theoretical, even philosophical, but not very practical. But it turns out to be both fascinating and practical. The question is extremely important to you and me and to our taxes, because we think we know how predictable the weather is in principle. The answer isn't three *days*; it's about three *weeks*.

We're not certain that the predictability limit is three weeks. But we *are* certain that there *is* a limit, and I'll tell you how we know. The limit might be 14 days or 18 days or 25 days or 30 days. It's not four days and it's not four months. It's a few weeks. That predictability limit comes about for the following reason. The atmosphere is not a regular, cyclical, periodic system like the Earth orbiting the Sun year after year, following the same path, taking exactly 365 and a fraction days, or like the Earth rotating around its axis in very close to 24 hours.

The atmosphere is not regular, it's erratic. It has a random component to it. It's unstable, the way a stream flowing down a mountain is unstable. If you put a leaf in the stream in one place, it might end up on one bank. If you put the leaf an inch away, it might end up on the other bank. And if you put the leaf in the stream at either place a few minutes later, it might end up somewhere else altogether. Or think of an old-fashioned pinball machine, before Nintendo or arcade games, the kind where you pull the handle and the pinball goes up the track and hits a peg. Depending on how it hits that peg, it goes either left or right. A very small change in the initial velocity of the pinball makes a big change in where it ends up.

Mathematicians call this "sensitive dependence on initial conditions." It's exactly how things happen in the pinball machine. If the pinball didn't depend so sensitively on the initial way you pulled back the spring and let it go, you could make the same trajectory pinball after pinball. Once you got it right and had your arm grooved in, you could just fire them up and win every time.

It's the same with a golf shot. A minute difference in the way you swing the club makes a huge difference in where the ball ends up. That's clear evidence of sensitive dependence on initial conditions.

We think the atmosphere is an example of a system that's unstable in that same way. We'll never know exactly what the initial state is, because it can be disturbed, poetically, by the simple flap of a butterfly's wings, and can end up in a very different state.

The flap of a butterfly's wings is a metaphor actually used by a scientist named Edward Lorenz at MIT. His metaphor is that if there were a planet exactly like the Earth, except that the new planet included one additional butterfly and the butterfly flapped its wings just once, then eventually the weather pattern on that other planet would look very different from the weather on Earth.

That image may seem farfetched, but as far as we know, it's a valid one. What it means in terms of practical forecasting is that any error in specifying the initial conditions—and errors are inevitable—is going to make the forecast go wrong after a certain time.

Sensitive dependence on initial conditions means that if the other planet, the one where the extra butterfly flapped its wings, is very close to Earth at the initial time, you might expect its weather to follow parallel to Earth's for a while, but eventually the two weather systems would diverge, until at some sufficiently long time in the future, the weather on one of the two planets wouldn't resemble that on the other at all, or at least not any more than two randomly chosen states of the atmosphere of a single planet would resemble each other. That's what we mean by sensitive dependence on initial conditions.

This is true for systems that are not regular and periodic and stable, but it's not true where what we're talking about is the location of the Earth in its orbit around the Sun on April 13. If the Earth is at that spot on April 13, we know that next year it will come around and be right there in almost exactly the same spot again on April 13. If we pick another year, or another planet or satellite in another orbit, the motion will once again be regular, periodic, cyclical.

The atmosphere is not periodic. It's irregular. There are an infinite number of possible configurations of the atmosphere. A storm could be anywhere. The temperature of any given molecule might be different from its actual value.

Just as two planets that were almost alike at some initial time would eventually evolve to having quite different weather, every weather forecast for Earth will eventually go bad. Even if the forecast were made with the perfect rules, even if we knew the equations that Mother Nature uses to make the atmosphere evolve, even if we had all the physical laws nailed down and a computer program that solved them exactly right and a computer that could handle all the arithmetic and make no mistakes, the forecast would eventually become inaccurate.

So, if not forever, how far in advance can we expect the best predictions to hold? That is to say, can we put a number on this kind of conjecture? Remember Kelvin's remark, that when you can describe something with numbers, you understand something about it. When you can't, you don't. In my experience, Kelvin's rule may characterize many scientific subjects, but there's much else that it can't handle. I don't think it describes love at all well, or the way roses smell.

What is the quantitative answer to this question of how far ahead you can predict? How would you go about trying to find that out? I'll tell you about two ways that have been tried.

One is to look back over all the weather maps, all the weather records, which go back many decades. These are the measurements taken to support weather predictions around the globe. That's an enormous data set—the same data used to produce long-term temperature records multiplied many times by wind measurements, humidity measurements, pressure measurements, and so on. All these data, taken all over the world for many decades, are carefully archived away. If you want to know what the weather map was for yesterday afternoon, you can look in the paper today. If you want to know what the weather map was for December 23, 1930, you can go look that up in the archives as well.

You could take all of those weather maps and search them to find two weather maps that look alike. You might even be able to program a computer to find the matching pairs for you. Is there in the archive some weather map that looks just like today's weather map, with the highs and lows in about the same places, in about the same intensities?

If you found a pair like that, one for today, the other for the atmosphere way back in the historical records at some time—say, September 2, 1941—that closely resembles today's weather map, then you could track the sequence that followed. You could look at September 3, 1941, and September 4, 1941, see how the atmosphere evolved then, and compare it to today's weather map, and then to tomorrow's and the next day's. Then you would have mimicked this experiment, not by having another planet with an extra butterfly, but by having two states from the archives for the same planet and seeing how long, as these two states evolved, they continued to resemble each other.

That's been done. There have been very extensive computer searches of the weather maps. The answer is, that after just a few weeks, the evolution from one initial state of the atmosphere tends to have drifted well away from the evolution from a second, but quite similar, state of the atmosphere. After two weeks, three weeks, four weeks, even the most similar maps no longer resemble each other. That's one approach.

The second approach to the same question is, "Okay, let's run a computer model twice." But we don't have a perfect computer model, we don't have a perfect simulation. Weather forecasts usually do go bad after a few days, so we're clearly doing something wrong. Still, let's use the best model we have and hope that it resembles the real atmosphere to a sufficiently close approximation. Let's run this computer model twice, once with one initial state and once with a slightly different initial state. We can start the computer off with any initial state we want. Remember, the computer program is a mimic of our atmosphere arrayed in a machine.

We can modify the initial state. We can make all the highs and lows slightly higher or slightly lower. Or we can speed up all the winds by

2 miles an hour. We can make a new initial state and run it with the same model. This brand of having fun with a computer is called an identical-twin experiment, because the same program is used to make the two evolutions. We simulate in the computer, as best we can, the evolution of the weather on one planet and the evolution of the weather on another planet, with the same rules. We use the same computer program with slightly different initial states. We then ask how long it takes for those two computer simulations—for the highs and lows, the major storms—to drift apart so that the two weather maps produced in the two evolutions, after the same amount of simulated time, no longer resemble each other.

The answer is that the two simulations diverge at about the same rate as the weather maps in the archives do. After a few weeks—two, three, four weeks—they no longer resemble each other at all.

The tentative conclusion we draw from this is that the atmosphere has a predictability limit caused by sensitive dependence on its initial conditions. That limit is a few weeks.

I've said that there are two causes of forecast error. One is not having the right rules to make a prediction. The other is not knowing today's weather well. It's possible to improve our knowledge of today's weather and thus make the initial state more accurate. You can spend more money to observe the atmosphere better, put up more satellites with more accurate instruments, pay more people to use more balloons, buoys, barometers, thermometers, hygrometers, and anemometers. By improving the initial state, you can make the weather forecast better.

But there comes a limit beyond which you cannot make it better, because there's a time beyond which Mother Nature herself doesn't know what she's going to do.

It's not really a butterfly flapping its wings that sets a system in motion, of course. It's the fact that a great big storm today was a little storm yesterday, a tiny storm the day before. The day before that, it was just a little ripple that could hardly be seen. The day before that, it wasn't there at all. How and where and when some speck of dust (or whatever) set it off, we cannot know.

Where that storm chooses to crop up is a random event. It depends sensitively on the tiny details of the embryonic little storm. It's initially just a gleam in something's eye. Just as the place where the pinball ultimately ends up depends very sensitively on how you shoot it up the channel. Just as the place where the golf ball ends up is determined by exactly how you swing at that precise moment when you hit the ball.

So we think the limit of predictability is a few weeks. Largely on the basis of this kind of theorizing, and these sorts of computer experiments, the countries of the world put together a major effort in the late 1970s called the Global Weather Experiment. Your tax dollars helped pay for it. For a period of about a year, the weather-observing system was significantly enhanced. In addition to the regular observing system, special new balloons and buoys, satellites, and ships were deployed. The weather-data system in much of the world was better in 1979, when this effort peaked, than at any time before or since. After that, people stopped taking the special measurements. Balloons popped, buoys sank, and the system degraded.

You can see what the effect of that upgrading was in parts of the world where the skill of the daily weather forecast—the same one we get in the paper and on television—depends critically on knowing what's just upstream. "Upstream" in this sense means the direction from which new storms and other weather systems are coming; in middle latitudes, "upstream" is just to the west.

Australia was one place where the additional observations made a big difference. West of Australia is a great, wide expanse of ocean that had been poorly observed. Before the Global Weather Experiment, Australian weather forecasts often went bad because just upstream was a storm, or a ripple in wind patterns, that hadn't been observed. Not necessarily a big storm, just something in the weather a bit upstream. Without the better instruments, meteorologists often didn't know about these events, so they often made poor forecasts. With the improved instrumentation, the forecasts got better. But after 1979, the forecasts deteriorated again.

We keep very accurate records of weather prediction. One of the reasons why some meteorologists (like me) go into theory, rather than something practical like weather forecasting, is that the people in weather forecasting keep score. Every day you know whether yesterday's forecast was good or bad.

The weather services of the world are very competitive, and they all keep records. We know where the best weather forecasts are made. We know which country is second best. Even in a given forecast office, we know which person is cleverest at interpreting the computer output and making predictions. It's a highly competitive business, and many sectors of the economy are sensitive to it. The governments of the world aren't willing to pay for satellites and supercomputers and all the other technology just to amuse scientists. They do so because weather forecasts have tremendous economic value. The weather-sensitive sectors of the economy—especially agriculture, but many other industries as well—often depend on accurate weather forecasts.

It's easy to demonstrate that the payoff is real. If we put a dollar into making the weather forecasts better, we get several dollars back in increased economic benefits. That's why governments are willing to make these investments in technology.

Experience has shown that predictability theory paid off. Predictability theory not only told you that there was a limit of a few weeks on how long you could ultimately hope to make useful weather forecasts, it told you something quantitative about how much you could improve if you got rid of some of the causes of error. You could do the experiment, for example, with *this* much difference in the initial state, or *that* much difference in the initial state. If you pay for only a limited number of field observations, your initial error is bigger. The forecast decays faster and becomes useless sooner. So you can make a trade-off. You can decide how much you're willing to spend to improve the forecast. As you do the experiment, you can refine your estimates of how sensitively the forecast skill depends on the initial error.

There is another very practical consequence to having this understanding of the limits of forecast skill. It provides you with a way of spotting quacks. If in principle it's impossible to make a detailed forecast of the weather three weeks or more ahead, and someone says, "I know what the weather is going to be on inauguration day after the next American presidential election"—there are people who have made those claims and have charged fees for those forecasts—you know that it's a fraudulent forecast. Not because the person isn't clever, but because it's impossible in principle to predict that well. Just as there are certain equations that have no solution, there are questions you can ask to which the answer is, "You'll never know." You'll never know a year ahead whether there's going to be a thunderstorm over Rome at 3 P.M. That's an example of a detail of the weather that's inherently unpredictable.

As far as we know, everything I've told you about predictability is absolutely true. The remaining questions are largely quantitative. Can we sharpen that estimate of predictability from three weeks, roughly speaking, to get it more exact? Can we tell what the limit is for predicting thunderstorms, versus the limit for hurricanes, versus the limit for tornadoes, versus the limit for very large, very broad-gauged events that last longer and have a longer predictability time? Does the three-week limit apply only to certain larger-scale features? Are there exceptions to these rules?

Many interesting questions remain, but the basic concept seems solid. For now, we can predict weather for at least three days. Actually, the standard these days is thought to be around a week for the largest-scale features: very large weather systems, highs and lows on continental scales, the things that dominate patterns of atmospheric pressure. When you look at a weather map, these patterns, which look like big finger-prints, are represented by isobars, lines connecting all the places with the same atmospheric pressure. These features seem to be predictable today for about a week. That's a measure of our current forecast skill. Those are the things we would hope to be able to predict for a few weeks. We're not there yet, but at least we have *some* skill in weather forecast-ing, we know some ways to improve the system, and we have some reason to think that extending our forecasts might be possible.

None of this, however, says anything about *climate*. There's a great difference between the predictability of weather, which is what we've just described, and the predictability of climate, which is what we're trying to do when we forecast the greenhouse effect. Remember, climate is the sum total of weather, over great expanses of time. Climate is average weather, but also extremes of weather and probabilities of particular weather features. We haven't said whether it's possible in principle to predict that *next summer* is going to be warmer than usual on average over, say, Western Europe. That's a different kind of concern than the forecast of a thunderstorm this afternoon over Paris.

These big questions, like how much warmer the planet as a whole will be 10 years or 100 years from now, may be answerable, because they represent a different kind of question. It's a question about the statistics of weather, about the overall effects of weather, about the totality of weather—about the totality that is climate rather than the specifics of weather.

So we're left with an unanswered question: How predictable is climate? Perhaps not very. We certainly don't have a track record of predicting climate skillfully. Though we do have some evidence that weather is predictable, when it comes to climate we don't have very much in the way of demonstrated skill. We have hints of some slight skill at monthly and seasonal ranges, but we have no track record at all in making predictions of climate change a decade ahead, let alone 50 years or a century ahead.

When we make a forecast (or a scenario or an outlook or whatever other weasel word we choose to give it) for the climate of the twenty-first century, we're doing something we've never done before. It's as if we went to the racetrack and somebody said, "I've got a hot tip on a horse in the next race. Put your bet on this horse." You say, "Hmm, before I put my money on it, I'd like to know something about your experience in this field. How well do you do at predicting horse races?" He says, "Well, I've studied this subject a great deal, I've theorized about it, I've amassed a good deal of data, and I think I've come to a considerable understanding. But this is the first race I've ever tried to forecast."

That's something to keep in mind. This is a new field. We don't have a track record in predicting climate. We don't have a theory of the predictability of climate that is anything like our theory of the predictability of weather. We don't yet have even a conceptual basis for knowing what might be predictable.

And in any case, we think it's a different kind of problem. The uncertainty of the forecast of weather derives from not knowing the initial state well and, in principle, never knowing it perfectly. Climate might not depend on the initial state. That is, the climate of the twenty-first century might depend only weakly, or not at all, on what the climate is today or later in this century. It might depend more on things like what the surface of the Earth will be like in the twenty-first century. How much of it will be bare ground and how much will be forest? What will the carbon-dioxide concentration be? How brightly will the Sun be shining? These are external conditions, outside features that help determine the climate.

In mathematical terms, the kind of problem that weather prediction represents is called an *initial-value* problem—predicting the future state of the system on the basis of its initial values, from what you observe it to be now. Climate prediction may be more of what mathematicians call a *boundary-value* problem. That is, it depends not on the way things were at some initial time, but rather on what's at the boundaries of the system. The Sun is one boundary of the climate system. The climate of the twenty-first century may depend in part on how brightly the Sun is shining, how much energy it's putting out. Carbon dioxide, too—if we think of it not as a basic component of the climate system, but as an influence that we exert on the climate—forms another boundary. The surface of the Earth is part of the boundary, if you think of it as something not part of the climate system (though clearly part of the surface *is,* for example, where there is ice or snow). But if you think of, say, deforestation in Brazil as something not part of the climate, but rather as an imposed external influence, then felling trees is making a change in the boundary values that can affect climate.

Richardson, the same profound Lewis Fry Richardson who invented weather prediction by computer techniques, had picturesque phrases for these kinds of problems. He called initial-value problems "marching problems." He said we're marching off into the future when we explore these problems, and where you end up depends on where you start. He called boundary-value problems "jury problems." He said it's as if what's on the boundary of the system is a jury. You have to satisfy that jury to find a solution to the problem.

This, too, is something to keep in mind. The question of weather prediction is a question of determining the future of a system from its present state. It's an initial-value problem. The predictability of climate, which may well be more of a boundary-value problem, is unsolved. We don't know what is forecastable in principle. We don't know how much of climate is random. We hope not all of it.

In that same sense, because climate is an enveloping term that includes a great many different features, the things that I mentioned earlier that interest us about the climate may have their own predictability features. El Niño is a good example.

What exactly is El Niño? Every few years, unusually warm water appears at the surface of the eastern tropical Pacific Ocean. Water temperatures there can be several degrees warmer than normal. This disrupts the fisheries off the west coast of South America. The phenomenon often appears around Christmas (El Niño means "The Child" in Spanish) and can last for many months, even a year or more. Research has shown that El Niño is part of a complex of changes in the atmosphere and ocean that involves the entire tropical Pacific region and can have far-reaching effects, producing drought in Australia and changing the patterns of rainfall in North America. Because El Niño lasts a long time, affects a large area, and produces effects in both atmosphere and ocean, it's not weather. It's an aspect of climate. Recent research suggests El Niño may well be predictable.

Similarly, a given hurricane is a weather event. But whether hurricanes in, say, a warmer world may be more rare or more frequent, more intense or less intense, or located in different parts of the world than they are today, involves questions of climate. There has also been some success in predicting year-to-year variations in hurricane climatology.

These questions are of central importance in predicting the climate of the future. One of the barriers is not knowing which ones are answerable in principle.

We thus have two questions to think about. First, how much can we know about the climate of the future? We already have some evidence that weather is partly random. At sufficiently long times, it's unpredictable. Second, once we understand what aspects of climate are predictable in principle, what data and models and other tools must we have to predict them? We're trying to be dispassionate, detached, and clinical about these questions, answering not with what we hope we can learn, but with what's really knowable.

It saves you a great deal of time if you can prove that something is unknowable, for then you don't waste time trying to find it. There are all sorts of mathematical questions to which you can prove there is no answer. For example, expressing pi as a finite series of digits— 3.14159 . . . —is impossible. We know that. We can prove it. Kids in school can prove it. In mathematical language, pi is an irrational number. (That didn't stop one group of lawmakers from trying to pass a law fixing pi at a nice round number. Such a law would have simplified trade and other things a great deal.)

Certain kinds of equations, too, can't be solved. There are geometrical constructions in Euclidean geometry—like squaring the circle— that are impossible. It helps to know that those things are impossible. It's impossible to make a perpetual-motion machine, for instance (though that doesn't stop people from showing up every year at the patent office with their latest attempt).

One of the things we'd like to know is what is predictable about the climate and what is not. Psychologically, you will find that people want things to be predictable. There seems to be something deep-set in the human psyche that abhors a random future. People want to know what the future will be, and that has kept all kinds of soothsayers, oracles, and astrologers in business for a long time.

Having learned at some point *what* is predictable about climate, we'd then like to learn *how* to predict it. And that brings us to our computer climate models.

Scientists have developed complex computer models to produce climate simulations. We'll consider typical models developed by research groups in various countries. Worldwide there are about two dozen prominent groups that have access to the scientists and the computing power needed to produce these simulations. I'll come later to what goes into the simulations. Let's look at the results first.

The models produce maps that are paintings of how the world of doubled CO_2 in the computer differs from the present-day world. These maps are produced by running the computer model twice—once with present-day values of CO_2, a second time with twice the CO_2—and subtracting the first set of results from the second. What you get is the difference between the doubled-CO_2 world and the present-day world. In other words, this simulates the effect of doubling CO_2 and waiting for it to have its effect on climate.

What do you think the effect would be? You might conjecture that something weird could happen to the climate. For example, the CO_2 might first raise the temperature a little bit, but then suddenly cause the Earth to be covered by clouds, rendering it highly reflective, with a resulting cooling that would plunge the Earth into an ice age. That doesn't happen in any of the models. Add CO_2 and the climate warms almost everywhere. All the models predict that.

In answer to our original *gedanken* experiment question of how much warmer the Earth would be in equilibrium if CO_2 were to double, the climate models indicate that, on global average, the planet in our thought experiment will be about 2.5°C warmer. But some models say 1° warmer, some say 2°, some 4°. There's a range of uncertainty of about 3°C. Computer models that are least sensitive to CO_2 might say 1.5°C, while other models might say 4.5°C. (To convert these numbers to Fahrenheit, multiply by 1.8.)

Remember that it's best to think of temperature as a *symptom*. It's just one way to measure climate, in much the same way that your body temperature, when you have a fever, does not adequately characterize the severity of your illness. It's merely one way of measuring its severity. We're using temperature here as an index or measure of the climate. If you move from Denver to Los Angeles, you can say that the average temperature is higher at your new home than at your old home, and that's one way to measure the severity of the climate. There are lots of other ways too—it's more humid in your new location, it doesn't rain as much in the summertime as it did in Colorado, it was windier and snowier there than here, and so on. We're using temperature as just one measure.

Remember the way to think about our *gedanken* experiment. Carbon dioxide is doubled and you wait a long time—at least several simulated decades, maybe a few centuries—for all its effects to take place. You wait until the climate has reached a new equilibrium. In this kind of experiment, we're not interested in the transient, real-world picture. This is a thought experiment, not meant to show what's going to happen in 2020 or 2050, but to obtain a measure of the sensitivity of the climate to CO_2.

Where on the planet do the models predict the greatest warming due to a doubling of CO_2? In the far north. Why? Where there are vast expanses of ice and snow—Canada, northern Europe, Siberia, the North Pacific, the Arctic Ocean, the North Atlantic, Greenland—the ice and snow start to melt. By the time you wait for all the effects to occur, a lot of the ice has melted. A large fraction of the sea ice—half of it, maybe three-fourths of it in some places, nearly all of it in others—melts.

In place of the ice and snow that exist in our present climate, there is now darker ocean, bare land, grass-covered land, or whatever was under the ice and snow in these models. All of these features are darker than the ice and therefore exhibit lower albedo, lower reflectivity. The sunlight, hitting the darker surfaces instead of being reflected by the bright-white snow or ice, is absorbed. There's a positive feedback that occurs in high northern latitudes called, not surprisingly, the ice-albedo feedback. That feedback is mainly responsible for the much stronger warming produced by a CO_2 doubling in the far north than elsewhere on Earth. It's called "polar amplification," in the jargon.

Thus, the broad-brush picture you get from these computer simulations of future climate is, first, that it warms everywhere, and second, that it warms most at high northern latitudes. (There's not as much warming at high southern latitudes because there's less land there to be snow-covered, and because the ice in Antarctica is too thick for all of it to melt.)

As we've noted, however, no two models produce exactly the same results. What's going on in each of these models is that the Earth is being divided up into a set of squares or rectangles, typically a few hundred kilometers on a side, much like Richardson's chessboard grid. The chessboard is laid over the whole Earth, and in each grid element a calculation is made of wind, pressure, temperature, clouds, humidity, rainfall, snowfall, ice or snow cover, and many other aspects of climate. There is a grid vertically too, with the atmosphere divided into a number of layers, typically about twenty.

The rule used in these computer models for computing future ice cover goes something like this. Add to the ice when rain or snow falls on a square. Subtract from the ice when water runs off into the sea, or percolates down into the land. Change the ice into water when the temperature rises above freezing, so that instead of ice and snow you have liquid water. Thus, the parts of the model are all interconnected. The precipitation part affects how much water falls on the ground. The temperature part affects whether it falls as snow or rain, and how long the precipitation *remains* as snow or ice.

The rules for calculating the effects of temperature and rainfall are slightly different in each of the models. There is, after all, no hard-and-fast rule that we can lay down that everyone can agree to on how fast ice forms, or how fast it melts. These are approximate representations of reality. We're going to come across quite a few of them: Thus, there are differences between models when it comes to predicting the effect of the ice-and-snow albedo feedback, which is the process that dominates the warming at high latitudes.

Well, then, how about in the tropics, where there isn't any ice? The models still differ. Let's look at Africa, for example. In central Africa, one model might predict 4°–6°C warming. Another might simulate a 2°–4°C warming. A third could forecast even less warming, say 0°–2°C. What could account for these differences? Not ice or snow. Instead, this might well be an example of surface reflectivity and soil-moisture effects, and probably the effects of clouds as well. We'll see some more good examples of the effects of clouds shortly.

Why is soil moisture important? If there's water in the soil, then part of the energy that reaches the surface from sunlight is spent in evaporating the water. If the soil is dry, the same amount of sunlight will raise the temperature more, because all of the energy goes to heat the ground rather than to evaporate water. So, a decrease in soil moisture will lead to an increase in temperature. But it's the ice-albedo feedback that dominates in the high northern latitudes.

Why is Antarctica not melting in these models? There's more than one reason. One is that, as I've noted, over the Antarctic continent itself, the ice is very thick, several kilometers thick. So you can melt some of the ice, but you still have more underneath it, and bare ground isn't exposed. Another reason is that in the doubled-CO_2 climate in the models, the hydrological cycle is more intense than at present; more water falls as snow in Antarctica, which stays too cold to melt.

One thing that climate models must do skillfully to get the doubled-CO_2 climate right is to simulate the present climate realistically. For example, the effect of CO_2 in the polar regions is largely dominated by whether there is ice and snow to melt. If there is, then we get a feedback effect, because when it melts, the darker, newly exposed surface absorbs more heat. The warming causes a change, and the change adds to the warming. That's a positive feedback.

When you drive down a straight road and notice that your car is going to the right, you turn your steering wheel to the left to bring it back. That's a negative feedback; you're damping the drift. If you notice that it's going to the right, you correct for that. You tend to keep your car in a straight line. If you were not functioning very well, or if you were driving one of those "dodge 'em" cars at the fair, you might turn to the right and say, "This is fun, I'll turn more to the right." That would be positive feedback. You wouldn't want to do that on the freeway, however. There you want a negative feedback. The thermostat in your house offers another good example of negative feedback. If it's cold in the winter, the thermostat senses the cold, turns on the furnace, and brings the temperature back up.

What we're looking at in the polar regions in climate simulations with doubled-CO_2 levels is positive feedback. The change in the ice due to the warming amplifies the warming.

The whole trick of climate modeling is getting the feedbacks right. Right now we can't blindly rely on the results of climate models because we're not yet sure about the extent or magnitude of the feedbacks. If there weren't any feedbacks, we could determine the Earth's temperature by means of a simple calculation; the result is that if you double CO_2, temperature goes up about 1°C. But some of these models show that Arctic temperatures could rise 12°C. That's due to enormous positive feedbacks. Other feedbacks come into play, and we'll be encountering them as well.

One of the points of this exercise is to show that it's understandable qualitatively, even at the nuts-and-bolts level, by those who aren't computer jocks or rocket scientists or mathematical whizzes. I haven't used a single equation and I'm not going to.

Let's consider precipitation and soil moisture briefly. The models agree with one another less in simulating precipitation and soil-moisture changes than they do in simulating temperature changes. The models tend to show greater precipitation, relative to that of the present-day climate, in the higher latitudes and in the tropics, and this is true throughout the year. In winter, the middle latitudes (the "temperate" zones) also show higher precipitation. But the models disagree sharply with one another concerning individual regions of the Earth, although most of them agree that the summer monsoon in India will be stronger in the doubled-CO_2 climate.

The soil-moisture simulations are especially interesting. A typical model treats soil moisture by keeping track of the amount of water in an imaginary bucket within each grid element. Precipitation adds water to the bucket; evaporation removes it. The bucket is assigned an arbitrary depth, typically 15 centimeters (6 inches). When the bucket fills, any excess runs off into the sea. Some more recent models include less simplistic rules, but the bucket concept is typical.

The models tend to show that doubling CO_2 leads to an increase in soil moisture in high latitudes of the Northern Hemisphere in winter. In summer, however, the middle latitudes of the Northern Hemisphere show a *reduction* in soil moisture and, in some models, an increased likelihood of drought. If these predictions were borne out, they would have substantial implications for agriculture.

In looking at part of the complex of climate, we've considered three variables so far—temperature, precipitation, and soil moisture. We haven't bothered with a lot of other variables. We haven't asked about wind speed or cloudiness. We haven't asked whether the precipitation is coming in sporadic heavy deluges or more frequent sprinkles or in any of several other ways we could think of. We haven't thought about whether the extra heat appears as severe heat waves or whether each day is just a little bit warmer. We're looking at each of these pictures as one slice of reality or, more humbly, as one slice of a much more complex computational climate simulation.

Yet, we can now begin to piece together a picture of what's happening in the models. We can get a feel for things by comparing the different simulations. It's easy to make fun of these models because they are fraught with such crudeness—soil moisture, for example, is not well represented by a bucket. We're looking at several different representations of the climate system, embodied in several different models. But these models are all thorough, well-intentioned attempts by hard-working, talented people. Expensive attempts, too: this is big science, a concept we will return to; each of these models uses up many, many computing hours on a multimillion-dollar machine. Yet we see that marked areas of agreement and disagreement among the different models remain.

Still, we can begin to get a feel—even though it can be hard to quantify, even though it can be hard to put your finger on the details of what seems to be agreed upon—for what is more reliable in these simulations and what is more conjectural. (We're using "details" in the sense that a scientist would, to indicate regional differences, not to indicate the trivial.)

I'll summarize the models we've examined thus far by noting that there's considerable agreement on temperature change. The world warms. Even quantitatively, there is considerable agreement on the pattern of the warming. It's a degree or two Celsius in the tropics, up to 10 or 12 degrees Celsius in the polar latitudes of the Northern Hemisphere. There's a clear rationale for that difference: the ice-albedo feedback.

Concerning precipitation, there's much less agreement. And when it comes to soil moisture, there are some areas where the models tend to agree, but still considerable areas where they disagree. Quantitatively, there are many regions where, from one model to another, we see strong disagreement.

The spread between the models, the variation in results that different groups of scientists have come up with, is one measure of uncertainty. When all models agree, then they are either all right or all wrong. When they disagree, at most one of them is right, and maybe none is, but in any case there's likely to be more uncertainty where there's broad disagreement.

Precipitation and related fields, like soil moisture, involve more uncertainty—lower confidence in the results—than does temperature. Regional, rather than global, results are clearly more uncertain still.

I think there's a lesson here about the importance of being able to speak quantitatively about things. It's one thing to say it'll get warmer or it'll get wetter. It's another to say that it will warm by 2 degrees or 10 degrees, that it will be 10% wetter or twice as wet, or that all the ice will melt or a fourth of the ice will melt. The quantitative aspects are important. We should keep Lord Kelvin's advice in mind.

Keep in mind also that thus far we've avoided trying to predict the transient picture, the picture of what will happen from decade to decade as we gradually change the composition of the atmosphere by gradually introducing more carbon dioxide and the other greenhouse gases.

What we've addressed up to now is how to get a handle on the simpler problem of climate *sensitivity* to the doubling of CO_2. We've put aside for the moment the question of how fast trace gases will increase. That problem involves predicting human activity, among other things, plus forecasting how the climate will respond to the gradual change. Instead, we're still using the thought experiment about what would happen if CO_2 were doubled. We're comparing today's world with a doubled-CO_2 world that's been left alone long enough to respond to the CO_2.

The IPCC Report of 1990, listed in the bibliography at the end of this book (under Houghton, the lead editor), is a synopsis of research on this topic, compiled by many scientists (IPCC stands for Intergovernmental Panel on Climate Change). The table on page 92 summarizes the consensus view on the basis of the kinds of results we've been seeing. The authors use a star system to express their confidence in these judgments. (I don't know who came up with the stars first; they probably originated in the French Michelin guide to restaurants, where one star is interesting, two stars is worth a detour, three stars is worth a journey.) Five stars, the most accorded in the table here, denotes a result the authors are really confident of—for example, that doubling atmospheric CO_2 will warm the Earth's lower atmosphere and surface. The IPCC Report expresses a mainstream viewpoint, but it is good to keep in mind that not all scientists agree with this "consensus." Even if they did, they might *all* be wrong.

If we had to pick one number to represent all the complexity and severity of climate change, we'd probably pick global average temperature change, the single most important indicator we can think of. In that single figure—not just in the patchy fields we've looked at, and not just in the regional picture, but in the *global* average temperature change—we've found that the models differ by about a factor of three. Why?

The question arises, why does science—objective, pure science—come up with different answers to the same straightforward question? Are the scientists confused? What's wrong with their models? Why don't they agree? That's an issue that perplexes science students and certainly perplexes policymakers. Where does the uncertainty come from? Why isn't science able to pin down the answer? Why don't we get one clear answer when we ask these computers what the climate's going to be?

We now know the answers to these questions, because we've done enough playing around with the models, turning the knobs, and exchanging the rules for feedbacks and other factors between the models. The main reason the climate models differ in global sensitivity to CO_2 boils down to one fact. They treat clouds differently. The dominant difference between the models—what makes one of them three times as sensitive to CO_2 as another—is clouds. From one model to the next,

Executive summary of equilibrium effects of doubling atmospheric levels of carbon dioxide, as simulated by a representative selection of climate models

Number of stars (*s) indicates degree of confidence in each assertion, as determined subjectively from three factors: amount of agreement between models; 1990 IPCC Report authors' understanding of model results; and authors' confidence in representation of relevant process in the models. Five stars indicates virtual certainty; two stars indicates low confidence.

TEMPERATURE

***** The lower atmosphere and Earth's surface warm;

***** the stratosphere cools;

*** near the Earth's surface, the global average warming lies between +1.5°C and +4.5°C, with a "best guess" of 2.5°C;

*** the surface warming at high latitudes is greater than the global average in winter but smaller than that average in summer (in time-dependent simulations with a deep ocean, there is little warming over the high-latitude southern ocean);

*** the surface warming and its seasonal variation are least in the tropics.

PRECIPITATION

**** The global average increases (as does that of evaporation); the larger the warming, the larger the increase;

*** precipitation increases at high latitudes throughout the year;

*** precipitation increases globally by 3% to 15% (as does evaporation);

** precipitation increases at mid-latitudes in winter;

** the zonal mean value increases in the tropics, although there are areas of decrease; because shifts in the main tropical rain bands differ from model to model, there is little consistency between models in simulated regional changes (the zonal mean of a quantity is the average of that quantity around latitude circles, averaged over all longitudes);

** precipitation changes little in subtropical arid areas.

SOIL MOISTURE

*** Soil moisture increases in high latitudes in winter;

** and decreases over northern mid-latitude continents in summer.

SNOW AND SEA-ICE

**** The areas of sea-ice and seasonal snow cover diminish.

SOURCE: 1990 IPCC Report

from what one research group thinks clouds should do to what another research group thinks they should do, there is a difference of a factor of three in the predicted global average surface warming in response to doubling CO_2. The models for which clouds change dramatically, so as to amplify the warming more, predict a temperature increase of about 4.5°C, sometimes even more. The models for which clouds change very little, sometimes even changing in such a way as to resist the warming, predict about 1.5°C.

The fact is, we don't know which is right. We don't even know if that spread of 1.5° to 4.5° is a good estimate. It's just the range by which the most complicated and ambitious models, the ones we think the most of today, differ from one another.

The effects of clouds and the effects of oceans are thought to be the greatest handicaps to creating accurate climate models. We just don't know how to represent these things. Keep in mind that clouds contribute to the greenhouse effect, by trapping heat, while at the same time contributing to the Earth's albedo, by reflecting sunlight away. In the present climate, as we have seen, the cooling effect dominates, but both effects are strong. Clouds have, in other words, powerful, competing effects on the heat balance of the Earth. That's why climate change can be sensitive to clouds and why clouds can provide an important feedback.

There are several sensitive questions whose answers we don't know— not just for our models, but for our planet today, the real world we live in. We don't know in any fundamental way why this Earth is about half-covered with clouds. We don't know why something like 30% of the received sunlight bounces off the planet. We do know that these questions are closely related. We do know that approximately 20% out of that 30% albedo is due to clouds. It's the clouds that dominate the albedo. And it's the clouds that are crucial to the greenhouse effect as well.

Models use comparably crude representations of the processes that go into clouds. Real clouds are complicated things. There are little water droplets in clouds. There are ice crystals in some clouds. Hail can form. Snowflakes can form, melting when it gets warm, freezing when it gets cold. All of that is represented in models by gross oversimplifications, partly because the scale of these models is huge—grid elements are hundreds of kilometers on a side—so that each cloudy area in the model represents the effects of many clouds. More important, we don't fully understand how all those intricate microphysical processes inside a cloud work. That's why the rules for clouds in these models can differ greatly from one model to the next.

To be concrete about it, a typical rule for specifying clouds in these models is to say that cloudiness simply depends on relative humidity. Keep track of the water vapor in each grid element, adding to it when additional water vapor blows in on the wind, subtracting from it when it blows out or precipitates. When relative humidity is above a given value, we'll say that a cloud is present. A typical rule is to predict the fractional area of the grid square that is covered by clouds. For example, the square is said to be clear if relative humidity is less than 80%, overcast if it's 100%, and partly cloudy if it's between 80% and 100% (at 90% relative humidity, for example, the square is half cloudy and half clear).

What happens to these clouds when carbon dioxide is doubled? Global climate model runs with doubled CO_2 tend to show more high clouds and much fewer low clouds, *and that's a positive feedback*. For reasons that we shall explore in a moment, this change in the cloud population *increases the warming that caused those changes in the clouds in the first place*.

So, what happens when we "remove" some clouds? In a doubled-CO_2 model atmosphere, we see that the rules in the model have effectively resulted in removing some clouds. The reasons for this are not obvious, but are bound up in the interlocking feedback processes in the models. On average there are fewer clouds present in the simulated greenhouse climate. Cloud cover is 50% in the present-day climate. Maybe it's 47% in the greenhouse climate, as simulated by the model.

Since the cooling effect of clouds dominates over the warming effect, when we remove clouds, we remove more cooling than warming. That's the first of the positive feedbacks.

We can do this to the real world just once. We're doing it now. We're putting CO_2 into the atmosphere, and if you'll just be patient and wait 50 years, you'll find out what will have happened in the real world. In the model we can do this trick of changing CO_2 levels and get the answer without waiting. That's the beauty of *gedanken* experiments.

In the global-climate model, in our computer simulation, we're doing the next best thing to putting the Earth in a test tube. We add CO_2 and end up with a world with slightly fewer clouds. That's positive feedback because, in the model as in the real world, the albedo effect of clouds dominates over the greenhouse effect of clouds. So, when we remove clouds, we do more to remove the cooling they cause than to remove the warming they cause. Hence, the reduction of total cloud amount adds to the warming. It's like the ice-albedo feedback, which adds to the warming in high latitudes. There's more. The average height of the clouds changes. Since removal of clouds in the models occurs mainly at low altitudes, the average cloud in the doubled-CO_2 world is higher than the average cloud in the present-day world. So, in addition to there being fewer clouds after doubling CO_2, the clouds are, on average, higher.

It's colder the higher you go. The temperature goes down by something like 6.5°C for every 1,000 meters you climb (or about 3.6°F for every 1,000 feet in elevation). Hence, higher clouds are also colder clouds. Colder clouds don't radiate as much heat. The desert radiates a lot of heat in the summer, because it's hot. An ice cube radiates less heat, because it's cold. Hotter things radiate more heat than colder things. It's a law of nature. For black bodies, as we saw earlier, radiation is proportional to the fourth power of temperature—a small increase in temperature produces a large increase in radiation.

So, when we raise the altitude of the clouds, we lower their temperature and they radiate less heat away. Higher clouds are less effective radiators. That means there is more heat left in the atmosphere, and that's a positive feedback too. That increases the temperature.

There's one more effect. Think of real clouds. When you look outside, the highest clouds you see are cirrus clouds. Cirrus are thin, wispy clouds, made of ice crystals. When you fly through them in airplanes, they are often quite transparent. They don't reflect much sunlight.

Lower clouds tend to be thicker, brighter, and whiter than cirrus clouds. They're much more effective reflectors of sunlight. Thus, when you replace lower clouds with higher clouds, which the models say happens to some extent in the doubled-CO_2 atmosphere, you not only make clouds cooler so that they radiate less heat, you also make more wispy cirrus clouds and fewer low, fluffy clouds. The result is that the clouds' ability to reflect away sunlight, their albedo, is reduced. The albedo of the planet, two-thirds of which is currently contributed by clouds, goes down, and more heat is absorbed.

In sum, the effect of the cloud changes in these models in a doubled-CO_2 world is threefold, and all three effects tend to increase the warming. There's a positive feedback from the reduction in cloud amount. There's a positive feedback in the fact that the average cloud altitude goes up, driving the average cloud temperature down. There's also a positive feedback from the reduced cloud albedo, the lowered reflectivity of the clouds.

I can't tell you if this is what will happen in the real world. The models differ from one another. The factor-of-three difference between the most sensitive and least sensitive models is due mainly to the different rules used for clouds. In the models that are most sensitive to CO_2, these positive feedbacks are especially strong. In the models that are least sensitive to CO_2, these positive feedbacks are quantitatively weaker, or are partially compensated for by negative feedbacks. Thus, the credibility of the model simulations depends to a great extent on whether the rules used for clouds are realistic or not.

We're not yet completely able to explain the climate record of the past, let alone that of the future. When we look at the temperature record of the last 100 years, it's difficult to explain the ups and downs. The Dust Bowl of the 1930s is hard to account for, it wasn't predicted, and in hindsight it still isn't fully understood. When we look further back in time, there were substantial climate changes then too. The Middle Ages, for example, brought to Europe a climate very different from today's climate, as we know from written records and from so-called "proxy" data, such as agricultural records, from which unobserved climate parameters can be inferred.

When we look still further back, we know that ice ages have come and gone one after another, typically lasting for periods of tens of thousands of years, and we don't have a way, you might say, to back that out of the equations. We don't have a computer simulation, a model of how the climate system works, that says there ought to have been ice ages, or there ought to have been a Dust Bowl. In short, we can't explain paleoclimates and we can't even look back and explain the climate just since the Industrial Revolution—during the last 100 years. That is, you can't take a climate model, add the carbon dioxide that we know has been put into the atmosphere since the nineteenth century, add the other trace gases, and come up with an explanation for the way that temperature has risen and fallen over the globe for the last century or so.

Weather forecasts are notoriously fallible, and I've already said that the models used to make climate simulations are the same kinds of models used to make weather forecasts. We know that tomorrow's weather forecast is sometimes not right, and the weather forecast for a week ahead is nearly always wrong. I don't know and you don't know whether next summer is going to be unusually warm or cool or wet or dry in any particular part of the world. If I knew the answer to that for, say, the coffee-producing regions, I could make a lot of money in the coffee-futures market. In fact, commodities trading houses have meteorologists on staff these days to try to do exactly that, but no one is consistently very good at it. We have a slightly-better-than-chance record of predicting some kinds of seasonal variations, and that for only certain parts of the world.

So, with this mixed record of scattered successes and considerable failure, how much trust should we put in the predictions of these same models for climate change due to doubling CO_2? What is our justification for believing the computer simulations? Is it merely hubris, a word that connotes excessive pride?

My personal answer to the question of the trustworthiness of climate models—and you must decide whether you agree or not—is that we should take them seriously, but not literally. What do I mean by that? The models, though they differ quantitatively, all agree that the climate will warm substantially due to a doubling of CO_2. This is a result to be taken seriously. Where the models differ most significantly, perhaps, is in the regional distribution of the effects, and it is there that we should be careful about taking them literally.

Remember, a climate model is actually just a computer program, a set of instructions to a machine, acting on a mountain of real and synthetic data, out of which comes a simulation of climate in the form of global maps of such parameters as temperature and precipitation. By analyzing the results of many such simulations in detail, we may improve our understanding of how the many different physical processes interact to determine climate. In conjunction with other kinds of climate research, like observational research to improve our knowledge of the actual, present-day climate, computer simulations can lead to insight into how the climate system works. Computer scenarios of future climate, like studies of past climate variability, offer clues about what might happen.

But our understanding is still too tentative and incomplete for us to place full trust in the models. Their promise is great. As science advances, and experience piles up, we can expect the models to become better and better mimics of reality. For the present, they are perhaps best thought of as fascinating *gedanken* experiments to guide and stimulate our thinking. Much has been learned from them already, but we're still far from possessing a complete understanding of the climate system and its variability and predictability. I'm often asked how much confidence we should place in the results of climate models. The question can be posed in various ways, but people clearly want to know whether the prospect of substantial climate change from an increased greenhouse effect is a bleak certainty or a highly unlikely possibility that can safely be ignored. My answer is that neither characterization is appropriate. Climate change is an unsolved scientific challenge. It's a research problem.

5

REACTING TO CLIMATE CHANGE

The theories and computer simulations we've been talking about lead us to believe that the planet may well experience global warming in the coming years and decades, and that such a climate change could have serious ramifications for Earth's inhabitants. If this is true, what, if anything, should we do about it?

There are two recurring points to keep in mind. One is the definition of the greenhouse effect. Remember that the natural greenhouse effect is itself very strong, as demonstrated by the difference in temperature between the Earth and the Moon. There are many other convincing reasons to believe in the greenhouse effect. People who don't believe in it are the sort of people who don't believe in *anything* scientific—people who still think the Earth is flat or that men never really walked on the moon.

The validity of the greenhouse theory is beyond question. What we're concerned about is not whether it exists, but rather how seriously people *increase* the effect by changing the concentrations of the various greenhouse gases. Even though carbon dioxide is a rare gas—in every million molecules, only about 360 are CO_2—still, if we double that 360 value to 720, we're effecting a 100% change in the concentration of CO_2.

Since we're introducing a big change in the atmosphere's chemical composition, we have every reason to suspect that we might be having a significant impact on climate. The argument swirling over greenhouse projections—or more correctly, the degree of uncertainty with which they are made—has to do not with the natural greenhouse effect, but with the anthropogenic, or human, influence on that effect. It's really a quantitative argument: How much change will there be, and where, and when?

The second point to keep in mind is that the term "global warming" is basically a misnomer. We've compared it to a fever, a symptom of a disease. Change in the average temperature of the Earth is not noticeable to anybody. What you notice is what happens near you, and that's true whether you are a person or a plant. What happens near you is measured not just by temperature alone, but by a lot of other factors as well. It's precipitation. It's sea-level rise—if you're living at the beach and the beach disappears, you notice that; if your whole country is close to a beach, as certain island nations are, and your country disappears, you surely notice that.

So when we say "global warming," we're not fully describing the many possible implications of an enhanced greenhouse effect. "Global warming" has a nice ring to it, but it doesn't convey the whole story.

Recall that a strengthened greenhouse effect may increase sea level, because warm water takes up more volume than cold water, and because ice melts. Sea level may rise by a meter, by 3 feet or so, over the next century. That's about what the Dutch are counting on as they plan to build and maintain their dikes, for example. Even a 1-meter rise in sea level translates into the loss of a great deal of low-lying land. Florida is in trouble, Venice is in trouble, a number of South Pacific island nations are in serious trouble, Bangladesh is in deep trouble. (They may not necessarily completely disappear under water, although the cover of one of the books on this subject has a picture of the Statue of Liberty with just the arm and the torch above the sea.)

There are other, less certain, potential consequences of an increased greenhouse effect and a warmer climate. Hurricanes may increase in intensity—the strongest hurricanes, the Hugos and the Gilberts, may become stronger still—because hurricanes get their energy from the warm tropical ocean, and warmer oceans can feed hurricanes more energy. El Niños, the Pacific phenomena that affect the climate in many parts of the world, will become more frequent in a warmer climate, according to some theories.

All of these scenarios are conjectural. They're hypothetical outlooks. Climate always varies from year to year. It's in the context of that natural variation that we're trying to discern the *long-term* results of changes in the greenhouse effect. We'll still see in the future, as best we understand these processes today, successions of wet years and dry years, just as we've seen in the past. We'll still see unusually cool winters and unusually warm summers from time to time. And we'll see the reverse in other years. Superimposed on that natural variability, however, we expect to see a long-term change toward a warmer climate, as well as other systematic changes. That warming, in other words, will be mixed in with the normal year-to-year variability. An engineer might call that the "signal embedded in the noise." The signal is the long-term rise in temperature; the noise is the normal year-to-year variation.

Until there is an incontrovertible basis for stating that adding carbon dioxide to the atmosphere increases the greenhouse effect, and that the increase in the greenhouse effect leads to climate changes that cause agriculture to suffer and people to lose waterfront property, it may be hard to motivate people and nations to do anything about it.

When we talk about the enhancement of the greenhouse effect, we're talking about a problem that's still very much in a state of active research. It's not something that was settled in the sixteenth century and sealed up in dusty books. We're talking about an understanding that's still being heightened and altered, bit by bit, week by week. Science is an active process, a continuing, evolving enterprise. The greenhouse effect is a wonderful modern example of that. It's a very exciting time to be a part of climate science as a participant, an exciting time to watch the science unfold.

As an example of this rapid scientific evolution, there are important differences between recent climate-model results and those of just a few years ago, when the models showed different climate changes over the oceans in response to doubling CO_2. One reason for these differences is that our ability to simulate oceans in the computer has increased. We have come to understand better what makes them tick, to predict better how the circulation of the sea will change as the climate evolves. We now realize that what's going on in the ocean involves not just the absorption of heat in the thin skin at the ocean's surface but also changes in the deep circulation of the ocean that represent longer time scales.

Compared to that of the atmosphere, the response of the ocean is slow and sluggish. It's a gigantic flywheel, a buffer for the climate system, because of its great heat capacity—it takes a lot of heat to change the ocean's temperature. This results in a lag in the climate's response to CO_2, because that response depends on circulation change, and ocean circulation is slow in comparison to atmospheric circulation. It's striking to think that because all the water in the ocean circulates, the water at the bottom of the sea will eventually get to the top of the sea. Later that water will descend again to the bottom. But this doesn't happen in an hour, or a week, or a month; it takes more like 1,000 years. It might be 800 years in one place, 1,200 years in another. Regardless, it's a very long time.

Even the upper ocean takes decades to respond to a stimulus like the doubling of CO_2. That's probably one reason why the actions that society has taken in putting greenhouse gases into the atmosphere, today and in the recent past, are not yet apparent in the observed climatic record. That's what introduces this very long time scale into the problem. When we put chlorofluorocarbons into the atmosphere, we see relatively rapid changes in ozone content. But with the other greenhouse gases, the process is stretched out, beyond the thinking horizon of many people and beyond the practical horizon for many politicians. The bad news emerges long after the next election.

Keep in mind, then, that while we're talking about CO_2 changes, other things are happening at the same time. I've mentioned that what we're dealing with is an ongoing modification of the evolution of an always-evolving planet. We've become actors in a play in which we were previously members of the audience. The play is still going on. The planet is still changing. It's been changing since the day it was formed. But now we're active participants in Earth's evolution, and no longer merely passive spectators.

As we begin to consider what decisions to make in view of the evidence we now have on the enhanced greenhouse effect, one of our first choices concerns the type of science to pursue. Here I will introduce a distinction between two kinds of science. I'll call them (as many others have) big science and little science.

Big science is a relatively modern development. It's big in the sense that it often involves teams of individuals. Big in the sense that it is often well organized. Big in the sense that its impetus may have come not from one person's brain, but from committees and government agencies and legislative hearings. And big, above all, in the sense that it's expensive. The classic example of big science is space science. It usually costs upwards of $100 million, and sometimes much more, to create a satellite and launch it. A multi-satellite program can run into billions of dollars. Astronomical telescopes and accelerators for particle physics are other examples of big science.

The big science I want to address first is the tool with which climate predictions are made, a tool we discussed earlier. The predictions involve gigantic computer simulations in very big computers. When we say a computer is big, what we really mean is that its memory capacity and speed are much greater than the memory and speed of ordinary computers, not that its physical size is particularly large. It can store a vast amount of numbers, and it can perform calculations very rapidly. Such computers are sometimes called supercomputers.

These computers tend to cost around $10 million each. That's been true for a long time, even though the big computers of today are much more powerful than the big computers of 10 or 20 or 40 years ago. Ten million dollars is a lot of money by anybody's standards. And the building to put the computer in and the staff to run it and gather data for it and all the rest of that can run the cost up to several tens of millions of dollars.

The kinds of computer simulations that we've discussed in studying the greenhouse effect come from machines of that class. And they're sometimes dedicated exclusively to this purpose. As you read on, think about how, if you were in charge of the money, you'd choose to spend the dollars. If you had $10 million, would it be better to buy one computer or to pay the salaries of a large number of individual scientists, one of whom might think of something that no committee or group or computer simulation could come up with? It's a practical, everyday problem, this question of how science gets funded and how we choose to do the kinds of science we do.

As an example, let's consider the federal agencies in the United States that support research in the area of global change. They include NASA (National Aeronautics and Space Administration), NOAA (National Oceanic and Atmospheric Administration), the Department of Energy, and the National Science Foundation, the primary supporter of basic research. These are some of the organizations whose dollars pay for the research that we've been talking about.

If you add up the budgets for global-change research of all those U.S. agencies, you will find that most of it goes to NASA, because space research—which yields so much of our observational data on global processes—is so expensive. It costs so much money to build space shuttles, to build satellites, to launch satellites, to build ground stations, and to hire people to process the data. It's a colossally expensive business—a business that didn't exist, after all, not so long ago. It didn't exist in the 1950s, when there *were* no satellites.

All this has changed the way we think about science, the way we do science, and the way we pay for it. It has made science expensive. We can do things we couldn't do before we had satellites, computers, and the other expensive tools. But there is a price to be paid.

There is a continual tension, a continual struggle, on many levels, including political levels, between big science and little science. In some ways, big science seems pedestrian—it's committee-like, bureaucratic—whereas little science has a great deal of inherent charm and emotional appeal.

In our story so far, we've heard about a number of "little" scientists, colorful individuals in many cases. Remember Richardson, the Englishman who first thought of the idea of computing the weather. And Keeling, the man who has devoted his life to measuring atmospheric carbon dioxide.

Recall Keeling's curve, the wiggly line rising from left to right showing the approximately 10% increase in atmospheric carbon dioxide from 1958 until the present. Keeling's instrument, the one he built in 1958, is still chugging away at the Mauna Loa observatory on the slope of a volcano on the big island of Hawaii. It's now surrounded by many other instruments. It might cost a few hundred thousand dollars a year to maintain Keeling's observatory on Mauna Loa. Keeling himself has had to spend a lot of his time convincing the government that supporting that observatory is still worthwhile. An amount less than the salary of a middling professional athlete in many sports is all it takes to maintain the longest, continuous atmospheric carbon-dioxide record on Earth. But the argument gets made all the time that there are better, cheaper ways of doing it, that you don't have to keep that old instrument chugging away alongside the newer ones.

Confronted with this argument, Keeling counters that we need to be sure that new data are calibrated with the old data, that consistency in the record is crucial. We don't want to have the problem with CO_2 that we have with global temperature, where for example the thermometer at the airport was out in the countryside 20 years ago, but today it's in the city because the city expanded to include the airport, thus introducing a spurious warming into the temperature record. We don't want the problem we have with ocean-temperature biases, where the sailing routes changed and the ships got bigger, so the engine intakes got deeper, introducing a bias because water is colder with depth. Keeling can go on like that for a long time. He's trying to convince the government that the integrity of these data is worth maintaining.

Keeling offers an acute example of the single-minded dedication of many individual scientists. He really wants to measure CO_2, and apparently always has. Humanity should be grateful for his dedication to his work.

Little science was crucial to our story of the ozone hole as well. Recall that if it hadn't been for Joseph Farman, who went with his colleagues to Antarctica every year, and first saw the ozone there disappear, we wouldn't have known of the ozone hole, at least not as many years back as we did. Remember that NASA's satellite data on ozone amounts were ignored by the computer "quality-control" program because they seemed too low. This was a case in which big science, in the form of satellite observations, was not as adept as little science. It was Farman, making measurements with simpler instruments from the surface, who brought ozone depletion to the attention of the world.

Incidentally, both Keeling and Farman began their observations in the 1950s as a result of the International Geophysical Year, or IGY. The IGY was an international effort that stimulated many areas of Earth science research, and it certainly qualifies as big science. But it was the perseverance and dedication of Keeling and Farman that sustained their continued measurements over the decades that followed the IGY. In this instance, big and little science played complementary roles.

The discovery that chlorofluorocarbons destroy ozone was a *theoretical* finding, by Molina and Rowland. The realization that CFCs were also greenhouse gases was also a theoretical finding, from a brilliant young scientist, Ramanathan, right after he earned his Ph.D. No committee went out and said that these were subjects worth looking into, and no heaps of money were granted to these projects. These were the private passions of a few good scientists.

So, great research and great results come from both little science and big science. We can never do without the insights of gifted, brilliant people. On the other hand, it's hard to imagine learning what we need to know about the Earth without being able to look at it from the satellites, or without being able to simulate its climate by supercomputers. It would appear that a balanced program, integrating both big and little science, is needed. Finding that balance is crucial.

We turn now to the policies we might need to implement to reduce the consequences of an enhanced greenhouse effect in the future. One of the first that comes to many people's minds is reforestation: planting lots of trees. Deforestation affects all of us emotionally. Everybody can relate to the felling of a tree. Everybody can lament the loss of a great tropical rainforest.

Deforestation does play a significant role in increasing atmospheric carbon dioxide. It's also environmentally significant in many other ways, because it does great damage to the region where the forest used to be. It wrecks soil quality. It leads to poor agricultural practices. It accelerates the loss of biological diversity by destroying habitat, making it impossible for many animals and plants to live where they once did. In short, it's the plundering of a valuable long-term resource for short-term economic gain, or perhaps, in some of the impoverished countries where this practice is common, out of perceived short-term economic necessity.

Compared to fossil-fuel consumption, however, deforestation is only a secondary source of CO_2. That's why you can't stop the growth of CO_2 simply by planting trees. Don't misunderstand. I'm in favor of planting trees and I urge people to do it. It makes you feel good, it raises your consciousness, it improves the neighborhood, and it makes a place for birds to nest. Doing it is a step in the right direction, just as recycling cans is a step in the right direction. But reforestation shouldn't be looked upon as a panacea for controlling CO_2. We're often enamored of the goal of a technological fix, and we try to find a way we can compensate for bad habits, in much the same way we'd like to have a pill to make us healthy even if we eat and drink too much.

In dealing with CO_2, we'll do better to cut down on emissions by conserving energy, increasing energy efficiency, and developing alternative sources of energy, than by looking for a way to get the CO_2 out of the atmosphere once we've put it there. Many of the proposals for planetary engineering on a grand scale are, in general, far-fetched and impractical. We would have to reforest an area the size of Australia to keep up with the CO_2 we're putting into the atmosphere. Beyond that, we would then have to find a way to sequester those trees, lock them up, so that their stores of carbon wouldn't just go right back into the atmosphere. For when trees are burned, they release CO_2 to the atmosphere quickly. When they die from other causes, they decay—or the houses or paper or furniture they are turned into eventually burn or decay—and through that decay the carbon is again returned to the atmosphere, on a longer time scale. In either case, short of encasing the trees in concrete and dropping them to the bottom of Lake Michigan—an alternative known as the "Chicago Solution"—the CO_2 stored in trees eventually returns to the atmosphere.

There are many good reasons to plant trees, but planting trees and doing nothing else will not solve the CO_2 problem.

There's also a proposal to put iron in the ocean as a way to counteract global warming. The theory behind the idea is the following. One of the things that happens to CO_2 when you put it in the atmosphere is that part of it is taken up by the ocean. Part of the mechanism for taking up CO_2 in the ocean, one of the ways in which CO_2 can leave the air and go into the sea, is that it is taken up by small plants called phytoplankton. In parts of the ocean, it seems likely that the rate of growth of the phytoplankton is limited by the available iron. Just like some older people, some phytoplankton need iron too. Many things—various nutrients, sunlight, temperature—can encourage the growth of plants. At least for some kinds of phytoplankton in some parts of the ocean, some of the time, what seems to be needed is iron. In the laboratory, when you put these kinds of little plants in a test tube and add iron, the plant grows better.

The theory is that if you put iron in the ocean, phytoplankton will grow bigger, stronger, healthier, and more plentiful. And so they'll take up more CO_2. And presumably, you'll have done something toward stabilizing or reducing the CO_2 concentration in the atmosphere.

That's an example of planetary engineering. It's one of a number of ways you could think of to manage the chemical composition of the atmosphere. All the gases we've been talking about have sources and sinks—the plants we just discussed are a sink for atmospheric CO_2. They're a place where it can go. If we had enough phytoplankton taking up enough CO_2, you might suppose that we would succeed in helping to reduce CO_2 concentration in the atmosphere. Or at least keep it from rising so fast.

The difficulty with that scheme right now is that we don't know how effective it would be. We don't know how much iron it would take. We're not sure what would happen, for example, if you started such a program and then stopped it. Suppose you got tired of sending tankers of iron to this part of the ocean. Then the phytoplankton might die off and the CO_2 they hoarded would go back into the atmosphere.

The idea, called iron fertilization, has now been tried experimentally on a small scale in the ocean. The researchers chose a patch of ocean, dumped some iron in, and watched what happened. What they found was that, at first, the phytoplankton grew rapidly, but in just a few days, the rapid growth ceased, perhaps in part because the iron did not remain in the region. So the remedy did not have the desired effect.

Doing this type of thing on a larger scale is one of a class of actions that you could contemplate taking if you knew well how the climate system worked, and if you were wise enough to try to manage it and clever enough to foresee side effects and possible unwanted consequences. It would certainly seem more prudent to do laboratory experiments and small-scale trials first.

There are many other such plans. They're being considered in various academic, industrial, and governmental situations all over the world. One plan actually proposes to put mirrors in orbit to reflect away more sunlight. Another class of plans involves modifying the surface of the Earth to change its reflectivity.

So far, no one has initiated any large-scale attempt to do anything like that. For a number of reasons, we need to tread very carefully before we start tampering with the planet in such ways. We've done badly enough with inadvertent tampering. If we do things intentionally, with the best of wills and great care, we may nonetheless find the results to be other than what we expected.

It would be irresponsible to conduct a massive international intervention on our planet without being certain that there would be no unwanted side effects. Complicated plans, even simple, small-scale plans, can go wrong.

In a way it's encouraging, if you're an optimist, to think that there are many ways out of the possible dilemma of inadvertent large-scale environmental degradation. If you're a pessimist, it's disheartening to think that there are even more ways in which even well-meaning people can mess up the planet.

Nonetheless, adding iron to the oceans is an idea that's being seriously considered. A number of very reputable people are interested in it. (Incidentally, this idea of "iron fertilization" involves adding iron in a form the phytoplankton can use, not as great girders or old warships.)

If you're an optimist, you can foresee the happy day in the future when technology is powerful enough and people are wise enough that we'll manage the planet just right. We'll get the planet we want. We'll stabilize our population at a sensible number, our overall quality of life will improve, and we'll develop a heightened ecological consciousness, so that we'll have not only the planetary temperature we want, but protection for the forests, lakes, streams, plants and animals, and everything else. We're a long way from that today.

There are many reasons to be optimistic. I share the viewpoint that there's a lot that people can do about climate once they care about it and know about it. And a lot of what's happening in science offers insight into the climate, into how to predict climate change, and how to cope with inevitable climate change.

Modern technology is impressive. We've all seen photos of the whole Earth as seen from a satellite. From space we can now monitor snow cover, for example, over North America, over northern Europe, over Siberia and China. Until very recently, we couldn't do that. We now have a bird's-eye view of the whole planet. We have a way of measuring the temperature over the whole globe, not just where ships happen to go, or where people happen to settle. We can measure the temperature with uniform accuracy and uniform coverage, and we can do so day after day, month after month, year after year. Several countries are committed to multibillion-dollar programs involving satellites that observe not just temperature, but ocean currents, sea ice, land-surface uses, and other features of the climate system.

We're fortunate that the greenhouse effect seems to act on a long natural time scale. There may be time, not only to change our ways and to use energy more sensibly, for example, but also to do research on the climate system, to understand it better, and to monitor it vigilantly for change. However, we ought not to become complacent. The sudden appearance of the ozone hole was a warning example. Nature might easily surprise us again.

We must remember, however, that there will always be random events. The whole question of climate predictability is fascinating, for random things *will happen*—volcanoes erupting, for example—that will forever limit our ability to make accurate forecasts.

Nonrandom, intentional things may happen as well. The burning of the Kuwaiti oil wells during and after the Gulf War comes quickly to mind as an example of environmental terrorism. Let's look briefly at how it affected the climate.

As soon as it became clear that enormous quantities of smoke were rising from the roughly 600 wells set afire in Kuwait in late February 1991, several speculations appeared in the press immediately. The general tone of many of them was that this was a small-scale "nuclear winter" scenario. Nuclear winter invokes the idea that one of the consequences of a large-scale nuclear "exchange" (to use the sanitized language favored by some people) would be large-scale fires and the injection of a great deal of smoke and soot and other material into the atmosphere. The result could theoretically block enough sunlight to plunge the planet into a severe cold spell—a nuclear winter.

There have been a number of inadvertent small-scale tests of this notion—small-scale only with respect to nuclear war, sufficiently large-scale if you were personally involved. One of them was the firestorms that occurred during World War II when certain cities were intensively bombed. Another is volcanic eruptions. Still another is forest fires. The burning oil wells in Kuwait, because of the extent and intensity of the fires and because they persisted so long, were in some ways a more serious test.

It may seem callous to look on this terrible disaster, a human and environmental tragedy, as a kind of fortuitous laboratory exercise. Nonetheless, people and instruments were rushed to Kuwait in an international effort to measure the effects of the fires. If this fiasco had a silver lining, it is that we've learned something about the consequences of such terrorism.

Initial speculation was that so much smoke would be put into the atmosphere that sunlight would be blocked over a large region, temperatures would fall, and crops would suffer. Perhaps the smoke might even affect areas far downwind, including the area of the Indian monsoon, an annual event that is critically important to the economy and sustenance of the region.

It seems that those early projections proved too pessimistic. There were no reports of serious large-scale disruption to the climate outside the local region. It's certainly true that immediately downwind and within the area of the fires, there was less sunlight and some cooling resulted, but these were local effects that lasted for only a limited time.

One of the uncertainties about nuclear winter, about that whole subject, is how long the smoke will stay in the atmosphere. How high up is it transported, how far does the wind take it, how long does it take the atmosphere to cleanse itself? We don't know yet.

The most immediate and most serious consequences of the Kuwait fires were not due to the smoke. There were many other horrible results. Toxic pools, for example, were everywhere. The smoke made things worse, but if you had to list the injuries to the environment of that region, worst injuries first, smoke wouldn't be at the top of the list.

In global terms, the carbon dioxide added to the atmosphere was modest compared to everything else. Even though these were huge fires that put a great amount of CO_2 and other things into the atmosphere, still, compared to what the other 5 billion of us were doing, their effect wasn't great. It appears that the fires contributed about 1% of the total global emission of CO_2 for that year. Remember, gases are dispersed very quickly; although the concentration of CO_2 and other combustion products was high locally, it was soon scattered by winds.

The Kuwait fires did serve to remind us that, in some respects, we live in an unpredictable world. It's difficult to include things like intentional mass burnings of oil wells among the parameters that drive computer climate simulations. But one thing that *is* predictable is that if we continue to burn fossil fuels, we'll continue to add CO_2 to the atmosphere, and we'll continue to exacerbate the greenhouse effect.

You may wonder if the problem won't eventually be solved automatically, when we run out of fossil fuels to burn, in the same way that an alcoholic's problem is solved if you send the person to Saudi Arabia. It's certainly true that fossil fuels represent a finite resource, but many projections of when they will run out have proved to be wrong. According to some older projections, we should have run out already. But prospecting continues. We're still finding substantial deposits of coal, oil, and natural gas.

Although readily recoverable cheap oil may be among the first fossil fuels to become scarce, coal won't be scarce for a long time. China, for example, is sitting atop literally mountains of coal. One of the big questions in predicting CO_2 levels in the atmosphere is what China will choose to do with that coal. Will it choose to industrialize along the Western model by massive use of coal to generate energy? China may not feel the need for luxuries in the near term, but may very well want to have at least what we would consider the basic necessities of an industrialized economy: rural electrification, energy to power factories, heat for homes, and so on.

So the real question in projecting future CO_2 levels is what will happen in what is now the less developed world, and how that world will choose to use the fossil fuels that will be available in this time frame.

For instance, today the United States produces more CO_2 than any other country. But that will not always be true. The population of the United States is about 260 million. China has more than 1 billion people—between four and five times as many people as we have. Even though the Chinese currently produce less CO_2 on a per-capita basis, they probably will eventually surpass the United States as a net producer of CO_2—by early in the 21st century, according to some estimates. So the United States may lose the dubious distinction of being the single worst contributor to the problem.

That means that CO_2 is an international problem—perhaps even more so than the ozone problem. Chlorofluorocarbons can be substituted for in the relatively few countries where they're used and produced, but every country produces CO_2. And since the action of the atmosphere mixes gases around the world uniformly, the concentration of CO_2 is about 360 parts per million just about anywhere you choose to measure it, unless you locate your instrument right behind the tailpipe of a car.

It's wrong to think that you can change your local climate by changing local emissions of CO_2. Air gets mixed throughout the whole world. The 1995 reading of 360 parts per million we get from Keeling's instrument is the result of all the CO_2 put into the atmosphere everywhere, all mixed together.

Clearly, this problem has an inherently international dimension, and therefore its solution, if there is to be one, must be inherently international as well. One country can't solve this. Even if the United States just shut down tomorrow morning, never put another molecule of CO_2 into the atmosphere, we'd still have a problem, because the United States has only a small fraction of the world's population. It's responsible for far less than half of the CO_2 produced globally.

It's apparent, then, why equity arguments arise between countries. Questions often take the form of, "Why must we in the Third World forgo the advantages of industrial development and become more conservative in burning fossil fuels than you in the advanced countries have been for the last century, when it is exactly that development that has made you advanced?" Or, "Who are you, having caused this problem, to tell us, who are trying to improve the quality of life for our people, how to generate energy?" Or, more bluntly, "If you want us, the Third World, to limit the rate at which we emit carbon dioxide and other greenhouse gases, how about supplying us with financial help so that we might develop the technologies that will enable us to take alternative paths?"

Those are samples of the questions that arise. Even more frightening questions, which one can easily imagine being asked, may be posed by countries suffering deleterious climate changes, such as the droughts that have afflicted sub-Saharan Africa. Affected countries may believe, rightly or wrongly, that the climate changes they're experiencing are due to an enhanced greenhouse effect. Such countries might ask for compensation for the harm caused by other countries. The international ramifications of this problem are potentially complex, severe, and dangerous to political stability.

I find it poignant, to use an analogy offered by Charles David Keeling, that if the forecasts are right, then as time goes on the U.S. Congress will become more and more convinced of the reality of global warming. Then, after some decades, you'll finally be able to muster two-thirds of the members of both houses of Congress to admit that the enhancement of the greenhouse effect is real. Perhaps it will take compelling evidence in the form of something as dramatic as the ozone hole to make people recognize that the climate has actually changed, and that we're the reason why.

6

GLOBAL-CHANGE CAUSES
AND REMEDIES

Up to this point, we've looked in depth at two of the most prominent issues of global change, stratospheric ozone depletion and an increased greenhouse effect. Before we take up other environmental problems, such as acid rain and air pollution, this is a good opportunity to step back and look at global environmental concerns in sum. Why are these concerns coming to the fore at this particular time in history? What can we as a species hope to do about the most pressing aspects of global change? These are the vital issues we shall examine next.

Let's discuss these global problems in terms of the number of people on the planet. If you're still wondering why the major global-change problems all seem to be arising now, a few facts will bring the fundamental reason home in a hurry.

What is remarkable about our time is the rate at which the world's population is growing. In the four seconds it takes you to read this sentence, there are 16 more people on Earth. In two days' time, the population of the planet will increase by enough people to populate another San Francisco. It took almost the entire history of the human race for global population to grow to 2 billion, a magnitude that was not achieved until the early 1930s. Since then, the rate of growth has been astounding, by any measure. The 3 billion mark was passed in 1960. Population exceeded 4 billion in 1974. The 5 billion figure was reached in 1987.

Global population in 1993 was about 5.6 billion, and the annual increase in recent years has been almost 90 million. The annual increase is the difference between the number of people who are born and the number who die each year. So each year, nearly 90 million more people are born than die. Thus, 90 million is the *net increase,* not the number of births. Incidentally, if you add together the current populations of Great Britain, Ireland, Iceland, Belgium, Denmark, Norway, Sweden, and Finland—nearly all of northern Europe outside of Germany—the total is not far from 90 million. Another way to dramatize the rate at which population is increasing is to realize that the demographic equivalent of another Switzerland is being added to Earth *every month.*

Even if this rate of increase—this nearly 90 million per year—were to remain constant, every decade or so we would continue to add almost another billion people to the Earth. Furthermore, most of the increase today is occurring in developing countries, such as India. During 1993, India's population increased by nearly 17 million. That was more than the combined increase of Europe, the former Soviet Union, all of Latin America, and the United States. In 1993, 94% of the world's population growth occurred in developing countries. Of the 5.6 billion people on Earth, more than three out of every four people now live in developing nations.

So there you see exponential growth in very dramatic terms. It's thus no accident that the enhanced greenhouse effect, acid rain, and the ozone hole, all of which are examples of planetary consequences of human activity, are occurring now. There just are more of us now. We're also living in ways different from our forebears; in particular, we use vastly more energy. All of these facets of global change are, in one way or another, by-products of the way we live and use energy.

How many people will there be in the year 2100? Demographers estimate that, barring catastrophe, there will be at least 9 billion human beings on Earth, no matter what is done in an effort to reduce population growth. Without any real attempt at serious measures to limit population, that number might be even more. The United Nations estimated in 1982 that world population would stabilize in 2100 at a level of 10.2 billion people. Today, that estimate appears to have been overly optimistic. The U.N. now expects population growth to continue beyond the year 2200, and that the total global population will reach 11.6 billion, more than twice the number of people alive today.

Africa is the fastest-growing region, and, because today 45% of Africans are not yet 15 years old, their childbearing years are still ahead of them, and there is little likelihood that African population-growth rates will soon decline sharply. In China, by contrast, population growth has slowed dramatically. There, the total fertility rate, the number of children borne by the average woman during her lifetime, dropped dramatically from 2.3 to 1.9 between 1991 and 1993. Much of this drop can probably be attributed to an increasingly harsh enforcement of the Chinese government policy decreeing strictly that each couple should have only one child.

If we were to assume that absolutely nothing affecting population would change, and that we would continue to experience these rates of population growth, how long could the Earth survive? The answer is that the Earth will be around, at best estimates, for several billion years. The more interesting question is: How much time do *we* have? "Saving the planet" is a sloppy use of language. What we're talking about is saving *us.*

My answer, and it is not from any special source of wisdom, is that the amount of time you have depends very much on who you are and where you live. The rich people in the developed countries have a relatively long time before they must face the consequences of a world with too many people on it, but the poorest people in the Third World are already in a disastrous situation. The Malthusian catastrophe of death by starvation and disease is already a reality. It's not happening in the fashionable neighborhoods of the great cities of Europe, Japan, or North America. It's happening in countries such as Chad, Somalia, and Ethiopia.

All of this is germane to the issues we've talked about. If the climate change that accompanies an increase in the greenhouse effect results in changing patterns of rainfall and drought, for example, the agriculture that may be best able to adapt is the well-developed agriculture of the First World, with irrigation, advanced soil science, genetically engineered crops, and the like. In regions where there's already too little food to feed too many people, and where there's no adequate infrastructure, the people and their governments simply do not have these options. There is no way for them to respond to the threats posed by climate change. Those are the areas that will be in the worst trouble.

Thus, the answer to the question, "How much time do we have?" is not a single number of years, but rather depends on several factors, just as the answer to the question, "What will the climate change be?" is not a single number, like 2, 4, or 6 degrees of warming. The answer to the climate question involves a whole complex of issues having to do with all aspects of climate, including frequency of droughts, rising sea level, extremes of temperature, and changes in El Niños and Indian monsoons. We use temperature in this context as a metaphor; I've compared it to fever, a symptom but not a description, of a human disease.

Expressing the number of years that we have left before an overpopulation catastrophe befalls us is a useful metaphor, and a way of making these issues concrete. But the real truth is that the repercussions of excessive population are likely to be highly uneven. And that is as it has always been. Throughout history, ordinary people have always been more vulnerable to natural calamities than the wealthy and privileged.

Some of us like to look at this situation optimistically. We like to think ours is a savvy species, that we can fix anything. If we caused a problem, then we'll find a solution for it. If you want to think optimistically in those terms—as I do—consider this: Perhaps the very fact that the planet *is* so teeming with people now, and the fact that the consequences of this heavy population burden are becoming clear in so many ways, will spur us to attack the fundamental problem of how to limit the number of people on the planet. How do we, to use the catch phrase of today, design a sustainable planet? How do we reach an equilibrium?

With that in mind, let's look at how a couple of countries compare in terms of what they do to the global environment. Let's use the problem of carbon dioxide adding to the greenhouse effect as our illustrative example. If we get our energy mainly from fossil fuels, and if that energy production is the source of the CO_2 we add to the atmosphere, then one way to estimate how much a given country increases the greenhouse effect is to calculate how much energy it uses. With these assumptions, the calculation is easy to do. We'll use approximate data from about 1990. The first country we'll consider is the United States.

There were about 250 million people in the United States in 1990, and they used about 280 gigajoules of commercial energy (energy that comes from a power plant as opposed to a wood stove) per person per year (*giga* means billion and a *joule* is a metric unit). An idle person, or a conscientious person trying to conserve energy, might use considerably less, whereas someone who flies often can easily be responsible for three or four times as much energy usage as the average American. But on average, the figure is around 280 gigajoules per person. Then the total energy usage (gigajoules per year per person, multiplied by number of people) is 280 times 250 million people, or 70 billion gigajoules per year.

Let's take another country. For India in 1990, population was about 835 million, more than three times the U.S. population. But per-capita commercial energy consumption for India was only around 8 gigajoules, compared to the U.S. value of 280. The product for India is, therefore, about 7 billion gigajoules per year, in round numbers, compared to 70 for the United States Thus, India, with more than three times the U.S. population, has only about one-tenth the U.S. effect on the environment, using the assumptions made above.

That remarkable result is at least qualitatively consistent with a number of other striking facts. For example, about 75% of the carbon dioxide put into the atmosphere now comes from rich First World countries, such as the United States, Canada, Japan, Australia, and the nations of Western Europe. By contrast, more than 75% of the world's people now live in developing countries, where per-capita energy usage is generally much lower than that in the First World. So 25% of the people are producing 75% of the problem. CO_2 is released whenever we make energy by burning fuels like coal, oil, and natural gas. To date, Indians are not for the most part driving many cars or heating and air conditioning large houses or using large amounts of electricity. Bearing in mind that nearly all the world's population growth is occurring in the Third World, the calculation of a country's CO_2 production that we just undertook should warn us about the likely future course of the enhanced greenhouse effect. It illustrates dramatically that the largest potential danger of massive additional CO_2 emissions is to be found not in the First World, but in the developing countries.

A calculation this simple can't be stretched too far. But we can test it to see whether its consequences make sense. Certainly, if it is CO_2 that we're interested in, and if the CO_2 comes from burning fossil fuels, then our calculation is probably a pretty good first estimate, because it just says that the amount of CO_2 released is going to be proportional to the amount of energy used. It assumes that we're producing energy by burning coal, oil, and gas to make the CO_2.

This sort of calculation does ignore the differences in CO_2 emissions among the various fossil fuels. For example, extracting a given amount of energy from coal produces more CO_2 than would be the case if you used oil, which in turn produces more than would be produced by natural gas. In fact, coal is about twice as "dirty" as natural gas, in terms of how much CO_2 is released to obtain a given amount of energy. These differences, which stem from differences in the carbon content per unit of energy from the various fuels, are not considered in this simplified calculation, but could be incorporated (and are, by scientists) if we wanted a more accurate result.

In doing this calculation, we're assuming additionally that the adverse effect of energy production on the environment lies simply in the amount of CO_2 emitted. That is indeed going to be the product of the population times the amount of CO_2 for which each person is responsible, which we have further assumed is proportional to the energy we use. For CO_2, the culprit we've been using as a paradigm global-change example, this is probably a fairly reasonable means of constructing a first idea of the magnitude of our contribution to increasing the greenhouse effect. Our technique, however, ignores all the other adverse environmental consequences of using fossil fuels as an energy source.

One of the advantages of a simple theoretical model, like this calculation, is that it helps to make clearer some of the things we've discussed before, and it allows us to evaluate the consequences of actions we might take. For example, the United States could make a serious effort to cut back its fossil fuel use, but even if it did so, this effort alone would not necessarily reduce the global problem in a major way. Why? Because just a slight increase in the per-capita energy consumption of developing countries with large populations could more than offset the U.S. action. As time goes on, Americans will contribute a smaller percentage of the world total of CO_2 emissions, and unilateral action to reduce U.S. emissions will have a proportionately lesser effect. Nevertheless, the United States and the other wealthy industrial countries must clearly play a leadership role if the developing nations are to avoid the inefficient and environmentally hazardous fossil-fuel route that the developed countries have generally taken.

Consider the probable future growth of population in India. If you make optimistic estimates about the success of birth control, which is a monumental problem in India—and for this purpose you can encourage birth control any way you want, through abstinence, contraceptives, or other methods—the *optimistic* estimates predict that India's population will reach at least 2 billion, over roughly the next century. Barring some unforeseen catastrophe, such as war or epidemic, this estimate implies that the population of India will inevitably grow by a factor of nearly two and a half, from, say, 835 million to 2 billion. It's frightening to realize that the population *of the entire world* in the early 1930s was

2 billion, and that the same number of human beings are now apparently destined to be crammed onto the Indian subcontinent.

Incidentally, it's now widely recognized that the key to reducing birth rates and lowering family sizes is not simply distributing condoms and birth-control pills, but also taking a range of other actions, always including educating and empowering women. Family planning must be combined with the provision of improved health care. Governments need to adopt and actively support policies that emphasize the desirability of small families, and a variety of contraceptive techniques must be made readily available. Infant mortality rates must be reduced, so that families won't produce many children in hopes that some will survive. In countries where total fertility rates are now highest, these conditions have emphatically not been achieved. It's still true today in some African nations that an average woman will bear seven or more children during her lifetime.

The great majority of the nearly 90 million people currently added each year to the planet live in the Third World, including China and India, the two countries with the largest populations. China's population is only slightly larger than India's, a little more than a billion right now. But in India there appear to be cultural barriers to population control that do not exist in China. And because there is no authoritarian central government in India, India's population may well overtake China's on the way to reaching the 2-billion mark. We're speaking about only a few decades; it need not take very long for India to become the most populous nation on Earth.

Thus, even with a relatively small increase in India's per-capita energy consumption—you needn't equip each Indian family with a large American-style house and air conditioning and three inefficient cars, but just allow it a modest increase in energy usage—the population multiplier is so great that it could easily swamp any effort to cut back fossil-fuel use in the United States, and global emissions of CO_2 could continue to increase.

What should we do about this? Once you have these kinds of numbers staring you in the face, what is the best response?

The appropriate response to the problem of climate change caused by an enhanced greenhouse effect must be global. This problem is unlike those that are solvable by relatively local means, like urban air pollution. It's also unlike global problems that have technological fixes, like ozone depletion, which can be stemmed by eliminating chlorofluorocarbons and related compounds.

The first principle likely to earn widespread support is that we ought not to use the lack of scientific certainty as an excuse for postponing all actions. When we analyzed the various climate-model predictions and saw how broadly they differed, we could agree that the large differences among them mean that at most one of these models is right, and more likely that none is exactly right. You could ask, given that level of scientific uncertainty, can we not postpone action altogether? The plain fact is that population and fossil-fuel use are increasing in the meantime, and we would be knowingly exacerbating the problem while waiting for the scientists to understand it better.

An analogy used by Paul Ehrlich of Stanford University is this: Suppose there is only a 5% chance that the environmental change is going to be gravely serious. Suppose, that is, that the science is so uncertain that there's only one chance in 20 that we will have, for example, a catastrophic rise in sea level or a catastrophic disruption of agricultural productivity. Would you get on an airplane if the chances were one in 20 that it would crash? Probably not. An eventuality that yields such serious consequences is well worth worrying about, low likelihood or not.

A second principle with wide appeal is to take actions that have other benefits, so-called collateral benefits. By this I mean the sorts of things that people agree are "win-win" propositions, the ones that would benefit humankind even if climate change were not a concern. For example, improved energy efficiency, additional energy conservation, and increased use of renewable sources of energy are at the top of almost everybody's list. Those measures would decrease environmental damage in other ways, even if there were no serious climatic change to worry about, even if the climate turns out to be robust and resilient in ways that we have not foreseen. The process of extracting energy from fossil fuels has many other adverse environmental consequences, like smog, like tanker accidents, and like what happens to a piece of the Earth where a strip mine operates. So reducing the use of fossil fuels reduces pollution in general. It also reduces acid precipitation and deposition (acid rain and its solid equivalent), which is mainly a product of the burning of high-sulfur coal.

Depending on how you go about reducing the use of fossil fuels, you have a chance to yield some other benefits as well. For example, the retail price of gasoline in Europe is much higher than in the United States, because gasoline is heavily taxed in Europe. The United States could consider the European stance carefully but then conclude that a $3-a-gallon gasoline tax imposed tomorrow morning in the United States would be unacceptably punitive, especially on people least able to pay it. It would be a regressive tax—the impact of sales taxes generally falls hardest on the poorest people.

But let's say the United States gradually phased in some sort of "carbon tax," and not necessarily a $3-a-gallon gasoline tax, over some considerable time, so that people got used to it. After all, Americans didn't get used to income tax immediately; it was phased in gradually over time, and now Americans think it's normal. If the United States introduced a carbon tax like that, and if it were one that people agreed was an equitable way to achieve a socially worthwhile goal, then the tax would not only motivate people to use less gasoline—by buying more fuel-efficient cars, living closer to work, walking or biking to work, car pooling, telecommuting, etc.—but it would also generate revenue. The United States could then use that revenue, for example, as is done in some other countries, to help promote mass transit, which would help relieve the burden on the people on whom the gasoline tax hits hardest. These same people might be the ones to gain the most benefit from buses, light rail, van pools, and other conveyances that could be bought with the money from the carbon tax. That's one scenario.

At the same time, Americans might find other economic benefits as well. Since a significant fraction of the fossil fuel used in the United States is imported oil, the country would decrease its trade deficit, reduce its balance-of-payments problem, and increase national security through lower dependence on foreign sources of energy. And those who would be spending less money on gasoline would have more money to spend on something else. A carbon tax might even promote activities that are healthful and socially worthwhile, too, like walking.

The rich countries generally do not have rapidly increasing populations. Some rich countries, notably Japan and certain Western European countries, have already effectively achieved zero population growth. And other countries are rather close to it. The United States, unfortunately, is an exception. In round numbers, the U.S. population is growing by about 3 million people per year. Of this number, approximately 2 million results from the excess of births over deaths, and about 1 million from immigration. In the early 1990s, the total fertility rate, the average number of children born by each woman in the United States, rose above 2.0 for the first time in 20 years. It's now about 2.1. That's regression, not progress toward a sustainable future.

For the wealthy countries, sustainable development—development that can be kept up for some considerable time—may not mean an increase in gross national product. It might mean a decrease in gross national product and an increase in quality of life.

To pick an example, if you think people are better off when they ride bicycles than when they drive cars, then every time you alter the transportation system away from motor vehicles and toward bicycles, you have increased the quality of life while decreasing energy consumption and carbon-dioxide production. That's an option that's open to rich countries.

The converse is the scary part. Even if you believe global population can soon be stabilized—and nobody thinks it can be at 6 billion, though some are sanguine about less than 10 billion—you're dangerously mistaken to think that you can enjoy perpetual economic growth based on fossil fuels as the primary energy source. If you think you can keep population constant in a country or in the world and just keep increasing the amount of fossil fuel that each person consumes, then you're being naive about the capacity of the Earth as a life-support system to handle the environmental consequences. Indefinitely continuing economic growth will require weaning humankind from its dependence on coal, oil, and natural gas.

If you agree with all that, then you'll agree that the global challenge is social and political as much as it is technological. It requires cooperation. The world has first to agree on what to do about this kind of problem, and then act on it.

When you consider the implications for our daily lives, the actions that we take individually are clearly helpful. It's helpful to use less water, bike to work, and conserve energy, and it's especially important for people in wealthy, industrialized nations to take such actions, because their per-capita energy usage is so much higher than in the developing world. People in the United States have the luxury of *choosing* to change their lifestyles, because few of them worry every day simply about feeding themselves. An additional benefit of taking individual action is that such action becomes an educational tool and a reminder, just as, for a religious person, a symbol like a rosary or yarmulke does not itself guarantee a good, moral, upright, religious life but, rather, reminds the person of the value of living such a life.

Recycling, for example, has the virtue of keeping people conscious of the importance of reducing the consumption of resources. But bringing resource consumption under control on a worldwide basis also requires that world opinion have an effect on the countries with the largest populations or rates of population growth, like India and China and several other countries in Asia and Africa.

Reforestation is also on everybody's list of good things to do. Forests are wonderful things: they provide habitats for many species; and the biological diversity of the Earth is largely concentrated in the tropical forests. The numbers are very uncertain, but biologists have classified about 1.4 million species of living things. But estimates for how many species have yet to be discovered range from about 10 million up to about 30 million. So even by the most conservative estimates, there are many more species yet to be discovered and studied and classified.

Why should we worry about that? Because of both practical benefits and long-term concerns. The species of plants and animals on Earth represent a kind of genetic treasure chest. They are the bank on which evolution draws for evolving further species, and once one of them is gone it cannot be replaced. Several species become extinct every day. The loss from deforestation alone has been estimated at 4,000 to 6,000 species per year. Although less than 10% of the land area of the world is in the tropics, the great bulk of the *variety* of land species is there. The tropical rainforest is an especially valuable part of the world. The rainforest, which is being lost at an alarming rate, perhaps as much as 10% per decade, supports a large fraction of the plant and animal species that will be gone before we learn anything about them.

Even if you take the especially self-aggrandizing and arrogant attitude that the purpose of the Earth is simply to serve human beings, there are many good, selfish reasons for wanting to preserve biological diversity. Pharmaceuticals derived from plants and animals are an example. Foods are another.

There are other benefits from reforesting. If we reforest on a sufficiently grand scale, we help stem the increase in atmospheric carbon dioxide, with all its possible climate consequences. We also reduce air pollution. Trees do make certain hydrocarbons, but they also take in chemicals that would otherwise be pollutants. Additionally, trees are powerful controllers of the local climate. The forest is also a source of timber, recreation, and so on. In short, reforesting, which has to be done on a very large scale to make any significant difference to atmospheric CO_2 concentrations, has side benefits that are worth pursuing, even if fixing the climate problem is not one of them.

Perhaps, then, we *should* carefully consider reforesting. But like recycling, reforesting is not a panacea for global-change issues. It cannot solve the problem of climate change caused by humans adding CO_2 and other greenhouse gases to the atmosphere. That problem is caused by how people live and how they produce and use energy. Solving that problem means adopting measures that promote energy efficiency, energy conservation, and a switch to renewable sources of energy, not to mention promoting reduced population. These are actions that must be taken globally and soon.

Consider the parable of the boiled frog. An alert frog dropped in a pot of boiling water will jump out. It will be shocked and traumatized, but it will survive. But if placed in lukewarm water and gradually heated, the wretched animal will adjust to the changing temperature without realizing it and end its days as frog soup. I don't know whether this is true or not; this is a parable, not an experiment that anyone has performed or should perform. The point is, the impact on the frog of a gradual warming is insidious.

Energy consumption from fossil fuels is growing slowly and insidiously too in many parts of the world. When we consider the consequences of China's industrializing on the Western model, using the centuries of coal supply that it possesses—which is both feasible technologically and tempting economically because China already owns the coal—we're recognizing that the world may be like the frog in the pan of lukewarm water that is gradually heating up. Then we'll be watching global population continue to increase and fossil-fuel use continue to increase, and the product of these two factors will increase more rapidly than either of them alone. If that pattern persists long enough, it is virtually inevitable that the carbon-dioxide increase will eventually have a substantial effect on climate.

The ultimate pessimistic viewpoint is that we as a species are *incapable* of change. A good many people, apparently sharing this viewpoint, claim that it's just impractical, unrealistic, and politically naive to expect people to make big changes in the way they live. They point to the U.S. auto industry, for example, as an industry on which many other industries and people are dependent, and one that historically has been based on the production of large, fuel-inefficient cars. And they point out the dominant nature of this industry: manufacturing automobiles is the largest industry in the world, and supplying the fuel for them is the second largest. Six of the top ten industrial companies in the United States are either oil companies or car companies, and these giants do not easily accept change.

One counterargument is that the auto industry has already dramatically changed. For example, the average new car in the United States now gets around 30 miles to the gallon, which is about double the fuel efficiency that was typical 20 or 30 years ago. And cars now feature numerous technological advances such as air bags, which we were told for years no one would buy, couldn't be produced affordably, and couldn't be made reliable. The state of the car today, with carburetors and distributors replaced by electronic fuel injectors and microcomputers, is unrecognizably different from that of only a few years ago. And recent technological developments are setting the stage for even more rapid and innovative advances. Cars planned for the not-so-distant future may perhaps best be thought of as computers on wheels. The most imaginative of them will not be made of steel or fueled by oil products. They are likely to be small, light, safe, and incredibly fuel-efficient compared even to today's cars. The counterargument, in short, is that change is inevitable, and the need for beneficial change spurs technological development.

Of course, energy conservation and energy efficiency are at the top of everybody's list as ways to cope with these problems. Perhaps the realization that the problems are real and that the time to act is now, not a generation or two from now, will spur progress in those areas.

At the same time, perhaps the situation will encourage us to hunt for the kind of political and technological solutions that we're finding for chlorofluorocarbons, but that, for carbon dioxide, seem still out of reach and beyond our collective vision. Can we, for example, encourage and accelerate the transition to alternative sources of energy, sources other than fossil fuels, sources that produce little or no carbon dioxide? Some energy sources, such as nuclear power, produce no carbon dioxide but have other serious side effects. As you know, there are no U.S. nuclear plants now under construction, largely because people are worried about reactor accidents and radioactive-waste disposal. A lot of people—I'm one of them—are concerned about these aspects of nuclear power.

I'm even more worried about the proliferation of weapons-sensitive plutonium. That's a problem you can't easily avoid using conventional reactor technology. The global population today consumes commercial energy at the rate of about 10 terawatts, or 10 trillion watts. If you were to produce all that energy in conventional nuclear plants, you would need 10,000 plants, because it takes 1,000 plants to produce a terawatt. Each such plant produces about 1,000 kilograms of plutonium every year, and it takes only 10 kilograms to make a bomb. Just ponder those numbers if you think the risks are exaggerated.

So we must face the consequences of millions of kilograms of plutonium being produced as a by-product of generating electricity from nuclear fission. Even if the reactors are fail-safe, built from passively safe reactor designs—so that you can't possibly have another Chernobyl or Three-Mile Island accident—they still produce plutonium. And a terrorist is going to hold up a truck or a train one fine day and get hold of some. That's one of the most serious concerns.

Plutonium is also incredibly unhealthy. A millionth of a gram can give you lung cancer. It's one of the most toxic substances known.

But the nuclear-weapons-proliferation issue is even more serious than the other issues. If you could somehow figure out what to do with nuclear waste, and if you could control all the other problems, then you would still have to maintain iron control over all the fingers on all the potential nuclear triggers. You really have to worry about what might happen when you start shipping substantial amounts of weapons-sensitive plutonium around the world.

There is hope in the long term for certain alternative energy sources. Nuclear fusion, one of the most prominently mentioned of these, could, in principle, allow us to tap virtually inexhaustible energy supplies with few harmful side effects. But this is a hope for the relatively distant future, not a practical reality for the present. Fusion energy is not available today. We don't yet even see a clear way to achieve it. And there is a pressing need for alternative energy sources now.

In my opinion, and that of many scientists, renewable resources such as solar, wind, biomass, hydropower, and geothermal energy are by far the best near-term hope for reducing reliance on fossil fuels. These alternative energy sources are increasingly competitive and feasible on a large-scale basis, even considering the many subsidies and policies that artificially lower the price of fossil-fuel energy by concealing its true costs. Furthermore, many renewable technologies are rapidly improving in terms of price. Even today, they are often economically competitive with energy from fossil fuels and are sometimes significantly cheaper. In general, the benefits of switching to renewable energy sources, like the benefits of improving energy efficiency, are far greater than most people and governments realize, and far easier to achieve.

To date, the U.S. government, in contrast to some Western European governments, has generally taken the view that it's more prudent to conduct further research and to delay the changes in the economic and social system that might result from massive changes in the way we produce and use energy. This view assumes that the risk of economic and social disruption is greater than the risk of waiting.

Many knowledgeable scientists and energy-policy experts vehemently disagree. They are convinced that an immediate and serious effort to reduce fossil-fuel use and initiate the transition to renewable energy sources is practical, economical, and in the best interests of the country and the world.

To close on a bright note, we belong to a species that has an incredible capacity for invention and adaptation. Many things that are taken for granted in the world today were unforeseen only a few decades ago. Once you recognize the nature of a problem, and once you convince enough people that there's something to be concerned about, you can initiate the process of coping with it. You can begin the transition to alternative energy sources, and you can start getting governments to think about how to reduce energy use and stabilize population.

There is of course a difference between knowing what must be done and bringing yourself to do it. Alternative energy paths are not a futuristic dream. They are available and attractive today. The global potential for improved energy efficiency and energy conservation is gigantic. Obtaining energy from renewable resources is demonstrably practical now, not at some vague future time. Done intelligently, switching from fossil fuels often actually saves money rather than costing more.

Thus, the task is in very large measure a consciousness-raising matter, in much the same way that a binding international agreement to rid the world of CFCs followed from the realization on the part of people in many countries that they all had a stake in eliminating them. Coping with the enhanced greenhouse effect and climate change is of course not as technologically simple as stopping ozone depletion, which has a single cause. But the ozone-depletion story demonstrates the resourcefulness that people and nations can bring to bear in facing a problem, once it has been recognized as a problem, by asking the right questions and provoking the right answers.

7

AIR POLLUTION AND ACID RAIN

We move now into areas of more direct local effect—air pollution and acid rain. One difference between these topics and the global effects of ozone depletion and greenhouse warming is that ordinary meteorology is crucial to many aspects of local pollution. Until now, we've managed to discuss global issues without getting into the basics of weather, without talking about fronts and storms and wind and rain. To understand air pollution, we must become a little more informed about what makes daily weather.

In simplest terms, if you analyze a pollution problem like Los Angeles smog, which is a classic urban air-pollution problem, you can think of it as a process that begins with sources of emissions. The most important source of Los Angeles smog is automobile exhaust, but of course there are other important sources, too. Each source emits its own mix of pollutants into the atmosphere, and the atmosphere is like a great big pot that contains this evil stew. It allows the pollutants to mix together and interact with one another. It exposes them to sunlight and transports them from place to place. And along the way it allows various changes to occur. The result is that pollution, that atmospheric stew, influences "receptors" like your lungs, the paint on your car, and crops in the field.

What goes on in the atmosphere is absolutely crucial to the situation. But so is location. If Los Angeles weren't where it is and if it didn't have the kind of weather regimes it has, it wouldn't have the air pollution it has, even though the main cause is people driving cars.

Health effects, an aspect of air pollution I'm not going to say very much about, is in some ways the most crucial. Although a great deal is known about the effects of air pollution on human health, like much medical knowledge our understanding is still incomplete in biophysical terms. We don't know with any certainty what happens to someone's lungs when sulfate particles invade them. It's true that air pollution can increase the chance of bronchitis and emphysema and so on, and there is a great deal of statistical evidence to support such claims. Smog alerts, in short, are a good idea. But the deeper you delve into the subject, the more you realize how incompletely understood it is at a fundamental level.

Here we'll concentrate on the meteorology and chemistry of air pollution. We begin with some aspects of meteorology. Let's consider circulation in the atmosphere, first in global terms, because it's relevant to what happens in Los Angeles.

What drives the large-scale circulation of the atmosphere is heat from the Sun. In the tropics, near the Equator, a given area of the surface of the Earth receives much more solar radiation on average than does an equivalent area at high latitudes, near the poles. Therefore, the warmest places on Earth are in the tropics. Especially over the tropical oceans, this warmth leads to convection in the atmosphere: the air closest to the surface absorbs heat from the surface, which is warmed by sunlight, and as that air is warmed, it becomes buoyant, and rises. A visible manifestation of that process, noticeable if you are in the tropics lying on the beach or flying over the area in a satellite, is impressive towers of convective clouds, which are typical, for example, of thunderstorms: tall, puffy white clouds, cumulus and cumulonimbus clouds. The presence of convective clouds is a sign of rising air. The rising air in this convection transports moisture and heat to higher altitudes.

The air that rises in the tropics has to come down somewhere. Thus, a circulation is established: the air rises near the Equator, flows poleward (northward in the Northern Hemisphere, southward in the Southern Hemisphere), descends in the subtropics (latitudes between about 20° and 30°), and returns to the Equator near the surface. This circulation, which resembles a gigantic sea breeze, is called the Hadley cell, after a scientist who studied it long ago.

This circulation is a statistical construct. What do we mean by that? If you go out one fine day to some point in the Northern Hemisphere tropics, say Martinique, and take measurements, you will not necessarily find that the wind that day blows from north to south (toward the Equator) near the surface and from south to north (toward the North Pole) at higher altitudes. But if you take many measurements, not just in Martinique but at many tropical locations, and you average them over days and weeks and months, you'll find that *on average* the circulation behaves in the sense implied by the Hadley cell, the motions being upward at the Equator, poleward aloft, downward in the subtropics, and toward the Equator near the surface. The statistical, long-term, average property of the atmosphere is such that in the tropics the large-scale north-south circulation is a Hadley cell, circling the globe.

A typical latitude of this descending motion in the subtropics is in the range from 20° to 30°. The reason why it is often sunny in these latitudes is that the descending motion of the Hadley cell suppresses atmospheric convection. Clouds generally require upward motion for their formation, and it is more difficult for a cloud to form if the large-scale vertical motion of the atmosphere is downward. Thus, the absence of convective clouds is a typical sign of descending air motions. All the great deserts of the world are in the subtropical latitudes. It's not an accident that the desert Southwest in the United States is about at this latitude rather than at, say, 45° north. It's no accident that the Sahara Desert is mainly in the 20°–30° north-latitude belt. The great Australian desert and Chile's bone-dry Atacama Desert are in the corresponding latitude belt in the Southern Hemisphere.

Though there are many variations from one longitude to another—not every place in the 20° to 30° latitude belt has a sunny, dry climate—on average, over the whole Earth, over many years, the basic feature of the large-scale, global-average, north-south circulation of the tropical atmosphere is the Hadley cell.

Why doesn't the Hadley cell extend all the way to the poles? Why don't we have a simple picture of rising motion in the tropics, with air flowing toward the poles at some altitude, descending near the poles, and returning toward the Equator close to the surface? Why does the Hadley cell extend only to about 30°? That's a profound question, the answer to which has been debated for centuries. Many wrong answers have been given by many thoughtful people. We know now that the answer is not simple. There is no relatively short statement you can make that shows exactly why the Earth causes this circulation to be what we observe it to be, rather than what we might think it ought to be.

We do know that the answer has to do with the fact that the Earth rotates: if the Earth didn't rotate, or if it rotated much more slowly, the circulation might well descend near the poles, instead of near 30°. The answer also has to do with other quantitative aspects: how far the Earth is from the Sun, and therefore how much energy it receives; how much moisture we have in the atmosphere; and how likely it is that water will change from one phase into another (solid, liquid, and gaseous water all occur in the atmosphere). The main factors causing the circulation of the Earth to be what it is are the temperature contrast between the poles and the Equator, and the rotation of the Earth. If the Earth rotated at a very different rate, there could be a very different circulation.

We do know that the circulations on other planets are markedly different from the Earth's circulation. This is a fascinating topic, one that really has come into its own only since the advent of space exploration. Analyzing the atmospheres of other planets makes us realize how different the circulations can be. In fact, no other planet in the solar system has anything like the same meteorology as the Earth. Why these things are as they are is another of those questions to which there is no simple answer. Rotation and heating are the critical elements. In these two respects, the planets all differ greatly from one another.

What we observe, first of all, is that the air that flows back near the surface of the Earth from the subtropics toward the Equator doesn't flow directly from north to south. Instead, it gets turned to the right (in the Northern Hemisphere) by a deflecting effect due to the Earth's rotation. This effect, called the Coriolis effect, arises because the rotation of the Earth produces an apparent acceleration that doesn't change the speed of the wind, but does affect its direction. The Coriolis effect needs to be taken into account in understanding many large-scale motions on the Earth, not just the meteorological patterns. For example, to calculate accurately how to launch a projectile, such as an artillery shell, from one location to another one far away, it's necessary to take into account the fact that, while the projectile is in flight, the target will appear to have moved because of the rotation of the Earth. Allowing for the Coriolis effect is unnecessary for rapid, short motions, but it's essential to slow, long ones, such as the large-scale winds.

North of about latitude 30° in the Northern Hemisphere, and south of about latitude 30° in the Southern Hemisphere, we have the belt that includes most of the United States, sometimes miscalled the temperate latitudes (it's often not very temperate there). These are the latitudes where we find the great migrating storms that characterize the weather of many parts of the United States. It's an area of complex atmospheric flow where the big highs and lows on the weather map migrate slowly from west to east.

The tracks of these storms often tend to follow the jet stream, an intense west-to-east band of rapidly moving air. The jet stream is found not near the surface, but at the top of the troposphere. It's the reason why it routinely takes less time to fly from the West Coast to the East Coast than it takes to fly back to the West Coast.

The jet stream can be thought of as resembling a river. In the river are eddies, and those eddies are associated with the storms, the highs and lows moving across the weather map. The storm systems tend to follow the jet stream. For a long time meteorologists called it the steering current, because it allows you to predict where today's cyclone will be tomorrow. On average, the jet stream appears as a narrow ribbon of fast-moving air, but in fact it meanders; its position changes a lot from day to day.

The weather in some areas is especially susceptible to variations in the jet stream. California is one. Often, whether a particular winter in California is a wet season or a dry season depends on the position of the jet stream. Southern California usually doesn't get very much rain. Most of the rain that does fall there comes from a few intense winter storms. There are winters when all the storms seem to go north, leaving Southern California dry. Sometimes you'll hear that called a blocking pattern. That means that a region of high pressure diverts the jet stream to the north. Why this happens is complicated, but that's a typical circulation during dry California winters.

The concept of fronts is more straightforward. Imagine that cold air is coming down from the north. As the cold air mass advances, it displaces warmer air. A front is just a boundary between air at one temperature and air at another temperature. So if this cold front is moving southward and you're in its path, then as time goes on the front will cross over you, and instead of being in the warm air, you'll be left in the cold. That's why it's called a cold front. Similarly, if the movement of the air mass is in the opposite direction, so that warm air is advancing, that's a warm front. If you're standing still and are initially in cold air, then after a warm front passes you, you'll find yourself in warm air.

In winter the temperature contrast between the Equator and the high latitudes, between the tropics and the polar regions, is strongest. For although the temperature in the tropics doesn't change very much all year, it's of course coldest in high latitudes in winter. It is that temperature difference between low latitudes and high latitudes that drives the entire atmospheric circulation. The Hadley cell, for example, is much more intense in winter than it is in summer. Storms in middle latitudes are, in general, also more intense in winter than in summer. These storms derive their energy from the temperature difference between high latitudes and low latitudes.

Land masses and mountain ranges have a powerful effect on all these weather patterns. We've been talking about the average conditions over the whole Earth, but it's clear that where you're located—whether, for example, you're on the west side or the east side of a continent—greatly affects your local weather. Storms generated in regions of great temperature contrast tend to form off the east coast of the continents. Air in middle latitudes usually moves from west to east, and when an air mass remains over a continent for a long time—in winter, when the continents are colder than the oceans—the air mass gets cold. Then, when the air moves eastward and hits the relatively warm ocean, it presents a strong temperature contrast. That change in temperature can produce an intense storm. That's why such storms form off the east coast of the United States in the region of the Gulf Stream and off the east coast of Japan and Asia in the region of the Kuroshio current. These are the regions where the greatest heat transfer from the ocean to the atmosphere occurs, and the regions where many of the storms in the middle latitudes tend to originate. The effects of mountains, like the effects of continents and oceans, are important as well.

The part of the Hadley cell that flows toward the Equator in the tropics at low altitudes is called the trade winds. In general, trade winds blow from east to west. By convention, we call a wind blowing from east to west an easterly wind. An easterly *comes from* the east; it doesn't *go toward* the east. So trade winds are easterlies. Because of the Coriolis effect, trade winds blow generally from northeast to southwest in the Northern Hemisphere and from southeast to northwest in the Southern Hemisphere, converging near the Equator.

The modern name for this region near the Equator where the trade winds from both hemispheres converge is the Intertropical Convergence Zone (ITCZ). You can see it very clearly in satellite photographs. Air arrives from the northeast in the Northern Hemisphere, from the southeast in the Southern Hemisphere, and where it meets it has nowhere to go but up. The result is intense rising motion. On a satellite photo, it is marked by cumulus convection.

The average position of the ITCZ is very near the Equator, but the ITCZ is almost never found at its average position! In the Northern Hemisphere summer, when the Sun is, on average, north of the Equator, this convergence zone shifts to the north. The Northern Hemisphere summer might have an ITCZ at, say, 5° or 10° north latitude. In the Southern Hemisphere summer (Northern Hemisphere winter), the ITCZ might be located at around 5° or 10° south latitude. So this pattern of deep cumulus convection, representing the upward-moving branch of the Hadley cell, migrates north or south of the Equator with the seasons. The annual average position is near the Equator.

At this point I need to remind you of something that's crucial when we come to talk about Los Angeles smog. In the troposphere, approximately the lowest 10 to 15 kilometers of the atmosphere, temperature falls off with height, usually. It's warmest at the surface, where the atmosphere is heated from below. Temperature decreases with height until at some altitude, typically around 10 to 15 kilometers, it reaches a minimum and begins to increase with height. The altitude where this temperature minimum occurs is called the tropopause. It's the boundary between the troposphere and the stratosphere. The lower region, the troposphere, is where all the weather is, where about 80% of the mass of the atmosphere is, and where all the people are.

The stratosphere, the layer just above the troposphere, contains nearly all the rest of the mass of the atmosphere. Temperature rises with height in the stratosphere, largely because sunlight is being absorbed by ozone. Up at 50 kilometers, 99.9% of the mass of the atmosphere is below you. Pressure at the surface is near 1,000 millibars; pressure at 50 kilometers is about 1 millibar. In this context, pressure is simply one way to measure the mass of air above a given altitude.

There are other regions above the stratosphere. The concept of temperature itself becomes strained at sufficiently high altitudes, because there are so few molecules of anything at those levels. The ionosphere, for example, is very important for radio communication, but there are very few molecules there, compared to the lower atmosphere.

In the lower atmosphere, in general, temperature decreases with height, typically at a rate of about 6.5°C per kilometer of altitude (or about 3.6°F for every 1,000 feet in elevation). But just as the circulation we looked at in discussing the Hadley cell was statistically an average circulation—the average of many observations over the whole atmosphere over many days, weeks, and months—so this picture of temperature is an average as well. That is, temperature doesn't always decrease with height at the same rate. Though the global long-term average decrease is about 6.5°C per kilometer, there are times and places where temperature decreases more rapidly or less rapidly with height, and there are times and places where it actually increases with height. And one of those is just above Los Angeles on a typical summer afternoon.

This situation has a name: inversion. The name comes from the fact that such a configuration, with cooler temperatures at the surface and warmer temperatures aloft, is the inverse of the normal configuration.

An inversion is a very stable configuration. It's very difficult for upward vertical motions to occur in an inversion. Convection frequently occurs in the tropics, because the air is hottest near the ground and is therefore buoyant. If air is coldest near the ground, with hotter air above, then the cold, heavy, dense air is already near the surface, and it will tend *not* to rise. An inversion thus effectively forms a lid that traps pollutants in the lowest level of the atmosphere and prevents them from dispersing. Keep in mind the difference between the long-term global-average picture and short-term local variations like this one.

Where you define the top of the atmosphere, by the way, depends on what your purposes are. By the time you reach an altitude of about 30 miles, or 50 kilometers, as we've seen, about 99.9% of the atmosphere is below you. From the point of view of someone who wants to breathe, if you're above 50 kilometers, you're in outer space. You need to carry an oxygen supply in order to breathe. In fact, you need pressurized air in commercial aircraft, which typically fly at a height of around 6 miles, which is only about 10 kilometers. At that point, if the pressure in the cabin fails, you need an oxygen mask to breathe. From that point of view, as soon as you're much above that height, you're outside the atmosphere.

But perhaps your point of view is that of a satellite, and you're interested in having a long lifetime. What brings satellites down is friction in the atmosphere. The higher the satellite, the less the friction. It's the occasional collisions of the satellite with the relatively few molecules that are up there that eventually slow it down. There's not much air there, but it's enough. In fact, the height of the atmosphere, or the height at which a given pressure level occurs, depends on the solar cycle: how much solar wind is coming from the Sun. Satellite-orbit designers actually have to take into account the 11-year sunspot cycle, because it affects the density of the upper atmosphere and hence the friction experienced by the satellite. Once a satellite begins to slow down because of friction, it will spiral downward into the Earth's atmosphere and eventually burn up.

So where you define the outside of the atmosphere is arbitrary. By the time you're at satellite altitudes, typically a few hundred kilometers, there's virtually no trace of atmosphere. There's gradual blending between an extremely thin atmosphere and the virtual emptiness of outer space. Yet that trace atmosphere can eventually destroy the satellite.

Remember how shallow this atmosphere is. The Earth's circumference is about 40,000 kilometers, around 25,000 miles. The thickness of the atmosphere, if we take it to be the altitude that includes 99.9% of the mass of the atmosphere, is only about 50 kilometers. We're clearly talking about a very thin skin compared to the size of the Earth itself.

As for the weather, almost everything that's interesting occurs in approximately the lowest 10 miles, or 16 kilometers. All the clouds we've been talking about occur in the troposphere. The troposphere is characterized by convection, or overturning. *Tropos* is Greek for "turning."

Occasionally, a powerful thunderstorm with intense upward air motion can reach the stratosphere, actually penetrating the tropopause, the boundary between the troposphere and the stratosphere. Because temperature increases with height above the tropopause, you might think of the stratosphere as one gigantic inversion. It's a stable region, with generally weak vertical motions, because temperature increasing with height means light air is found above heavier air.

We need now to learn more about the physics of radiation. There are many different kinds of electromagnetic radiation, which we distinguish according to their wavelengths. The kind you can see, visible light, occupies a small region of the electromagnetic spectrum that includes wavelengths between about 0.4 and 0.7 micrometers. A micrometer (formerly called a micron) is a millionth of a meter. Light can be thought of as vibration, a rapidly fluctuating electromagnetic wave. Similarly, very long wavelengths we call radio waves, and very short wavelengths we call X-rays and gamma rays.

We know that each of these bands of wavelengths has its own properties. X-rays, for example, unlike visible light, can penetrate people. But it's a very small portion of the spectrum that we're concerned with when we talk about climate.

The distribution of the radiation that the Sun gives off has a maximum at around 0.5 micrometers in the visible. It extends down to small fractions of a micrometer, and it extends to longer wavelengths too, but it drops off to very little amplitude when the wavelength is longer than about 2 micrometers. There's a lot of energy in the visible part of the spectrum. That's why the sun looks so bright!

The Earth, on the other hand, gives off radiant heat, or infrared (IR) radiation. It peaks at around 12 micrometers, in the infrared. Your eyes are not sensitive to IR, so you can't see the Earth at night. Of course, you could see the Earth from space in the daytime, if you were fortunate enough to be an astronaut, but what you would be seeing is not the radiant heat the Earth gives off, but rather reflected sunlight. At night, with the Earth between you and the Sun, you could not see the Earth.

When you look up at the Moon, you're not seeing radiation that the Moon itself gives off. You're seeing sunlight reflected from the surface of the Moon.

The science of light, incidentally, began in antiquity. Infrared radiation, however, was discovered only in 1800 by Sir William Herschel, an English astronomer. A good deal later, a remarkable pair of physical laws came along to explain why the Earth radiates mainly in the infrared and the Sun radiates mainly in the visible. The difference has to do with temperature. One law says that colder bodies emit radiation with longer wavelengths than do hotter bodies. The quantitative statement of that law is that the maximum wavelength is inversely proportional to the temperature. You can find out what that wavelength is by dividing the number 3,000 by the temperature in degrees Kelvin. That gives you the wavelength in micrometers. The law is called Wien's displacement law. Wien, a German, formulated it in 1893.

The temperature of the outside of the Sun is about 6,000° Kelvin. So if you divide 3,000 by 6,000, you get about 0.5 micrometers, which is the wavelength at which the Sun's radiation is maximum. The temperature of the surface of the Earth is about 288°K, or 15°C, roughly 60°F. The Earth, however, emits not only from the surface but also from the atmosphere, especially the troposphere, which is colder than the surface. The Earth's average effective radiating temperature thus turns out to be a little more than 250°K. Divide 3,000 by about 250 and you get a number around 12. That's why the maximum radiation of the Earth occurs at a wavelength of around 12 micrometers.

Wien's law is a nifty formula. It works backwards, too. You can take any body in the universe, and if you know the wavelength at which its radiation is at a maximum, you can figure out its temperature. You can discover that some stars are hotter than the Sun, because they radiate at a still shorter wavelength. You and I are radiating, incidentally. People give off about the same amount of energy as a 60-watt incandescent light bulb.

The other law is one we came across earlier. It tells you how much energy a body—actually a "black body," a perfect radiator—gives off in terms of its temperature. This equation says that the flux of energy is some constant times the fourth power of temperature. It means, for example, that if you double the temperature of a body, you don't just double the amount of radiation it gives off, you multiply it by 2^4, or 16. This law, by the way, is called the Stefan-Boltzmann law. Stefan formulated it first, in 1879, from experiments; Boltzmann deduced it theoretically five years later.

Because $6,000°K$ is much more than $250°K$, 6,000 to the fourth power is a great deal more than 250 to the fourth power—more than 300,000 times as much, if you do the arithmetic. So each square meter of the Sun gives off more than 300,000 times as much energy as each square meter of the Earth. Hotter bodies give off more energy than colder bodies, and they give it off in shorter wavelengths.

Sunlight is intercepted by the Earth. Remember, about 30% of the sunlight that hits the Earth is reflected away—that's the albedo—mainly by clouds, which account for about 20%. Another few percent are scattered away by particles in the atmosphere. A tiny bit of what gets all the way down to the surface isn't absorbed but is reflected. Most of what gets down to the surface is absorbed. In round numbers, 30% is reflected away, 50% is absorbed at the surface, and the other 20% is absorbed in the atmosphere.

When we say that the greenhouse effect operates because the atmosphere is transparent to incoming sunlight, that's a rough approximation. Twenty percent of the incoming sunlight does not pass through the atmosphere, but instead is absorbed in the atmosphere. Some of the incoming sunlight powers chemical reactions: some of it photodissociates oxygen, some photodissociates ozone, and, in Los Angeles, some makes smog. Sunlight is a key ingredient in making smog.

The structure of many of the molecules in the Earth's atmosphere is such that they can absorb light of particular wavelengths. For example, when oxygen absorbs sunlight, a molecule of oxygen absorbs some of the energy from the sunlight, and that energy can sometimes serve to break the bond that holds one oxygen atom to the other, resulting in two free atoms of oxygen. Not just any old sunlight will do that, but only sunlight in particular wavelengths, determined by the structure of the oxygen molecule.

What about the other 78% or so of the atmosphere that consists of nitrogen? Is there a reaction that breaks ordinary nitrogen into N + N? No, there isn't. The chemical bond between the two atoms of nitrogen in the N_2 molecule is so strong that no sunlight, not at any wavelength that the Sun emits, is sufficiently strong to break up that bond. Another way to describe this property of nitrogen in the atmosphere is to say that it's photochemically inert.

Some of the infrared radiation emitted by the Earth has a good chance of being absorbed by gases on the way out. The Earth emits energy chiefly in the wavelength range from around 6 micrometers up to 14 micrometers. Between those two wavelengths, there is a "window" in the spectrum, so called because the gases in the atmosphere don't absorb much energy from the radiation in that part of the spectrum. The atmosphere can thus be said to be transparent to IR radiation in that band of wavelengths, and it is in that window that the Earth does most of its emitting to space.

There is another window in the visible part of the spectrum, which is why sunlight reaches Earth's surface. That's why we see the Sun. In a part of the electromagnetic spectrum where the Sun emits strongly— from 0.5 or 1 up to about 2 micrometers—the atmosphere is partially transparent. There are regions of spectral absorption by water vapor, and where a little bit is absorbed by oxygen and ozone, but most of this "visible window" is clear for the penetration of sunlight.

It's because the Earth is emitting in the infrared part of the spectrum, and because water vapor and carbon dioxide and other gases are absorbing in the infrared, that we have a greenhouse effect. The more of these gases there are in the atmosphere, the stronger the effect. That's why these gases—methane, nitrous oxide, ozone, carbon dioxide, water vapor—are the gases we talk about in reference to the greenhouse effect. They just happen to have a molecular structure that absorbs in the part of the spectrum where the Earth emits. Perhaps it's a coincidence. If we had different gases so that this was a clear window, or if we had an Earth at a different temperature so that it radiated at considerably different wavelengths, we wouldn't have the same greenhouse effect.

Consider the reaction by which O_2 + sunlight results in O + O by means of photodissociation, the breaking apart of the oxygen molecule by light. Photodissociation of oxygen tends to occur in the high atmosphere, in the stratosphere and in the region above it called the mesosphere. Why? Because that's where the sunlight first contacts the atmosphere, and because the reaction absorbs sunlight at just the wavelengths needed to break up the oxygen molecules, so that down in the lower atmosphere not much sunlight in those particular wavelengths remains.

Photodissociation of the O_3 ozone molecule occurs in the same way, but requires a different band of wavelengths of sunlight. Ozone can photodissociate in the presence of sunlight into ordinary oxygen (O_2) and a free oxygen atom (O). The free oxygen atom gains some energy from sunlight in the process, and is therefore at a higher energy level than before. For it to recombine with O_2 oxygen to form ozone requires the presence of a third molecule, a mediator molecule, which has a purely mechanical role in this process. The mediator, which might be oxygen or nitrogen, is present when the free oxygen atom and the oxygen molecule collide, essentially in a three-body collision. The mediator molecule's function is to carry away the extra energy. If the free oxygen atom and the ordinary oxygen molecule just slammed together, they would immediately fly apart again because of the extra energy carried by the oxygen atom, unless a third body were present to carry away the energy.

Ozone photodissociation also occurs mainly in the stratosphere, where most of the ozone is. Many of the free oxygen atoms resulting from the photodissociation reaction combine quickly with ordinary oxygen to form new ozone. In other words, this reaction is reversible. The rates at which these reactions occur depend on the availability of the molecules, the availability of sunlight, and the availability, in this case, of the mediator molecule, whose only function is to carry away energy.

Because ozone is very rare, while oxygen and nitrogen are abundant, the mediator molecule is often oxygen or nitrogen. Since there are many, many more of those molecules than there are ozone or odd oxygen molecules, the chances are good that an oxygen or nitrogen molecule is nearby when this reaction occurs.

This same energized or excited oxygen molecule can also interact with water vapor. Water is a stable molecule—it doesn't fly apart of its own volition—but in the presence of an excited oxygen atom, water can break up into two OH molecules. These are called hydroxyl molecules. Hydroxyl, a very reactive molecule, is the garbage collector of the atmosphere. It has the function of scavenging many molecules. It can react with all sorts of hydrocarbons, for example, such as methane. It can also react with NO_2 to form nitric acid (HNO_3).

Another thing that the energized odd oxygen molecule can do is attack nitrous oxide (N_2O) to form two nitric oxide (NO) molecules. And that's an important reaction too, as we shall see.

Remember that the atmosphere is made up of roughly 78% nitrogen (N_2) and 21% oxygen (O_2). Nitrogen cannot be photodissociated by sunlight—there is no sunlight energetic enough to break apart nitrogen molecules. But an ordinary molecule of nitrogen can, in the presence of heat, break apart and recombine to form two nitric-oxide molecules. So we have here another way of forming nitric oxide.

Where does this commonly occur? It happens all the time in your car's engine. There's plenty of this stuff around, because your engine takes in a lot of air. Gasoline is mixed at roughly the ratio of one part gasoline to 15 parts air in your carburetor or fuel-injection system before it's ignited. So your car processes an enormous amount of air. One of the things that happens in that engine is that combustion breaks apart the molecules and recombines them in this way. The temperature inside the combustion chamber of your car is about 2,000°K, hot enough for this reaction to occur. In fact, this is a crucial reaction in smog.

What you need to make smog is lots of tailpipes and other sources putting out products like nitric oxide and carbon monoxide; you need sunlight providing the energy for reactions; and you need a vessel, a cooking pot, to keep these pollutants from escaping.

The sad fate of Los Angeles is that it offers all three of these things. The vessel that it lies in is part meteorology and part topography. Above Los Angeles you often find temperature inversions, in part because the city has cold air blowing inland from the ocean on sea breezes. So cold air often underlies warm air there, with temperature increasing with height.

The sea breeze brings winds blowing toward the land at low levels—where the people are—during the daytime, when tailpipes are putting out exhaust, and pushes everything from the ocean onto the land. There is also a wall in the form of the mountains on the east side of Los Angeles, which keeps things from escaping. You thus have a situation in which the pollutants can't escape. If you took the inversion away, they could escape by convection. If you took the mountains away, the winds could disperse the pollutants. (This actually happens, to some extent: there is Los Angeles smog in the Grand Canyon, because there are gaps in the mountains—Los Angeles basin is not a perfect containing vessel.)

The situation is different in different places at different times of the day. Los Angeles has not only pretty bad smog but pretty variable smog. We know a lot about how much it varies from hour to hour and from place to place. The thing to keep in mind is that because the pollutants are produced during different parts of the daily cycle, and because it takes time for all these things to occur, different effects happen at different times of the day.

Carbon monoxide (CO) is a direct pollutant—it comes straight from a source, like your car. It's poisonous, and it affects people. The worst place in Los Angeles for carbon monoxide is where the biggest concentration of vehicles is: on the west side, for example, where several freeways meet. The worst time of day for CO is early in the morning, during rush hour.

The other pollutants occur later in the day and in different regions. For example, the worst place for ozone in Los Angeles is on the east side of the basin. So if you think you are sensitive to a given pollutant, you might try to locate yourself so as to maximize your own well-being. That's a macabre calculation, but there are plenty of data to rely on.

The inversion acts as a lid all the time, but as people go to work in the morning, there's a maximum in emissions. The sea breeze generally packs the pollution up against the mountains, but in the morning the sea breeze hasn't fully developed yet, because it depends on the temperature contrast between the land and the ocean. Hence, early in the morning, there's no big transport of pollutants out from the most densely populated areas, such as along the coast or downtown Los Angeles. In the early morning, then, the worst area to be in is where the traffic concentration is, and the pollutant to worry about the most is carbon monoxide.

By midmorning, however, the sea breeze has picked up, because the Sun has warmed the land a little, and the pollutants start to move inland, from west to east. At that point, the secondary pollutants, known usually as NO_x (nitrogen combined with an odd number of oxygen atoms), begin to pick up, because it takes time for them to be produced. In general, they aren't the primary pollutants that come out of tailpipes, because to form, they require reactions.

The region of maximum pollutant concentration moves inland as the day progresses and as the sea breeze pushes the whole ugly stew from west to east. By midafternoon, there's typically a very strong sea breeze, and the most heavily polluted air gets pushed right up against the mountains. With the Sun shining on a typical warm, smoggy August day, ozone, which depends on sunlight to form, is at a maximum. That explains why cities on the east side of the Los Angeles basin have reputations for very bad air quality.

Such is the typical pattern of different pollutants occurring at different times of the day. Nighttime, incidentally, is the best time. Because traffic declines then, there's less source. Sunlight departs, thereby eliminating the reaction that forms ozone. And what was a sea breeze reverses and blows out to sea. But in the morning, the cycle repeats.

Turning now to another form of airborne pollution, acid rain, let's begin by defining pH, which is a measure of the acidity of a substance. The lower the pH number, the more acidic the substance is. The pH level is measured on a logarithmic scale, which means that every step on the scale represents a factor of 10. Thus, something with a pH of 8 is 10 times more acid than something with a pH of 9, which in turn is 10 times more acid than something with a pH of 10.

The difference between natural rain and acid rain is a factor of between 10 and 100 in acidity. Natural rain has a pH of between 5 and 6 and the most acidic acid rain has a pH of around 4. Even natural rain is slightly acid; the basis of its acidity is partly carbonic acid, H_2CO_3, which is formed from the same CO_2 that's in the atmosphere. The CO_2 gets washed out of the atmosphere and combines with water to form the carbonic acid. The neutral number on the pH scale is 7. That's the number that separates acids (lower numbers) from alkalines (higher numbers), sometimes called bases. Distilled water, actually pure water, H_2O—nothing else but the water you would find in a laboratory, which is close to the water you buy in the store—is neutral, with a pH of 7. Keep in mind that naturally occurring acids (sulfuric, nitric and others) make natural rain somewhat acidic.

The state of the science of acid rain is better than that of the ozone hole or the greenhouse effect. Our knowledge of acid rain is incomplete but still less fragmentary than our understanding of ozone loss or climate change. Yet, we need to learn more about acid rain. Ironically, the pace of research in this area has slowed in recent years, in part because new laws have reduced the emissions of chemicals that cause acid rain. These laws make the subject seem less urgent.

There's obviously research to be done. But the question of "solving" the acid-rain problem is considered largely a problem of politics, economics, and human behavior. It's not a mystery, and in that sense it's unlike any of the other things we've addressed thus far. The ozone hole, remember, was unsuspected for years. It was discovered 50 years after we put into the atmosphere the first chlorofluorocarbons, these chemicals which, when first invented, we thought were a miracle chemical, whose harmful side effects were not even suspected. What we know about ozone depletion we have learned only in recent years. And each year we're learning more about how it works. For the greenhouse effect, too, many of the answers are not yet at hand.

Acid rain is not in that category at all. We understand exactly how it's formed. It occurs because we've been interfering with the natural workings of nature. Consider the role of sulfur, for example. Sulfur gets into the atmosphere naturally, partly from volcanoes. When a volcano erupts, it brings up a great deal of sulfur from deep in the Earth. Sulfur also comes from the decay of organic matter, dead plants and animals and compost heaps. It comes out of the ocean too, partly as hydrogen sulfide, a chemical that has an intense smell of rotten eggs when present in high concentrations, and partly as dimethyl sulfide.

The sulfur that goes into the atmosphere eventually gets rained out. It combines with water in the atmosphere, forms sulfuric acid, rains out, returns to the ocean, and so completes its cycle.

The anthropogenic, or human-caused, sources of sulfur lie almost entirely in the burning of fossil fuels, and the greatest contributor is high-sulfur coal. Coal has a substantial sulfur content, ranging from about 0.5% in low-sulfur coal, which happens to be expensive, to as high as 7% in plentiful low-grade coal.

Sulfur dioxide, SO_2, is the major pollutant that leads to acid rain. In the global aggregate, we annually release about 100 million tons of sulfur dioxide and about half that much, about 50 million tons, of NO_x, which also creates acid precipitation. The natural production of sulfur is smaller than the anthropogenic, or human-caused, source. There is a potentially important climate connection too. The sulfur emissions form particles (aerosols) that can reflect sunlight and alter clouds.

Furthermore, sulfur dioxide and NO_x emissions are strongly localized. Unlike carbon dioxide, which gets mixed around the whole world very rapidly, acid rain can have a very localized effect. There are well-documented cases of strong ecological damage in the vicinity downwind of power plants.

The effects of acid rain are much more severe in some areas than in others. This has led to many of the political problems that accompany acid rain. The smokestacks from power plants in the Midwest, burning sulfur rich coal, can produce acid rain in the lakes of Maine. A few trace studies have been done; people have tagged particles, followed them in the wind, and modeled them numerically. So we can know where the source of acid rain is, and that leads to heated disputes. One that has gone on for many years is between the United States and Canada. There are many such disputes in Europe. There is acid-rain damage to lakes and forests in Sweden that has sources in England. Acid rain brings heavy political costs, for the benefits of the power and the costs of the acidification often fall on very different people.

There's a long list of things that can be done about the acid-rain problem. The right mix depends on many factors, including local politics and global economics.

One solution is to use low-sulfur coal. But high-sulfur coal is far cheaper than low-sulfur coal, as it happens. That has to do with the economics of mining it and transporting it and so on. If you want low-sulfur coal, you must pay more.

Another possible solution is to treat high-sulfur coal chemically before you burn it. And an enormous technology has been developed in so-called *scrubbers,* which are mechanical and chemical devices for removing the sulfur, not from the coal before it's burned, but from the stuff that goes up the smokestacks after it's burned and before what remains is released to the atmosphere.

It's also possible to disperse the emissions. One way to do that is just to build taller smokestacks. Part of the acid-rain problem has been that in some regions where powerplants are located, there are consistent inversions. Recall that inversions are temperature structures in which light, warm air overlies cold, dense air. When that kind of meteorology settles on a region where a smokestack is situated below the level of the inversion, the emissions are trapped below the inversion. But if you build a taller smokestack, get its top above the inversion, you improve the ability of the stack to disperse the emissions. And in general, the higher you are, the stronger the wind, which helps disperse emissions as well. Of course, this may only relocate the problem.

Alternative energy sources are of course the long-term solutions. If you don't want acid rain, don't burn sulfur-rich fuels. In many cases, the economics of coal-fired powerplants are very attractive, except for the necessity of dealing with emissions. In many cases, legal requirements have been placed on plants to encourage them to move away from the use of sulfur-rich fuels.

Locating powerplants strategically is a viable strategy, too, because in many cases, where you put the powerplant determines where the stuff that emerges from the stack ends up. You can make wise or foolish choices regarding the location of each powerplant.

Another possibility is to buffer the lakes, treating the problem at the other end. That is, take a lake that has already had its acidity increased by acid precipitation—or acid deposition, technically, since the compounds can come down either in the form of rain or as solid particles— and add some substance such that when you mix the whole stew together, you get something with a more nearly neutral level of acidity.

Interestingly, and fortunately, when you buffer a lake, over time an amazing number of things often get restored. In many lakes that are otherwise healthy ecosystems, once you have done away with the cause of the problem, you can engineer the lake back to health. However, lakes are complex, and buffering is often not effective. There's an enormous range of experience with the problem, and success depends on a great many factors other than the acid.

It's much harder, by the way, to "buffer" a forest. Damage to plant life comes from precipitation that falls, but it also comes from ground water drawn up in the root system, which carries nutrients and minerals and the rest of the things that come in solution. But it's really hard to get in and change ground water or change precipitation. So right now, these end-use mitigation strategies are applicable to lakes but not to forests. A great deal of research remains to be done on the means of dealing with acid rain.

Often the fights about acid rain are not so much scientific in nature as they are political and economic. The challenge is to find the right combination of balancing the interests of the generators and users of affordable and reliable electricity with the interests of the people who suffer the consequences of acid deposition. It becomes very straightforward: How much are you willing to pay?

It's like the old story in stock-car racing. A wealthy playboy decides he wants to take up stock-car racing, so he asks, "How do you get into this?" He is told, "Well, you go buy a car and find an engine builder and he builds you an engine, and you're in business." He then asks how much it will cost. The reply is, "Speed costs money; how fast do you want to go?"

That's the situation here. Neutral lakes cost money; how neutral do you want to go? The difficulty in the political arena is that in many cases there are interjurisdictional equity arguments. The laws that govern the polluter are from a different entity or even a different country than the laws that govern the polluted.

One of the issues in solving the acid-rain problem is the argument about what an affected lake would have done by itself anyway. Fish in a lake die, and the fellow who is producing energy from high-sulfur coal in the Midwest says, "You can't pin that on me, because a lot of other things can happen in lakes too." A lake 10 miles away from a sick lake can be healthy, for instance. So you can argue about that.

You can't argue, in general, that acid rain has no effect. That is a flat-Earth kind of argument. Damage from acid rain is clear in many places. But it's also true, when you argue about damage suffered by one particular area, that although the atmospheric chemistry may not be very complicated, the biology of the lake or the region or the forest *is* complicated. So when it comes to taking a sick tree and tracing back to which pest or which disease caused that sickness, and how the progress of that pest or disease was or wasn't influenced by all the chemical consequences of what kind of worm grew up in its roots or what kind of rain fell on its leaves, that can be tricky.

Thus, there are points over which there are legitimate controversies and unsettled issues. But in general, the argument that acid rain has no effect, that there's no large-scale damage anywhere on the planet from sulfur emissions or smokestacks, is untenable.

Acid rain often gets mentioned in the same breath as ozone depletion and the greenhouse effect. And in some sense it belongs there; after all, why is there acid rain? Because there are so many people using so much energy. But acid rain differs from the ozone and greenhouse problems in the sense that we do know what to do about it. We simply have to find the political will to do it. If you don't want to have acid rain, don't put sulfur dioxide and NO_x into the atmosphere. That's really the best solution. In many cases, a great deal has been done about acid rain. There are examples of lakes that were once acidified and are now restored to a neutral state and good health. The problems that remain are problems of economics and politics.

The issues we've examined in this chapter may seem somewhat out of place in a discussion of global change. After all, loss of stratospheric ozone and the possibility of climate change due to an enhanced greenhouse effect are issues that are truly planetary in scope. But air pollution in Los Angeles and acid rain in Sweden or Canada are purely local problems, aren't they?

No, they aren't. Not at all. They are genuinely global problems, because there are so many cities with polluted air, and because there are so many sources of acid rain. Humankind is the only animal that fouls its own nest, and it's been exceptionally ingenious in devising ways to do so.

The sad fact is that Los Angeles is not an unusual example. Urban air pollution affects many cities. Traffic police in Tokyo have sometimes sought relief by wearing oxygen masks. Mexico City, with the biggest urban concentration of people on the planet, perhaps 20 million inhabitants, has some of the dirtiest air on Earth. It has the triple misfortune of high altitude, overpopulation, and few effective controls on emissions. The growing prosperity of many densely populated cities in the developing world is vividly apparent in their filthy air. The traveler whose plane descends toward Delhi or Calcutta or Bombay sees not the India of legend promised by the guidebooks, but a dark cloud of pollution.

Everything we know about current trends tells us that many of these aspects of global change will inevitably intensify in the future. Almost all of the population increase in the developing world, which means the great bulk of all of the population increase on the planet, will occur in cities. The cities of 2025 may have three times the population of those of 1990. Planetary population grows, but urban population grows at a faster rate.

Acid rain is a problem in the United States and Canada, but in Eastern Europe it's a disaster. The former Communist governments there ranked environmental protection low in priority. Acid rain has affected more than half a million acres in Poland, even more in Czechoslovakia.

Local problems, if sufficiently numerous and severe, are global problems too.

8

THE FUTURE OF PLANET EARTH

All of the major topics we've concentrated on—ozone depletion, enhanced greenhouse effect, air pollution, and acid rain—can be traced
directly to a common source in population, affluence, and technology.
These environmental effects are all happening at the same time, in our
lifetime, on a global scale, and not by chance, but rather because they
have a common cause—namely, the number of people on Earth, the
way we live, the amount of energy we use, and the way we generate that
energy.

We began with ozone. There are many memorable aspects of the
ozone-depletion story. One is the fact that ozone loss was first predicted
theoretically by two scientists and then discovered, in the spectacular
form of the ozone hole, by another. Since the discovery of the ozone
hole, we have put together, within less than a decade, a fairly complete,
credible, agreed-upon picture of how ozone loss comes about.

The observation of severe ozone loss over Antarctica wasn't predicted. The prediction was that chlorofluorocarbons could decrease
ozone; and the theory, developed by Rowland and Molina, envisioned
a gradual loss over many years. First came the realization that chlorofluorocarbons, because of their long lifetimes, and because they're
nearly inert, provide a vehicle for lifting chlorine from the surface, where
we emit it, up to the stratosphere, where it might remain chemically
inactive for decades. Once there, the chlorine is released through a very
complicated process involving the meteorology of the polar stratosphere. We've also learned that the Antarctic circulation system provides
a containment vessel—a closed vortex in which the ozone-rich air is

trapped—where this process can take place at increased levels because of the presence of frozen surfaces on clouds on which some unusual chemical reactions can occur.

After this long process, we now have a theory that appears to be credible. A lot of thorough scientific work has been done validating this chain of events and providing enough convincing evidence—enough of a "smoking gun"—that the governments of the world have agreed to ban chlorofluorocarbons.

The ban on CFCs, incidentally, will have considerable economic consequences. Some of them will be quite pleasant, for some fortunate people. CFC substitutes are going to make a lot of money for their producers. If you have to have a different kind of air conditioner in your car, if you have to buy a new kind of refrigerator, because CFCs are no longer tolerable, then the people who make that car air conditioner and that refrigerator, and the people who sell them and transport them and maintain them, are going to make money. Just ask the people who invested in compact discs (does anybody remember phonograph records?). Those people made money, because a brand-new technology came along and music lovers switched over. Money can be made on energy conservation and energy efficiency, too, and money can certainly be made when environmental concerns mandate a major change in technology. Change is opportunity. Environmentalism can be profitable.

Turning now to the greenhouse effect, recall the work of Lewis Fry Richardson, the individualistic, pacifist, Quaker, ambulance-driving mathematician. Recall how he carried out a laborious hand calculation and then lost it, and how, when he found it, knowing full well how mistaken it was, had the courage to publish it anyway. Of all the scientists we've studied, he is probably the most idiosyncratic. He makes ordinary obsessive scientists, and even strongly motivated ones like Keeling, look normal by contrast. Richardson was truly a special case in the spectrum of humanity, and it was because of his vision, early in this century, that today we have the technology for making the weather forecasts that are so economically beneficial to agriculture and many other sectors of the economy. And it was because of Richardson's lonely research that today we have global-climate models, from which our best estimates of future temperature change have come.

Climate modeling remains largely an unsolved problem. I've said that we ought to take the model results, the climate scenarios of the future, seriously but not literally. We know that the models are complicated by how intricately the processes interact with one another, and by how strongly these interwoven processes influence climate stability. We also know that we don't yet have a track record in this area, because we don't have a history of predicting climate. We didn't predict the climate trends that have already occurred.

A distinguished environmental scientist, Dean Abrahamson, has re-marked, "When my grandfather was born, environmental concerns were almost all based on housekeeping and trash in the backyard. By the time I was born," continued Abrahamson, who is now approaching middle age, "there were demonstrable regional impacts. The birth of my children coincided with entire river systems and air sheds being affected. Now . . . major global systems, upon which society depends for its welfare, are being destroyed."

That's a remarkable summary of the change we've seen within this century, within the space of just three or four human generations. First there were local concerns: we mentioned that there was smog in Lon-don centuries ago, and the backyard problem has always been there. But concerns that were regional and national are now global in nature.

The other aspect of the problem we face today is that these changes require a behavioral response. We caused them, and what gets done about them depends on us. You can contrast this realization with an attitude that was prevalent in Western society as recently as the 1970s. That was a time of worry over running out of finite resources. Many predicted at that time that soon there would be little readily recoverable oil, for example. We do know, of course, that we will run out eventually, even though the schedule isn't what was foreseen then. But the prob-lems we face today don't arise from the scarcity of resources. China, as I mentioned, sits atop an immense reserve of coal, enough for centuries. The fear today is not that the Chinese will run out of coal, but that they will use it.

We're worried not so much about a lack of those kinds of resources, but instead about what you might call a global waste-disposal problem: what to do with the by-products of the civilization we've built. They include carbon dioxide from fossil fuel and deforestation, but they also include many other things that we've touched on: CFCs, acid precip-itation, air pollution, and so on. We're worried about the side effects of the way we've chosen to live, and the responses required to solve these problems are both global and behavioral.

There are reasons to be optimistic, and one of them is the growing awareness of the problem on the part of many people. Thirty years ago you wouldn't have seen *Time* magazine naming Earth as planet of the year in place of a person of the year.

I think this change has come about in part because of space exploration, in particular manned space exploration. All astronauts have something in common, something that's been noticed by many people; you can uncover it yourself by going back through the comments made by astronauts from all countries. Astronauts, who are technical people—pilots and engineers who say things like "10-4" and "affirmative" when they mean "yes"—waxed absolutely poetic when they were in space. The word you heard from all of them was *beautiful*. Alan Shepard, the first of the American astronauts, said, "What a beautiful view!" The Soviet cosmonauts said the same thing: "Our planet is uncommonly beautiful and looks wonderful from cosmic heights." There probably aren't any astronauts who haven't said words to that effect.

Because of space exploration, we've all become vicarious astronauts, taking on the perspective of the Earth from space. That represents great progress in terms of human awareness of the changes in the planet and the causes of those changes.

I think another kind of awareness comes simply from the proliferation of knowledge. The Keeling curve, showing the concentration of atmospheric CO_2 rising, has become an icon. Keeling's data on carbon dioxide from Mauna Loa provide unmistakable evidence that the chemical composition of the atmosphere is being altered by humanity. In a sense, every discussion of global change tacitly cites those data. They've become widely known. People in the street know that atmospheric CO_2 levels are rising, strengthening the greenhouse effect. The subject has earned widespread concern.

Harlan Cleveland, a statesman of science, has advanced the notion of a "global commons," in a book with that title. The commons, historically, meant the part of the town that belonged to everybody. Boston Common is a commons. It was a place in the middle of the town where everybody could graze their cows, at least in an earlier day, if not now.

Cleveland sees a global commons with four components. First is the oceans, which belong to no nation and on which ships of all nations may sail. Second is the atmosphere, which respects no boundaries; the weather system that affects the United States today may have been over the Pacific last week and over China the week before that. Third is outer space, which is international, which no nation can stake a claim to; although Americans planted a flag on the Moon, no one suggests that it therefore belongs to the United States. Fourth, finally, is Antarctica, which by international agreement is peaceful—there is nothing of a military nature on Antarctica—and relatively pristine, a park where scientists can be observed doing science, a place where, most of the time, only scientists and penguins and precious little else of large size are on the ice.

Cleveland takes those examples—the ocean, the atmosphere, space, and Antarctica—as the global commons, the common heritage of all humankind. I think we might wish to extend that list to things like the tropical rainforests, which in a strict sense belong to the countries where they're located, but which benefit all of us.

Once you've accepted the idea that there is a commons that everyone benefits from and that everybody is responsible for, then you're not far from the idea that we ought to devise fair and equitable ways of protecting it.

We can cite examples of efforts toward realizing those goals. One is the Montreal Protocol, a remarkable document—or a remarkably successful series of treaties, if you count the amendments that were later enacted. The Montreal Protocol and its amendments have already led to a dramatic reduction in the rate at which chlorofluorocarbons are being put into the atmosphere.

These actions have far-reaching and long-term consequences. Chlorofluorocarbons have such long lifetimes that their concentrations will continue to increase for some time. But they will eventually begin to decrease, because of the actions we're taking today.

Recall the poignant plea of the 17-year-old Australian, Zanny Begg, an observer at the London conference that amended the Montreal Protocol. "You are making history" she said to all the diplomats and scientists and delegates attending this historic conference. "Have the courage to save the ozone layer."

Her challenge is echoed in an extraordinary essay by a woman much more widely known. This essay appears as an appendix to the book *One Earth, One Future,* which is not a typical environmental manifesto, but rather a publication of the very staid U.S. National Academy of Sciences. The essay is by Gro Harlem Brundtland, prime minister of Norway, who headed an international commission that produced a report called *Our Common Future*. In her essay, she said, "The interplay between scientific process and public policy is not new but has been a characteristic of most of the great turning points in human history. One need look no further than the dawning of the nuclear age to see that."

Brundtland makes some recommendations. She says, "We need a global consensus for economic growth in the 1990s." The reason for that, she continues, is simply that "it is politically, economically, and morally unacceptable that there is a net transfer of resources from poor countries to rich ones. Nearly a billion people live in poverty and squalor, and the per-capita income of some 50 developing countries has continued to decline over the past few years." These trends must be reversed. Brundtland goes on to say:

> We need concerted international action. There are certain imperatives that must be vigorously pursued:
>
> · We must agree on regional strategies for stabilizing and reducing emissions of greenhouse gases. Reforestation efforts must be included as a vital part of the carbon equation.
>
> · We must strongly intensify our efforts to develop renewable forms of energy. Renewable energy should become the foundation of the global energy structure during the twenty-first century.
>
> · We should speed up our efforts on international agreements to protect the atmosphere. There are different views on how to proceed on this issue. I urge that negotiations to limit the emissions of greenhouse gases begin immediately.

The history of carbon emissions from fossil-fuel burning illustrates her point. Consider the carbon added to the atmosphere in the form of carbon dioxide in three recent years: 1950, 1965, and 1985. Remember, we're putting out nearly 6 billion tons a year today, about 1 ton for every person on Earth. Only a few pounds for each resident of India, quite a lot of pounds for each North American. The approximate amounts were 1.5 billion metric tons a year in 1950, 2.9 billion in 1965, and 5.1 billion in 1985. So the amount of CO_2 being added to the atmosphere by people more than tripled over this 35-year period. During this same period, world population approximately doubled. Thus, CO_2 emissions increased sharply in both absolute and per-capita terms.

But what's extraordinary here is how the relative roles of different parts of the world changed during that period. Consider the portion emitted by North America. In 1950, that portion was nearly half of the global total. Fifteen years later, North America emitted more CO_2 than it did in 1950. But instead of being about half the global total, the contribution from North America was about a third. In 1985, when the global total was larger still, North America contributed only about a fourth of it.

The carbon emitted by China and other developing countries was barely discernible in 1950, but by 1985 it had exceeded that of North America. China's portion of global emissions may grow to surpass the emissions of the United States (which comprise most of the North American total) within only a few decades or less, because there are more than a billion people in China, and they have unlimited coal for near-term purposes. By the early 1990s, Chinese carbon emissions had already begun to exceed 50% of U.S. emissions. Incidentally, global carbon emissions have been on a plateau of around 5.9 billion tons since about 1987, owing in part to the economic contraction in the former Soviet Union and to stagnant economic conditions worldwide. Rapid industrialization in Asia has been largely responsible for the fact that global emissions did not actually *decrease* during this period.

If China continues to industrialize by using coal as a fuel, its contribution of CO_2 emissions will inevitably grow. Although the United States still contributes more CO_2 than any other single country, China is now second, ahead of Russia. In coming years, the U.S. share of the global total will almost certainly continue to decrease. But the United States can and should lead the way in reducing emissions of CO_2. Its per-capita contribution is shamefully high. A single American can do far more to reduce CO_2 emissions than can a single Indian. Acting alone, however, the United States cannot solve the CO_2 problem. All countries need to do their part as well. Global problems require global solutions.

Some countries are beginning to act. For example, a 1991 meeting of European ministers in Brussels approved in principle an energy tax designed to cut down on carbon-dioxide emissions. Their plan was to implement a tax increase that would raise the price of gasoline in Europe by about 6% and the price of electricity by about 14%.

These European countries also planned to tax other fossil fuels by equivalent amounts, and even to tax other energy sources that don't produce CO_2, so that in France, for example, even though electricity comes mainly from nuclear power, there would still be incentive for conservation.

The European Community generates only a small fraction of the world's carbon dioxide, far less than the United States does. But it is clearly serious about taking action.

As you might suspect, some European ministers have occasionally had critical things to say about the United States. At the Brussels meeting in 1991, the Dutch environmental minister noted that the European Community cannot reduce global warming by itself. He expressed the hope that the United States, which produces about twice as much CO_2 per capita as Western Europe, would join the campaign. Although he admitted that recent talks between the United States and European officials had produced no movement, at least Western Europe decided not to wait.

Remember, we're talking about industrial democracies here, with governments that are not composed of professional environmentalists but that are nonetheless responding to the pressures of their electorates. So, if you want to be optimistic about the chances of real progress toward a sustainable future, there's considerable evidence that a massive change in attitudes and policies, which was once unthinkable, may be coming to the fore today.

9

ON SCIENTISTS
AND DOING SCIENCE

Of the issues we've considered, ozone depletion is perhaps the one that offers us the most hope that people collectively will behave intelligently to help assure a healthy future for our Earth. Fortunately, in the case of stratospheric ozone, the problem was quickly recognized, and decisive action did eventually occur. Otherwise, the outlook for future decades would have been far more bleak. As humankind continues to discuss even more difficult global environmental issues, such as possible climate change from an increase in the greenhouse effect, we will necessarily be concerned with determining which actions are wise and prudent, given incomplete scientific information. In some cases, there may well still be time enough to act, to avoid serious planetary change. Often, the critical time scale—running neck and neck with the rate of growth of the problem—may be the time required to inform people, to build a political consensus, and to muster an international willingness to take action.

When making projections into the environmental future, or in talking about what the climate may be like in the middle of the twenty-first century, when some of us and many of our children will still be alive, that time scale must be kept in mind. The environment changes, but many other things change too. It's good to keep in mind that much of what we take for granted today was unforeseen, except by a few visionary people, not so long ago. Developments ranging from color televisions to pharmaceuticals to personal computers were difficult to imagine not so very long ago. Technology is powerful, and there may be technological measures for coping with many of these problems. Agriculture, for example, can sometimes evolve and adapt through improved technology.

In the case of climate change, just as with ozone depletion, our past actions may well have already committed the Earth to future change. If the theories of how climate will respond to an increased greenhouse effect are even approximately valid, then we've already committed our planet to substantial climate change. And, because scientific understanding is still seriously incomplete, we'll inevitably be making decisions that may have far-reaching consequences without having at hand all the scientific knowledge that we'd like.

We've found compelling reasons to believe that the world should accelerate a transition to nonfossil primary energy sources. Should the countries of the world follow the model of France, which generates about three-fourths of its electricity from nuclear power? There are serious disadvantages to nuclear power, as we've seen. Should humankind instead put increased efforts into developing renewable energy resources, like solar, wind, hydroelectric, geothermal, and biomass, all the sources of energy *other than* nuclear and fossil fuels? Should governments emphasize energy conservation and efficiency, which have many side benefits? I think so, though others disagree. After all, if you change your choice of cars and drive one that uses less fuel, or if you drive less, you not only help slow the increase in the greenhouse effect by putting out less carbon dioxide from the tailpipe, you may also help reduce smog and save yourself some money—and perhaps even improve political stability in the Middle East. So there are many ramifications to these choices.

But the scientific element in these discussions is critical. You can't make a sensible decision about how to have an environmentally sustainable planet in the future if you don't have an understanding of the consequences of actions today—actions such as releasing CFCs into the atmosphere or burning fossil fuels and making carbon dioxide. The role of science here is central.

It's interesting to note that Molina and Rowland's 1974 paper, the theoretical work that pointed out the catalytic cycle that affects ozone, did not specifically predict the Antarctic ozone hole. Molina and Rowland were initially concerned not about Antarctic ozone, but rather about the gradual destruction of the ozone layer globally. One of the lessons of the ozone story is that the ozone hole itself was unexpected.

No theory predicted a 50% ozone loss over Antarctica. It was a surprise discovery, made serendipitously by Farman and his group, who had been going to Antarctica every year.

Farman and his colleagues didn't go to Antarctica to validate Molina and Rowland's notions. You wouldn't want to go to a bleak and desolate spot to do that. You could measure ozone in Monte Carlo. Farman was in Antarctica because Antarctica is a natural laboratory. It's relatively pristine, a good clean place to do lots of kinds of science. Farman had been making measurements there for decades. The ozone hole was discovered simply because people were making measurements they thought would be useful. They weren't expecting to find the ozone hole. Even when they did measure it, they were skeptical of their data. In fact, they waited several years for the ozone hole to recur in succeeding years before they published their findings.

Molina and Rowland are justly given much credit for having done the critical theoretical work on ozone depletion. It's good to keep in mind that no committee or government agency told them to do research on whether chlorofluorocarbons are a threat to ozone. It was pure science, done out of intellectual curiosity, done because they thought it was important and interesting. In fact, Rowland had been working on other topics when he first became interested in finding out what happened to CFCs once they were put into the atmosphere. He wrote a research proposal asking for money to pursue his new interest. The government agency that was supporting Rowland's work turned down his request for new funding, but did give him permission to divert some of his existing research funds to study CFCs. We should all be grateful for that. Rowland was just following a hunch. He might have been wrong.

In that way, science is inefficient. I believe that to be a fair generalization. Some bright ideas turn out in retrospect to have been brilliant. And Molina and Rowland's was. Some experimental work turns out to be extremely productive—you learn something very valuable from it. And the observational work of Farman's group at Halley Bay fell in that category, too.

Incidentally, neither of these examples of research was particularly expensive. The annual cost of Farman's observations in the early 1980s was about $18,000. Theoretical work, such as that of Molina and Rowland, is usually cheap, too. The main cost is the salary of the scientists. The crucial breakthrough in the theory of ozone depletion was made quickly. In October 1973, a young Dr. Molina arrived at the University of California, Irvine, to begin a postdoctoral fellowship, working with

Professor Rowland. By December, they had completed the crucial theory. The paper was written in January, and it appeared in June 1974. Over the next two decades, the immense significance of this research gradually became undeniable. In 1995, Molina and Rowland, together with Paul Crutzen, a Dutch scientist who had also done pioneering work on atmospheric ozone, were awarded the Nobel Prize in Chemistry.

Keeling's measurements of carbon dioxide have a good deal in common with Farman's measurements of ozone. Both began their work in the late 1950s during the International Geophysical Year (IGY). Both thus owe a debt to "big science," the large organized research enterprise marked by committee management and governmental involvement. But both Farman and Keeling continued their work for decades after the IGY, motivated only by their own curiosity and a hunch that their observations would turn out to lead to something worthwhile.

But it's exactly this kind of work, done on individual initiative by scientists who think it important, that can so often lead to profoundly important results. Along the way, the ozone controversy had an effect on the decision not to build an American supersonic transport aircraft to compete with the Concorde. Although that decision was probably dominated by economic rather than environmental factors, nonetheless, on the basis of this kind of science, the environmental impact was at least taken into account in deciding whether to fly supersonic airplanes in the lower stratosphere.

Still, every working scientist knows that for every brilliant idea you come up with, you may have ten that lead nowhere, maybe even 100 if you're honest with yourself. Scientific research is an inherently inefficient process, and its results are serendipitous and difficult to predict. That makes particular projects really hard to justify to politicians, to budgeteers, to taxpayers. And that's why it's easy to make fun of science projects that have seemingly bizarre titles.

We're at the end of this story, insofar as we know it at the moment, but it's a story that never really ends. To me, one of the most fascinating aspects of scientific research is that no branch of it is ever neatly tied up and finished. No science is dead. Science isn't something that was carried out long ago and is finished now and can be presented in sterile textbooks, like Latin grammar. It's alive, it's evolving, it's different today from what it was yesterday, it's being done by people who have both egos and imperfections, and—fortunately for all of us—it's changing all the time.

GLOSSARY

All of the technical terms employed in this book are defined or characterized on first occurrence in the text, and in many cases on later occurrences as well. Most of these terms are also defined here, usually in more detail, and many are listed in the Index. A few additional terms, not used in the text, are included here to round out certain interrelated groups, and all technical terms employed within the definitions in the Glossary are also defined in the Glossary. Time spent browsing and cross-referring in the Glossary should thus help to fix meanings and relationships in mind. The Glossary concludes with a list of some commonly used chemical symbols.

Absolute humidity is one of several measures of atmospheric moisture content. It is the mass of water vapor per unit volume of the air containing the water vapor, typically expressed as grams of water vapor per cubic meter of air. (Compare **relative humidity,** and see also **humidity.**)

Absorption is the conversion into heat of a fraction of the radiation that is incident on an object.

Acid deposition is the combination of dry deposition of acidic substances (coal ash, etc.) plus precipitation (rain, snow, etc.) made acidic typically by the addition of sulfur dioxide and nitrogen oxides into the atmosphere as a result of fossil-fuel burning. Automobile exhaust and the emissions from coal-fired powerplants are two significant causes of acid deposition. In severe cases, acid precipitation kills fish and other aquatic life and damages and/or destroys trees, crops, and other vegetation. In some instances, it has rendered entire lakes and forests nearly lifeless.

Acidic (see **pH**).

Acid precipitation is rain (or snow) with a pH less than about 5.6, usually because of the presence of nitric and/or sulfuric acid. Because natural rain is slightly acidic, rain with a pH value somewhat less than the strictly neutral criterion (a pH of 7) is not generally referred to as acid rain.

Adiabatic means occurring without the exchange of heat. In meteorology, an adiabatic exchange usually occurs between an air parcel under consideration and its surroundings.

Advection, in meteorology, is horizontal movement of air, or horizontal transport by air of any property, such as heat or humidity.

Aerosol is a gaseous suspension of fine liquid or solid particles in air.

Air mass is a large volume of air, typically thousands of kilometers in horizontal dimensions, that is relatively uniform horizontally in its properties, especially in temperature and moisture content.

Albedo is the total fraction of light (or, more generally, of electromagnetic radiation flux) striking a surface that is reflected by that surface, often expressed as a percentage. Light-colored, light-reflecting surfaces, such as snow and ice, have a high albedo, while dark, light-absorbing surfaces have a low albedo.

Alkaline (see **pH**).

Antarctic ozone hole (see **Ozone hole**).

Anthropogenic means caused or created by human beings. For example, anthropogenic carbon-dioxide emissions are those caused by such human activities as the burning of fossil fuels.

Anticyclone is a weather system characterized by relatively high atmospheric pressure compared with its surroundings, together with winds blowing clockwise in the Northern Hemisphere and counterclockwise in the Southern Hemisphere. (Compare **cyclone.**)

Atmosphere is the envelope of gases that surrounds a planet. Earth's atmosphere is one of the five basic interrelated components of the Earth system. (See the other four components: **biosphere, cryosphere, hydrosphere,** and **pedosphere.**)

Atmospheric pressure is the force exerted by the air on each unit of area of a surface, essentially equivalent to the weight of the overlying atmosphere. High atmospheric pressure generally leads to stable weather conditions, whereas low pressure can result in storms.

Atom is the smallest unit of a chemical element that can take part in a chemical reaction. An atom is composed of a nucleus, which contains protons and neutrons, surrounded by electrons.

Barometer is an instrument used to measure atmospheric pressure.

Biodiversity is a general term that describes several aspects of the variety inherent in the complex web of living things, and it has different specific meanings. **Species diversity,** the most common use of the term, is the total number of biological species occurring in a particular area. **Habitat diversity** is the variety of places, or types of places, where life exists. **Genetic diversity** is primarily the variety of populations comprising each species, where population is seen as a group of members of a species that live together and so can mate with one another.

Biomass is the total dry weight of living material in a particular area.

Biome is a distinctive ecological system, characterized primarily by the nature and composition of its vegetation.

Biosphere, one of the five basic interrelated components of the Earth system, is the region on land, in the oceans, and in the atmosphere inhabited by living things. (See **atmosphere.**)

Biota is all living things, collectively, including animal and plant life.

Black body is an idealized or theoretical object that absorbs all of the radiation incident upon it and emits the maximum possible radiation for its temperature at every wavelength.

Blizzard is snow falling with winds faster than 35 miles per hour and visibility of a quarter-mile or less over an extended time period.

Business-as-usual, in the context of global-climate change, is a scenario for future world patterns of energy use and greenhouse-gas emission that assumes there will be no significant change in people's and governments' attitudes and priorities.

Carbon cycle is the exchange of carbon between land, atmosphere, and oceans. About one-fourth of the total quantity of atmospheric carbon (in the form of carbon dioxide) is cycled in and out of the atmosphere each year; approximately half of this amount is exchanged with the land biota, and the other half, through physical and chemical processes, passes across the ocean surface.

Carbon dioxide (CO_2) is a colorless, odorless gas that is a trace constituent of the Earth's atmosphere and one of the major greenhouse gases. Anthropogenic CO_2 results mainly from burning fossil fuels (coal, oil, natural gas) and from deforestation.

Celsius is a temperature scale, also called the Centigrade scale. Its fixed points are the freezing point of water ($0°C$) and the boiling point of water ($100°C$). To convert from Celsius to Fahrenheit, multiply the Celsius temperature by 1.8 and add $32°$.

Chlorofluorocarbons (CFCs) are synthetic compounds invented by Thomas Midgley, Jr., in 1928 as refrigerants. CFCs destroy stratospheric ozone and are also greenhouse gases. The primary use of CFCs today is as a coolant in refrigerators and air conditioners. CFCs are also used as solvents, foam-blowing agents, and aerosol propellants, though the use of CFCs in aerosol cans in the United States was outlawed in the late 1970s. Substitutes for CFCs are under development, and some are already available. The Montreal Protocol for the Protection of the Ozone Layer is an international agreement that requires that parties to the agreement in developed nations phase out the production of CFCs by 1996.

Climate is, collectively, the temperature, humidity, precipitation, winds, radiation, and other meteorological conditions characteristic of a locality or region over an extended period of time. Compared to weather, climate involves longer times and deals not only with the atmosphere but also with oceans, land, and biosphere. The essential characteristic of climate is that it is a statistical concept embracing the sum total of weather, thus including not only average conditions but also probabilities of extreme events and other descriptions of the variability of meteorological conditions.

Climate sensitivity is the magnitude of the climate change expected to result from a particular change in external influences. One description of climate sensitivity is the rise in global average temperature expected to result from a doubling of carbon dioxide in the atmosphere.

Climatology is the scientific study of climate, particularly of its variability and its dependence on factors that influence its behavior.

Cloud is a visible aggregation of condensed water-vapor (liquid or ice) particles.

Cold front is a zone of transition marking the boundary between advancing, relatively cold and dense air and retreating, relatively warm and less dense air. (Compare **warm front.**)

Compound is any substance, for example carbon dioxide (CO_2), formed from two or more elements chemically combined in fixed proportions. (Compare **element.**)

Condensation is the process of changing state from gas (or vapor) to liquid, as in the formation of water droplets in clouds.

Condensation nuclei are small particles in the air that attract water and encourage condensation.

Convection is, generally, vertical motion in the atmosphere or ocean generated by temperature differences and resulting in the transfer of heat.

Coriolis effect is an apparent deflective force due to the Earth's rotation, affecting relatively large-scale, slow motions of the atmosphere and ocean, causing a deflection to the right in the Northern Hemisphere and to the left in the Southern Hemisphere.

Cryosphere, one of the five basic interrelated components of the Earth system, is that portion of the Earth's surface with average temperatures below the freezing point of water. The bulk of the cryosphere is at or near the poles, but cryospheric regions also exist atop high mountain ranges on all continents. The cryosphere is composed of snow, permanently frozen ground (permafrost), floating ice, and glaciers. (See **atmosphere.**)

Cumulus clouds are clouds exhibiting significant vertical development, often due to convective updrafts.

Cyclone is a weather system characterized by relatively low atmospheric pressure compared with its surroundings, together with winds blowing counterclockwise in the Northern Hemisphere and clockwise in the Southern Hemisphere. (Compare **anticyclone.**)

Deforestation is destruction of forests, usually by cutting or burning. Deforestation enhances the greenhouse effect in two ways. First, when wood is burned or decomposes, it releases carbon dioxide. Second, trees that are destroyed can no longer remove carbon dioxide from the atmosphere in the process of photosynthesis.

Demography is the study of the nature and structure of human populations, including their distribution, age structure, composition, lifestyles, and change.

Desertification is degradation of land characterized by reduced soil moisture and reduced vegetation, including crops, and by soil erosion. Like deforestation, desertification can affect climate in several ways, such as by altering the water cycle.

Developing countries, sometimes called less-developed countries (LDCs) or "Third World," are those characterized in general by low personal income, little industrialization, high rates of illiteracy, and poor public health. Most developing countries are in the Northern Hemisphere.

Dew point is a measure of humidity, given in terms of the air temperature at which dew begins to form, as water vapor condenses into liquid.

Dobson unit (DU) is a measure of ozone abundance. Ozone varies naturally, especially with latitude and season, ranging typically from about 250 to 460 Dobson units. (Gordon Dobson was a researcher at Oxford University who, in the late 1920s, built the first instrument, now called the Dobson meter, for measuring total ozone from the ground.)

Drought is an extended period of abnormal dryness for a particular region.

Drylands are areas of the world where precipitation is low and where rainfall typically consists of erratic, short, local, high-intensity storms.

Earth system (see **atmosphere**).

Ecology is the science that deals with the interrelationships between living organisms and their environments.

Ecosystem is a distinct system of interdependent plants and animals, together with their physical environment. An ecosystem may be as large as the entire Earth, or as small as a pond.

Electromagnetic radiation is energy transfer by waves having both electrical and magnetic properties.

Electromagnetic spectrum is the range of types of radiation, ordered by wavelength or frequency, and includes all forms of electric, magnetic, and visible radiation.

Electron is a negatively charged component of an atom.

Element is any substance, for example iron or oxygen, that cannot be separated by chemical means into two or more simpler substances. (Compare **compound**.)

El Niño is a warming of the surface waters of the eastern tropical Pacific, occurring at irregular intervals of about 2 to 7 years, usually lasting from several months up to about 2 years, that has a significant influence on regional and global climate. El Niño has been linked to colder, wetter winters in parts of the United States, drier, hotter summers in South America and Europe, and drought in Africa, as well as reduced numbers of fish in South American Pacific coastal waters due to reduced upwelling of nutrient-rich waters. (See also **El Niño-Southern Oscillation.**)

El Niño-Southern Oscillation (ENSO) is the closely linked phenomena of El Niño (see above) and a global-scale shift in atmospheric pressure called the Southern Oscillation (SO). In the so-called warm phase of ENSO, El Niño warming extends over much of the tropical Pacific and becomes clearly linked to the SO pattern. Many of the countries most affected by ENSO events are developing countries with economies that are largely dependent on their agricultural and fishery sectors as a major source of food supply, employment, and foreign exchange. New capabilities for predicting the onset of ENSO events can thus have important human impacts. ENSO is fundamentally an aspect of the combined ocean-atmosphere system and cannot be understood as either entirely meteorological or entirely oceanographic in nature. Although ENSO is a natural part of Earth's climate variability, whether its intensity or frequency may change as a result of global warming is a concern. Recent progress toward predicting the occurrence and characteristics of ENSO events shows great promise.

Endemic means occurring naturally *only* in a certain region, as a species that is endemic to a particular place.

Environment is the complex of physical, chemical, and biological factors in which a living organism or community exists.

Environmental refugees are people obliged to leave their traditional or established homelands because of environmental problems (deforestation, desertification, floods, drought, sea-level rise, nuclear-plant accidents), on a permanent or semipermanent basis, with little or no hope of ever returning. Though no formal accounting has been taken, there may currently be about 25 million environmental refugees in the world, according to one estimate, and it is likely that the number will rise.

Equator is an imaginary circle around the Earth that is equally distant from the North and South poles and defines the latitude 0°.

Evaporation is the process of changing from a liquid state to a gaseous state, or vapor.

Evapotranspiration is the discharge of water from Earth's surface to the atmosphere by evaporation from bodies of water, or other surfaces, and by transpiration from plants.

Exotic means originating outside of an area, as for example an exotic species.

Fahrenheit is a temperature scale based on the freezing point of water (32°F) and the boiling point of water (212°F) under standard atmospheric pressure. To convert from Fahrenheit to Centigrade, subtract 32° from the Fahrenheit temperature and divide the resulting quantity by 1.8.

Feedback is a sequence of interactions in which the final interaction (or some set of interactions) influences the original one. In such a sequence, a cause produces a result, and the result then in turn influences its cause. As a system changes, it may generate processes that affect the original change. If one of these processes amplifies the change (global warming, for example, may cause a change in cloudiness, which then adds to the warming), it is called a *positive feedback*. If it dampens the change, it is called a *negative feedback*.

Fog is a cloud in contact with, or close to, the surface of the Earth, reducing visibility to less than one mile, or about 1.6 kilometers.

Food chain is a series of plants and/or animals that depend, one on another, as food sources (that is, a plant is eaten by a small fish, which is eaten by a larger fish, which is eaten by a bird, and so on, the series thus represented constituting the chain).

Fossil is the hardened remains or traces of particular plant or animal life from a previous geological period, preserved in the Earth's crust.

Fossil fuels, basically coal, oil, and natural gas, are fuels created by the decomposition of ancient animal and plant remains. They are finite (limited) resources, and they release carbon dioxide and other gases when burned.

Front is a narrow zone marking the boundary between two air masses of significantly different meteorological properties, usually the properties of temperature, humidity, wind speed, and wind direction.

General Circulation Models (GCMs) are computer models of Earth's climate that are used to improve our understanding of factors that influence climate and enhance our ability to forecast future climate patterns. One reason GCMs are so useful is that they allow researchers to vary individual factors and observe the results, isolating processes in a way that is not possible in the physical world. GCMs are also sometimes called "Global Climate Models," a more accurate and more descriptive characterization. "General circulation" is an older technical term in meteorology that originally referred to the long-term average aspects of large-scale atmospheric behavior. In modern usage, a GCM can be an atmospheric model or an oceanic model or a model of the coupled climate system involving the atmosphere and ocean and other components as well.

Geoengineering is the intentional artificial modification of Earth systems to counteract anthropogenic effects such as global warming or stratospheric ozone depletion. An example of geoengineering aimed at reducing global warming is the "iron hypothesis," which suggests that adding iron to the oceans could stimulate the growth of small plants that would photosynthesize at greater levels, thus removing carbon dioxide from the atmosphere. In general, geoengineering proposals would be costly and logistically difficult, and before any were to be undertaken, it would be prudent to be certain that unanticipated adverse consequences would not occur.

Geosphere is, collectively, the physical elements of the Earth's surface, crust, mantle, and interior. (Compare **pedosphere.**)

Geostationary, or **geosynchronous,** describes an orbit in which a satellite is always in the same position with respect to the Earth. The satellite travels around the Earth, in the same direction and at the same speed as the Earth's rotation, completing one orbit in a 24-hour period, thus remaining above the same point on the Earth's surface. All geostationary satellites are directly above Earth's Equator and are at the same altitude, namely about 36,000 kilometers, or 22,300 miles, above the Earth's surface.

Geothermal energy is energy obtained by the transfer of heat to Earth's surface from its depths. A natural hot spring is one such example, and significant amounts of electricity are generated by power plants that pump superheated fluids from the depths.

Glacier is a multi-year accumulation of snowfall in excess of snowmelt on land, resulting over time in a mass of ice covering at least a tenth of a square kilometer, that shows some evidence of movement in response to gravity. Glacial ice is the largest reservoir of fresh water on Earth, and second only to the oceans as the largest reservoir of total water. Glaciers are found on every continent except Australia.

Global change is change in the Earth system that is either a global phenomenon or occurs regionally but strongly enough and often enough to be of global significance. The leading current global-change issues include climate change due to an enhanced greenhouse effect, stratospheric ozone depletion, acid precipitation, urban air pollution, and loss of biodiversity.

Global warming is a predicted warming of Earth's climate due to increased concentrations of greenhouse gases in the atmosphere. The Intergovernmental Panel on Climate Change (IPCC), composed of many of the world's leading authorities on the subject, estimates that if atmospheric carbon dioxide were to double, global average temperature would eventually increase by 1.5° to 4.5°C (about 3° to 8°F), with a "best guess" of 2.5°C (about 4°F). The IPCC also estimates that about half the magnitude of this warming will have occurred by the year 2030.

Greenhouse effect is the natural process whereby gases in Earth's atmosphere act like the glass in greenhouse, letting the Sun's energy in, but preventing some of the Earth's radiation from escaping to space. Were it not for this natural effect, Earth's climate would be about 33°C (60°F) colder, and life as we know it would not exist. The "enhanced greenhouse effect" refers to an increase in this natural heat-trapping phenomenon caused by anthropogenic emissions of greenhouse gases.

Greenhouse gases are water vapor, carbon dioxide, methane, tropospheric ozone, nitrous oxide, CFCs, and other gases that absorb some of the long-wave thermal radiation emitted from Earth's surface, thereby contributing to the greenhouse effect and warming the atmosphere. With the exception of water vapor, these are also called "trace gases," since they total less than 1% of the atmosphere.

Green revolution is a dramatic increase in global or regional food production, primarily as a result of the development of new strains of crops.

Ground truth is information collected at the Earth's surface at the same place and time as a remote sensor gathers analogous data. Ground-truth information is used to interpret and calibrate remotely sensed data from satellites.

Gulf Stream is the warm, swift ocean current that flows from the Gulf of Mexico, along the coast of the Eastern United States, across the Atlantic to the European coast, and makes Ireland, Great Britain, and the Scandinavian countries warmer than they would be otherwise.

GWP, which stands for Global Warming Potential, is the ratio of how much a gas contributes, molecule for molecule, to enhancing the greenhouse effect, compared to the contribution of carbon dioxide.

Habitat is the environment in which an individual or population of humans, plants, or animals occurs.

Hadley cell, a feature of the tropical general circulation of the atmosphere, is characterized by rising air near the equator, poleward flow aloft, sinking air in the subtropics, and return flow toward the Equator near the surface.

Hail is precipitation composed of lumps of ice. Hail is produced when large frozen raindrops, or other particles in cumulonimbus clouds, grow by accumulating supercooled liquid droplets. Violent updrafts in the clouds carry the particles up through the freezing air, allowing the frozen core to accumulate more ice. When the piece of hail becomes too heavy to be carried by rising air currents, it falls to the ground.

Halocarbons are halons, chlorofluorocarbons, hydrochlorofluorocarbons, and other chemicals that deplete the stratospheric ozone layer. The term "halocarbons" is used in the Montreal Protocol on Substances that Deplete the Ozone Layer.

Halons are a class of ozone-depleting compounds containing bromine.

HCFCs. (See **hydrochlorofluorocarbons.**)

Horse latitudes, the regions near latitude 30° in both hemispheres, are associated with high pressures and weak winds, because of subtropical anticyclones. The term originates from the days of sailing ships, from which, according to legend, horses were either thrown overboard or eaten as food ran out when the ships were becalmed.

Humidity is the amount of water vapor in the air. The higher the temperature of the air, the greater the number of water molecules it can hold. (See **absolute humidity, relative humidity.**)

Hurricane is an intense warm-core tropical storm with winds exceeding 74 miles per hour. Hurricanes originate over the tropical and subtropical North Atlantic, Indian, and Pacific oceans (in the latter they are known as *typhoons*), because high sea-surface temperatures are essential to their formation.

Hydrocarbons are compounds containing only carbon and hydrogen.

Hydrochlorofluorocarbons (HCFCs) are replacements for chlorofluorocarbons (CFCs) that are less ozone-depleting than CFCs but not totally nondepleting. HCFCs are also greenhouse gases, and thus contribute to global warming.

Hydrologic cycle is the natural sequence through which water evaporates from the ocean, land surface, and plants into the atmosphere as water vapor, falls to Earth as precipitation, and largely returns to the ocean through pathways including rivers and ground water.

Hydrosphere, one of the five basic interrelated components of the Earth system, consists of all of Earth's waters, including the oceans, fresh waters, and water vapor in the atmosphere. (See **atmosphere.**)

Hydroxyl is a chemical group consisting of one atom of hydrogen and one atom of oxygen.

Ice Age is a geological time period during which sheets of ice cover extensive parts of the Earth.

Image resolution is the level of detail in an image, and is determined by the area represented by each pixel (picture element). The smaller the area represented by a pixel, the more detailed the image and the higher the image resolution. For example, if a U.S. map and a world map are printed on the same-sized paper, one square inch on the U.S. map will represent far less area and provide far more detail, relatively, than one square inch of the world map. The U.S. map would thus be said to have higher resolution.

Indigenous means occurring naturally in an area, as for example an indigenous species of animal or plant.

Infrared radiation is electromagnetic radiation at wavelengths longer than red visible light, but shorter than microwaves. Most radiation emitted by the Earth is infrared, and it is this radiation that is involved in the greenhouse effect.

In situ (Latin for "in original place"), usually refers to data collected at the actual location of the object or material measured, as opposed to remote sensing.

Insolation is the striking, by solar radiation, of a particular horizontal surface on or above Earth's surface.

Ion is an atom or molecule that has acquired an electric charge by the loss or gain of one or more electrons.

Ionosphere is an electrified region of the upper atmosphere.

Isothermal means of or indicating equality of temperature. In meteorology, isotherms are lines on a weather map connecting points of equal temperature.

Kilometer is a metric unit of distance approximately equal to 3,280.8 feet, or 0.621 miles.

Lightning is a discharge of atmospheric electricity accompanied by a vivid flash of light. During thunderstorms, static electricity builds up in clouds. A positive charge builds in the upper part of the cloud, while a negative charge builds in the lower portion. When the difference between the charges becomes great, the charge jumps from one area to another, creating a lightning bolt. Most lightning bolts strike from one cloud to another, but they can also strike the ground. Such bolts can occur when positive charges build up on the ground. A negative charge or "leader" flows from the cloud toward the ground and then a positively charged stroke (called the return stroke) runs from the ground to the cloud. What appears as a lightning bolt is actually a series of downward and upward strokes, all taking place in less than a second. (See **thunder**.)

Mean is the scientific term for arithmetic average, as in "global mean temperature."

Mesosphere is an atmospheric layer above the stratosphere, at an average elevation between 50 and 80 kilometers above the Earth's surface.

Meteorology is the science of the atmosphere, in all its ramifications.

Microwave is a comparatively short electromagnetic wave, typically with a wavelength between about 1 millimeter and 1 meter.

Modeling is an investigative technique that uses a mathematical and/or physical representation of a system or theory to test for the effects that changes in system components may have on the overall functioning of the system. Mathematical modeling using computers plays a major role in climate research, by simulating how Earth's climate will respond to changes in the atmospheric concentrations of greenhouse gases.

Molecule is two or more atoms of one or more elements chemically combined in fixed proportions. For example, atoms of the elements carbon and oxygen, chemically bonded in a 1:2 proportion, create molecules of the compound known as carbon dioxide (CO_2). Molecules can also be formed of a single element, as in ozone (O_3).

Monsoon is a particular seasonal weather pattern in subtropical regions, especially when characterized by periods of heavy winds and rainfall. Monsoons are caused by a pronounced seasonal change in wind direction. Winds usually blow from land to sea in winter, whereas, in the summer, this reverses, bringing precipitation. Monsoons are most typical in India and elsewhere in southern Asia. They also occur in Africa and Australia.

Montreal Protocol on Substances that Deplete the Ozone Layer is an international agreement that prescribes a timetable for ending the production of chlorofluorocarbons (CFCs) and related compounds. Begun in 1987, this unprecedented international treaty is a unique example of scientists and industry working with governments to seek a global solution to the human-caused environmental challenge of ozone depletion. After the original agreement was signed, new evidence arose proving that deeper and quicker cuts in CFC production were necessary to protect the ozone layer. The 1990 London amendments and the 1992 Copenhagen amendments sped up the halocarbon phaseout and controlled several other chemicals that were not in the original agreement: methyl chloroform, carbon tetrachloride, methyl bromide, and hydrochlorofluorocarbons. The revised agreement now calls for the phaseout of CFCs to be complete by 1996. The treaty also attempts to make the phaseouts fair to developing countries by setting up a fund, paid for by developed nations, to assist developing countries in making the switch to ozone-safe chemicals.

Negative feedback (see **feedback**).

Neutron is a component of most atomic nuclei that is without electric charge, and is of approximately the same mass as the proton (the positively charged component).

NO_x is the common pollutant gases nitric oxide (NO) and nitrogen dioxide (NO_2), considered collectively.

Nuclear winter is the combination of climatological and related phenomena that are the hypothetical environmental consequences of nuclear war, consisting especially of a sudden and severe cooling due to a reduction in the amount of sunlight reaching Earth's surface, because of heavy smoke concentrations in the atmosphere arising from fires caused by nuclear explosions.

Orbit is the path of a body, such as a planet or satellite, in its periodic revolution around another body in space. For example, artificial satellites that orbit Earth near latitude 0° are said to have equatorial orbits, since they remain above the Equator. Satellites with inclinations near 90° are said to be in polar orbits, because they cross over or near Earth's North and South poles as they revolve around the planet.

Ozone is a gaseous molecule consisting of three atoms of oxygen (O_3). Ozone in Earth's stratosphere forms a protective layer that shields Earth's inhabitants from damaging ultraviolet radiation from the Sun. Ozone occurring in the troposphere, near Earth's surface, on the other hand, though identical, is a harmful pollutant resulting from the interaction of anthropogenic emissions of nitrogen oxides, volatile organic compounds, and sunlight.

Ozone depletion is the thinning of the stratospheric ozone layer that protects life on Earth from excess ultraviolet radiation from the Sun. Anthropogenic halocarbons are primarily responsible for this reduction in the amount of ozone in the stratosphere.

Ozone hole is a region of the atmosphere over Antarctica where, during the Southern Hemisphere springtime, a substantial fraction of the stratospheric ozone disappears, owing primarily to catalytic destruction by halocarbons of anthropogenic origin.

Paleoclimatology is the reconstruction of ancient climates by using evidence such as tree rings and air trapped in ice cores. Researchers use such evidence to understand natural climatic shifts, which can help us in understanding and eventually predicting future climate trends.

Pedosphere, one of the five basic interrelated components of the Earth system, is the solid portion of the Earth's surface. The pedosphere rides on continental structures that evolve over millions of years as a consequence of the tectonic motions of Earth's land masses. (See **atmosphere;** compare **geosphere.**)

pH is a measure of the acidity or alkalinity of a solution. A value of 7 is neutral, values less than 7 are acid, and values over 7 are alkaline or basic. A change of one unit on the pH scale represents a factor of ten in acidity; for example, a solution with a pH of five is ten times as acid as one with a pH of six.

Phenology is the science dealing with the relationships between climate and periodic biological phenomena that are related to or caused by climatic conditions, such as the seasonal budding of trees and the migration of birds.

Photochemical smog, present in many large cities, is formed by chemical reactions involving nitrogen oxides and hydrocarbons (from human activities, including automobile use) taking place in the presence of sunlight, typically in still, stagnant air. An important component of photochemical smog is tropospheric or ground-level ozone. The term "smog" is misapplied in this sense; its original meaning was a combination of smoke and fog.

Photosynthesis is the series of chemical reactions by which plants use the Sun's energy, carbon dioxide, and water vapor to form materials for growth, and in the process release oxygen.

Photovoltaic (PV) means capable of converting solar radiation directly into electricity. A photovoltaic or solar cell, often made of silicon, is a device for that purpose.

Phytoplankton are minute forms of plant life in the oceans at the base of the marine food chain.

Pixel is the smallest element of an electronically coded image. "Pixel" is a contraction of the words "picture element." (See **image resolution**.)

Plate tectonics is the concept that Earth's crust is composed of rigid plates that move over a less rigid interior. The movements of these plates cause geological events such as earthquakes and continental drift and, over long periods of time, can cause significant shifts in the relative positions of Earth's land masses.

Positive feedback (see **feedback**).

ppbv stands for parts per billion by volume, a measure of abundance.

ppmv stands for parts per million by volume, a measure of abundance.

Precipitation, in meteorology, is liquid or solid forms of moisture that fall from clouds, including rain, snow, hail, and sleet. Raindrops typically form around condensation nuclei, which are often particles of salt or dust. Under appropriate conditions, water or ice droplets forming on these particles can attract more water and continue to grow until they are large enough to fall out of the cloud.

PV (see **photovoltaic**).

Radiation budget is an accounting of the radiation that enters and leaves a planet's atmosphere. On global average, the quantity of solar radiation entering the atmosphere from space should be balanced by the thermal radiation leaving the Earth's surface and atmosphere.

Radioactive decay is the spontaneous breakdown of certain atomic nuclei (for example uranium) into one or more nuclei of different elements (for example radium from uranium).

Rainforest is a basically evergreen woodland of the tropics distinguished by a continuous leaf canopy and an average rainfall of about 100 inches (250 centimeters) per year. Rainforests play an important role in the global environment for several reasons. Though encompassing just 6–7% of Earth's land, they are the most biologically diverse biome on the planet, thought to house nearly half of its species. Rainforests also take up carbon dioxide, helping to balance anthropogenic emissions. When rainforests or other forests are cut or burned, the opposite occurs: they release stored carbon dioxide, adding to the greenhouse effect.

Rain gauge is a calibrated container that measures the amount of rainfall occurring during a specific period of time.

Relative humidity is the amount of water actually in the air compared with how much the air can hold at its current temperature. For example, 50% relative humidity means the air holds half the water vapor it is capable of holding. (Compare **absolute humidity** and see also **humidity**.)

Remote sensing is the process of obtaining information from a distance, especially from aircraft or satellites. Modern remote-sensing technology has greatly expanded our ability to see and understand the Earth and its systems and to observe changes. It has become a critical tool in activities ranging from the verification of arms-control treaties to the provision of emergency aid to disaster-stricken regions. Through remote sensing we learn about problems such as droughts, famines, and floods; we obtain information about agricultural practices, weather conditions, transportation systems, river flows, and terrain changes. We use remote sensing to locate Earth's natural resources, and can then use that information to exploit or protect them.

Renewable energy is energy from sources that are not depleted by use. Examples include using passive solar energy to heat buildings, solar thermal energy to heat water or turn turbines to produce electricity, photovoltaic cells to convert sunlight directly to electricity, wind power, and hydroelectric energy.

Sequestration is the natural removal of a substance from one regime and its storage in another (the sink), as when carbon dioxide is sequestered from the atmosphere by plants via photosynthesis.

Sink is the place of storage of substances removed naturally from another regime (see **sequestration**). Plants, for example, through photosynthesis, transform carbon dioxide from the air into organic matter which is then "stored" in the plant or in the soil. Plants are thus said to be "sinks" for carbon. One of the key uncertainties regarding climate is that the quantity of carbon held in the various sinks and the rates of exchange between them are not well known.

Smog (see **photochemical smog**).

Solar constant is the average total radiation reaching the top of Earth's atmosphere from the Sun. The numerical value of this constant, about 1,370 watts per square meter, is not, in fact, truly constant; variations of about a tenth of a percent have been measured during the last two decades.

Solar radiation is energy emitted from the Sun. It is the main energy source for Earth's climate system, heating the surface of the Earth and driving currents in the oceans and winds in the atmosphere. Ordinary visible sunlight is the most obvious form of solar radiation, but other forms are significant, too; for example, see **ultraviolet radiation.**

Sonde is a device sent up into the atmosphere, typically borne on a balloon, to obtain information about atmospheric conditions above the Earth's surface. Radiosondes, for example, measure temperature, pressure, and humidity and then transmit these data to Earth by radio.

Southern Oscillation (see **El Niño-Southern Oscillation**).

Spectral band is a segment of wavelengths within the electromagnetic spectrum.

Stratosphere is the region of the atmosphere between the troposphere and mesosphere, having a lower boundary approximately 8 kilometers above sea level at the poles and 15 km at the Equator, and an upper boundary at an altitude of approximately 50 km above sea level. This is the region that contains the ozone layer that protects Earth's surface from excess ultraviolet solar radiation.

Sustainable development is development that meets the needs of the present generation without compromising the ability of future generations to meet their own needs. Some people believe that the concept of sustainable development should include preserving the environment for other species as well as for people.

Synoptic means simultaneous. For example, a synoptic weather map displays meteorological conditions observed in different places at a single time. "Synoptic" also refers to a large or general view of something. For example, an aerial photograph provides a "synoptic," or "bird's-eye" view of an area.

Tectonics (see **plate tectonics**).

Terrestrial means pertaining to the Earth, as distinct from other planets (as in extraterrestrial life). It also means pertaining to the land, as distinct from the water or air (as in a terrestrial, as opposed to aquatic, ecosystem).

Thunder is the sound that results from lightning. A lightning bolt produces an intense burst of heat that makes the air around it expand explosively, producing the sound we hear as thunder. Since light travels faster than sound, we see the lightning before we hear the thunder. The difference in time between the two can tell us how far away from us the clouds producing the lightning and thunder are. (See **lightning**.)

Thunderstorm is a local storm resulting from rising, warm, humid air, which produces lightning and therefore thunder, usually accompanied by rain or hail, gusty winds, and strong updrafts.

TOMS (see **Total Ozone Mapping Spectrometer**).

Tornado is a strong, rotating column of air extending from the base of a cumulonimbus cloud to the ground. These twisting, spinning, often violent funnels of low-pressure air, created during powerful thunderstorms, are the most unpredictable weather event.

Total Ozone Mapping Spectrometer (TOMS) is a remote sensing instrument, first flown on the Nimbus-7 satellite, whose primary function is to monitor global ozone. TOMS is a major contribution from NASA to the monitoring of the Earth. The original TOMS instrument began delivering ozone data in November 1978, providing high-resolution mapping of total ozone, from the ground to the top of the atmosphere, on a daily basis. TOMS provided the first maps of the ozone hole. The TOMS instrument on Nimbus 7 failed in May 1993, after a remarkably long and productive lifetime. Subsequent TOMS and other instruments continue to monitor ozone depletion and variability.

Trace gases (see **greenhouse gases**).

Trade winds are global-scale winds in the tropics that blow generally toward the west in both hemispheres (from the northeast in the Northern Hemisphere and from the southeast in the Southern Hemisphere). These relatively steady winds came to be called "trade winds" because they provided trading ships with a sailing route to the "New World," America.

Transpiration is the transfer of water from plants to the atmosphere; water is taken up by the roots of plants and released as water vapor by the leaves.

Tropical cyclone is a low-pressure weather system in the tropics in which the central core is warmer than the surrounding atmosphere. A tropical storm is designated a cyclone when its winds are from 39 to 74 miles per hour; when winds exceed 74 miles per hour, the cyclone is called a *hurricane* or *typhoon*.

Tropics are the region of Earth from latitude 23.5° north (the Tropic of Cancer) southward across the Equator to latitude 23.5° south (the Tropic of Capricorn). This region has relatively small daily and seasonal changes in temperature, but great seasonal changes in precipitation.

Tropopause is the boundary or transition zone separating the troposphere, the lowest major layer of the Earth's atmosphere, from the stratosphere, which lies above it. Temperature generally decreases from the Earth's surface up to the tropopause, and then is approximately constant or increases with height above the tropopause. The altitude of the tropopause is variable, typically ranging from somewhat less than 10 up to 15 or more kilometers above sea level. The tropopause height is usually higher over the tropics than in polar regions, and higher in summer than in winter.

Troposphere is the region of the atmosphere that extends from the Earth's surface to about 7 miles (12 kilometers) above sea level, on average. (See **stratosphere.**)

Tropospheric ozone is ozone (O_3) in the troposphere. As opposed to stratospheric ozone (the "good ozone" that protects us from excess ultraviolet radiation from the Sun), tropospheric ozone, or "bad ozone," results from the interaction of nitrogen oxides (NO_x), volatile organic compounds, and sunlight. Most of the pollutants that lead to the formation of tropospheric ozone come from automobiles, powerplants, and other human activities. In many cities, ozone is a significant health problem. Ozone also causes 3 to 5 billion dollars a year in lost crop production and substantial losses in forest products. Tropospheric ozone is also a significant greenhouse gas.

Typhoon is a tropical cyclone with winds 75 miles per hour or greater, occurring in the northwest Pacific Ocean. In other parts of the world, such storms have different names, such as *hurricane.*

Ultraviolet radiation (UV) is the energy range just beyond the violet end of the visible spectrum. Most UV is blocked by Earth's atmosphere (particularly the stratospheric ozone layer), but some solar UV penetrates and aids in plant photosynthesis and the production of vitamin D in humans. Too much UV can burn the skin, cause skin cancer and cataracts, and damage vegetation.

Volatile organic compounds (VOCs) are precursors of tropospheric ozone and photochemical smog. They are produced by human activities, including the use of dry-cleaning solvents.

Volcano is a naturally occurring vent or fissure at Earth's surface through which erupt molten, solid, and/or gaseous materials. Major volcanic eruptions inject large quantities of dust, gas, and aerosols into the atmosphere and can thus cause temporary climatic cooling.

Warm front is a zone of transition marking the boundary between advancing, relatively warm and light air and retreating, relatively cold and dense air. (Compare **cold front.**)

Water vapor is the invisible, gaseous form of water.

Weather is the state of the atmosphere at some place and time, particularly as characterized by variables such as temperature, cloudiness, wind, humidity, and precipitation.

Wind is a natural motion of the air, especially a noticeable current of air moving in the atmosphere parallel to Earth's surface.

Some often-used chemical symbols

CFCs	chlorofluorocarbons
CH_4	methane
Cl_2	molecular chlorine
CO	carbon monoxide
CO_2	carbon dioxide
H_2	molecular hydrogen
HCFCs	hydrochlorofluorocarbons
H_2O	water
N_2	molecular (ordinary) nitrogen
N_2O	nitrous oxide
NO	nitric oxide
NO_2	nitrogen dioxide
O	free oxygen
O_2	molecular (ordinary) oxygen
O_3	ozone
OH	hydroxyl radical
SO_2	sulfur dioxide

BIBLIOGRAPHY

I have tried to include here the most significant, the most informative, the most accessible, and the most readable works bearing on the issues taken up in this book. That these issues are all of relatively recent origin is borne out by the fact that all but four of the works listed have been published since 1983. All but one are books, and only a handful are cited in the text. For those who want to learn more, some browsing in this list will thus be well rewarded.

Abrahamson, Dean Edwin (ed.). *The Challenge of Global Warming.* Washington, D.C.: Island Press, 1989.
  Twenty-one chapters by different authors cover a range of issues, from the physical climate system, to biology, to international policy and global security. The caliber of the chapters is generally high, and this is a good single-volume summary of the issue of climate change due to the enhanced greenhouse effect.
Abrahamson, Dean, and Peter Ciborowski (eds.). *The Greenhouse Effect: Policy Implications of a Global Warming. Proceedings of a Symposium Held in Minneapolis, Minnesota, May 29–31, 1984.* University of Minnesota: Center for Urban and Regional Affairs, Publication No. CURA 88-8, 1988.
  This volume stresses not the physical climate system, but possible policy strategies, ranging from alternative fuels to coping with rising sea level. A good introduction to the interface between global-change science and the world of socioeconomic and political realities.
Ahrens, C. Donald. *Meteorology Today: An Introduction to Weather, Climate, and the Environment, Fifth Edition.* Minneapolis/St. Paul: West Publishing Co., 1994.
  A leading introductory college-level textbook on atmospheric science. This is a big book (almost 600 pages), crammed with facts and color illustra-

tions. It is exceptionally clearly written, and the science it reports is up to date and accurately described.

Ashford, Oliver M. *Prophet or Professor? The Life and Work of Lewis Fry Richardson.* Boston: Adam Hilger, Ltd., 1985.
A charming biography of Lewis Fry Richardson, a pioneer in computer simulations of the atmosphere. Today's global-climate models are a vindication of Richardson's vision, developed during World War I. The author, a meteorologist, was a close friend of Richardson.

Balling, Robert C., Jr. *The Heated Debate: Greenhouse Predictions Versus Climate Reality.* California: Pacific Research Institute for Public Policy, 1992.
The "consensus" among scientists concerning climate change and the greenhouse effect is not unanimous. This book includes ideas of several greenhouse skeptics who do not avoid provocative statements and debatable issues. Many experts strongly disagree with some of the opinions expressed in this book. Scientific truth emerges when conflicting theories and interpretations compete openly and can be evaluated objectively against the reality of observations. This book is contrarian and controversial, but alternative viewpoints deserve a fair examination.

Bohren, Craig F. *Clouds in a Glass of Beer: Simple Experiments in Atmospheric Physics.* New York: Wiley, 1987.
Teachers especially will enjoy this delightful book, which describes practical classroom demonstrations and laboratory experiments that illuminate a broad range of atmospheric phenomena. The author, a meteorology professor at Pennsylvania State University, is a gifted teacher whose enthusiasm for his subject shows on every page. Not to be missed.

Bolin, Bert, Bo R. Döös, Jill Jäger, and Richard A. Warrick (eds.). *SCOPE 29, The Greenhouse Effect, Climatic Change, and Ecosystems.* Chichester, England: Wiley, 1986.
SCOPE stands for Scientific Committee on Problems of the Environment, an international organization, and this book summarizes the state of the subject as presented in a conference in 1985. The topics are familiar: greenhouse gases, models and observational studies of climate, the effects on ecosystems and agriculture. Most of the chapters are written by leading authorities.

Broecker, Wallace S. *How to Build a Habitable Planet.* Palisades, N.Y.: Eldigio Press, Lamont-Doherty Geological Observatory, 1985.
An iconoclastic textbook by a world-famous geochemist, this undergraduate text traces "the development of the Earth from its roots in the Big Bang to its future in man's hands." The scope of Broecker's erudition is impressive. A valuable and profoundly original book.

Brooks, C. E. P. *Climate Through the Ages.* New York: Dover Publications, 1970.
A true classic. This is a reprint of a 1926 textbook, revised in 1949. One of many good reasons for studying this and other "obsolete" texts is to remind ourselves of the fallibility and changeability of science. In this book, for example, the notion of continental drift is treated as a theory

that is unlikely to deserve acceptance. In addition to promoting humility in scientists, this classic text is still full of valuable information and is a model of clear writing.

Brown, Lester R., et al. *State of the World*. New York: W. W. Norton, 1984–94.

This annual report from the team of the Worldwatch Institute is must reading for those who monitor and teach the state of the planet. It is not necessary to share all the environmental viewpoints of the authors to appreciate their valuable scholarship and up-to-date data.

Brown, Lester R., Christopher Flavin, and Sandra Postel. *Saving the Planet*. New York: W. W. Norton, 1991.

A highly readable introduction to the complex task of achieving a sustainable global economy. Topics range from energy policy to population stabilization to "green" taxes.

Brown, Lester R., Hal Kane, and David Malin Roodman. *Vital Signs*. New York: W. W. Norton, 1992–94.

An annual compilation of current facts and figures on trends in everything from food production to energy usage to population increase. An invaluable data source for a myriad of indicators of planetary health.

Cagin, Seth, and Philip Dray. *Between Earth and Sky: How CFCs Changed Our World and Endangered the Ozone Layer*. New York: Pantheon Books, 1993.

This big book (430 pages) is a major achievement in contemporary Earth science history. It tells the story of CFCs and ozone depletion in rich but readable detail. The authors talked at length with virtually every major scientist involved in the topic, as well as with industrialists, environmentalists, and many others. Their book is completely nontechnical, but extensive notes allow the interested reader to substantiate virtually every statement in it.

Cleveland, Harlan. *The Global Commons: Policy for the Planet*. Lanham, Md.: The Aspen Institute and University Press of America, Inc., 1990.

This short and eloquent monograph by a modern scientific statesman is a jewel: thought-provoking and unsettling. Must reading for planetary policy-makers, this book begins with a quote by E. B. White, "I own one share of the corporate Earth, and I am uneasy about the management."

Ehrlich, Paul, and Anne Ehrlich. *The Population Explosion*. New York: Simon and Schuster, 1990.

The population of the Earth was 3.5 billion people in 1968, when Paul Ehrlich's *The Population Bomb* was published. In the following quarter-century, world population increased by some 2 billion. This powerful book chronicles the explosive growth of humanity and its implications for our common future.

Ehrlich, Paul R., and Anne H. Ehrlich. *Healing the Planet*. Reading, Mass.: Addison-Wesley, 1991.

In this companion volume to *The Population Explosion*, the Ehrlichs explain how too many people using inappropriate technology contribute to environmental degradation. The chief topics include energy, global warming, ozone loss, and pollution and abuse of water and land. Extensive references to the primary scientific literature make this book especially valuable to readers who wish to explore these subjects more deeply by consulting original papers.

Ehrlich, Paul R., Anne H. Ehrlich, and John P. Holdren. *Ecoscience: Population, Resources, Environment.* San Francisco: W. H. Freeman, 1977.
With more than 1,000 pages, this wide-ranging and clearly written textbook is a vast mine of information.

Firor, John. *The Changing Atmosphere.* New Haven, Conn.: Yale University Press, 1990.
A superbly readable introduction to global-change issues by a scientist with a broad understanding of both the underlying research and the policy implications. A special virtue of this book is its evenhanded treatment of complex scientific issues. Firor provides a good overview of current understanding, together with many references to the scientific literature for those who wish to dig deeper.

Gore, Al. *Earth in the Balance: Ecology and the Human Spirit.* Boston: Houghton Mifflin, 1992.
Long before he became a candidate for vice president of the United States, Senator Gore was deeply interested in environmental issues and was one of the most active environmentalists in Congress. A former journalist, Gore required no ghost writer; he is responsible for this book himself. Not everyone will agree with all of Gore's conclusions and prescriptions for the planet, but we can all recognize the achievement represented by this book: a prominent American politician has produced a serious and readable treatise on the global environment.

Graedel, T. J., and Paul J. Crutzen. *Atmospheric Change: An Earth System Perspective.* New York: W. H. Freeman, 1993.
An excellent college textbook on Earth system science, with strong emphasis on environmental chemistry. This book is authoritative, clearly written, and copiously illustrated. The reader is assumed to have studied introductory college-level mathematics, physics, and chemistry, but a determined high-school graduate will find nearly all of the book comprehensible.

Gribbin, John (ed.). *Climatic Change.* New York: Cambridge University Press, 1978.
A valuable collection of articles by a broad range of scientists, although badly out of date.

Gribbin, John (ed.). *The Breathing Planet.* New York: Basil Blackwell & New Scientist, 1986.
A collection of 46 short papers from the journal *New Scientist.* Especially valuable in tracing the evolution of controversies surrounding topics such as drought, ozone depletion, acid rain, and the greenhouse effect.

Harte, John. *The Green Fuse: An Ecological Odyssey.* Berkeley: University of California Press, 1993.
A work of literature as well as of science. Harte is a fine scientist and an ecological visionary. This book is a personal pilgrimage and a voyage of

discovery through the linked worlds of the physical climate system and the even more complex universe of living things.

Houghton, John. *Global Warming: The Complete Briefing*. Oxford: Lion Publishing, 1994.

The best one-volume treatment of the science of climate change due to an increase in the greenhouse effect. Houghton draws heavily on the results of the Intergovernmental Panel on Climate Change (IPCC) reports. A leading figure in international meteorological circles, Houghton formerly headed the United Kingdom Meteorological Office and played a major role in compiling the IPCC scientific assessments. This book is readable, up to date, and authoritative, with extensive references to the research literature. Both scientists and nonscientists can learn from it. The viewpoint adopted is that of the mainstream scientific consensus, although the author is careful to cite examples of some representative dissenting opinions.

Houghton, J. T., G. J. Jenkins, and J. J. Ephraums (eds.). *Climate Change. The IPCC Scientific Assessment*. World Meteorological Organization/ United Nations Environment Program, Intergovernmental Panel on Climate Change. New York: Cambridge University Press, 1990.

The famous "IPCC Report." Crammed with tables, charts, and maps, this is a one-volume definitive summary of mainstream climate science. It is surprisingly readable as well as comprehensive and authoritative. The results of global climate models are summarized succinctly in this report. Never forget, however, that global climate models are imperfect and may be misleading in important respects. Not all scientists subscribe to the "consensus" outlined in this report.

Houghton, J. T., B. A. Callander, and S. K. Varney (eds). *Climate Change 1992. The Supplementary Report to the IPCC Scientific Assessment,* World Meteorological Organization/United Nations Environment Program, Intergovernmental Panel on Climate Change. New York: Cambridge University Press, 1992.

This update of the original IPCC Report does not change the main conclusions of the earlier volume. Nevertheless, at 200 pages, the 1992 "Supplementary Report" is more than half the length of the original, and that fact alone is eloquent testimony to the pace of research in this field.

Kondrat'ev, K. Ya. *Changes in Global Climate*. Leningrad: Gidrometeoizdat Publishers, 1980; published in English by Amerind Publishing Co., New Delhi, 1984.

Although Western scientists are often poorly informed about developments in the former Soviet Union, the reverse is not true. This book, one of many by Kondrat'ev, is an overview of climate and radiation problems, surveying both the Russian literature and (mainly) contributions from the West.

Koopowitz, Harold, and Hilary Kaye. *Plant Extinction: A Global Crisis*. Washington, D.C.: Stone Wall Press, 1983.

An extremely readable summary of the threatened loss of many plant species, this book describes many examples of this aspect of biodiversity. A collaboration between a biologist and a journalist, this is a fascinating work.

Leggett, Jeremy (ed.). *Global Warming: The Greenpeace Report*. New York: Oxford University Press, 1990.
This collection of 19 articles emphasizes policy responses. Some, but not all, of the authors support the Greenpeace position that governments can and should do much more to deal with "the greenhouse threat."

Levine, Joel S. (ed.). *Global Biomass Burning: Atmospheric, Climatic, and Biospheric Implications*. Cambridge, Mass.: MIT Press, 1991.
The proceedings of a 1990 conference, this big book contains 63 serious scientific papers and is not for the faint of heart. It is the best one-volume treatment of this subject. Biomass in this context means forests, grasslands, and agricultural fields after harvesting. Biomass burning not only produces carbon dioxide, thus potentially affecting climate, but also has many other implications for planetary ecology.

Lorenz, Edward N. *The Essence of Chaos*. Seattle: University of Washington Press, 1993.
The fact that the atmosphere has a finite predictability is what limits the maximum range of weather forecasts. This phenomenon, due to sensitive dependence on the initial state, is an example of chaos. Lorenz is arguably the world's most eminent dynamic meteorologist, the discoverer of chaos, and the father of modern predictability theory. This book traces not only the scientific aspects of the topic, but the historical development of it as well. Most of the book is nonmathematical and readily accessible for the general reader.

Lyman, Francesca, et al. *The Greenhouse Trap*. Boston: Beacon Press, 1990.
A World Resources Institute product, this short book by a journalist is an extremely readable overview of the greenhouse climate issue. It includes suggestions for how governments and individuals can help. No scientific background is assumed.

MacCracken, Michael C., et al. (eds.). *Prospects for Future Climate. A Special US/USSR Report on Climate and Climate Change*. Chelsea, Michigan: Lewis Publishers, 1990.
At their summit meeting in December 1987, a call for an assessment of current understanding in climate was made by Presidents Reagan and Gorbachev. This book is the result. Scientifically up to date, with an extensive bibliography, it covers much of the same ground as the IPCC Report, but is a good deal more readable and less detailed.

Mathews, Jessica Tuchman (ed.). *Preserving the Global Environment: The Challenge of Shared Leadership*. New York: W. W. Norton, 1991.
A collection of ten papers by an international array of authors, assessing global environmental trends and their policy implications.

Meadows, Donella H., Dennis L. Meadows, and Jorgen Randers. *Beyond the Limits*. Post Mills, Vt.: Chelsea Green Publishing Co., 1992.
This sobering book is a sequel to *The Limits to Growth*, which sold nine million copies in 29 languages some 20 years earlier. Using computer-

modeling techniques, the authors advocate a decrease in consumption and
population so as to reach a sustainable society. Though this type of computer modeling may still be in its infancy, the results of the simulation are
extremely thought-provoking.

Moran, Joseph M., and Michael D. Morgan. *Meteorology: The Atmosphere
and the Science of Weather, Fourth Edition*. New York: Macmillan College Publishing Co., 1994.
The latest version of a standard text, this substantial book (over 500
pages) is aimed at college students who are not science majors. It is somewhat less technical than the book by Ahrens, but covers much of the same
material.

Oppenheimer, Michael, and Robert H. Boyle. *Dead Heat: The Race Against
the Greenhouse Effect*. New York: Basic Books, 1990.
Oppenheimer, a scientist with the Environmental Defense Fund, and
Boyle, a writer, have collaborated to produce a very readable book on the
science and politics of global change. The style of this book is breezy and
journalistic, but it is full of valuable information. It is easy reading, with
no technical background assumed. One need not agree with all the conclusions of the book to benefit from reading it.

Reisner, Mark. *Cadillac Desert*. New York: Viking, 1986.
The story of water and the American West, researched in detail and told
with passion. A powerful achievement of investigative journalism, this
book will make you understand why "water flows uphill, toward money."

Roberts, Walter Orr, and Henry Lansford. *The Climate Mandate*. San Francisco: W. H. Freeman, 1979.
A successful collaboration between a scientist and a journalist. This very
readable book is concerned with connections between climate variation,
food production, and population growth. The book is nonmathematical
and written for a general audience.

Rosen, Louis, and Robert Glasser (editors-in-chief). *Climate Change and
Energy Policy. Proceedings of the International Conference on Global Cli-
mate Change: Its Mitigation Through Improved Production and Use of
Energy, Los Alamos National Laboratory, October 21–24, 1991, Los
Alamos, New Mexico*. New York: American Institute of Physics, 1992.
This up-to-date volume is the proceedings of a conference held in Octo-
ber 1991 in Los Alamos. Experts from many countries explored connec-
tions between climate, energy technologies, and policy.

Sagan, Carl, and Richard Turco. *A Path Where No Man Thought*. New York:
Random House, 1990.
Surely there is no more terrifying possibility of change on planet Earth
than nuclear war. Even a "small" nuclear war, in addition to its own hor-
rors, might well generate a sudden and severe climate change due to the
smoke from many fires, which might block sunlight and lead to lower
temperatures. This possibility is called "nuclear winter," and this is the
best one-volume treatment of the subject, by two scientists whose research
has done much to advance our understanding of it.

Schneider, Stephen H., and Randi Londer. *The Coevolution of Climate and Life*. San Francisco: Sierra Club Books, 1984.

Yet another collaboration between a scientist and a writer. Schneider is a climatologist with a marvelous flair for describing science to nonscientists. He is a prolific author and has done much to educate politicians and reporters about climate. For a scientist, he is an unusually eloquent public speaker and is especially adept at communicating via the mass media—he is what the French call *médiatique*. If you read only one of his books, make it this one.

Schotterer, Ulrich, and Peter Andermatt. *Climate—Our Future?* Minneapolis: University of Minnesota Press, 1992.

Containing a few well-chosen words and many magnificent pictures, this book is a work of art. It is a translation into English of a work that first appeared in Switzerland, and is an attempt to convey the essentials of the 1990 IPCC Report to a wider audience. A true masterpiece of scientific communication. As the author remarks, "Images tell the story, figure captions enhance the essentials."

Scientific American (Special Issue). *Managing Planet Earth*. New York: Scientific American, Inc., September 1989.

This special issue contains 11 articles by noted authorities on topics relevant to global change. There are especially good articles on atmospheric chemistry, climate change, water, biodiversity, and population. A superb collection that merits careful study.

Scientific American (Special Issue). *Energy for Planet Earth*. New York: Scientific American, Inc., September 1990.

This collection of articles includes readable and authoritative accounts of the prospects of solar, nuclear, and fossil-fuel energy. Other articles cover particular segments of the energy picture, including the developing world, motor vehicles, and industry.

Senior, C. A., and J. F. B. Mitchell. "Carbon Dioxide and Climate: The Impact of Cloud Parameterization." *Journal of Climate*, vol. 6 (3), 393–418, March 1993.

This is a technical publication, appearing in a specialized research journal, intended for scientists active in climate research, rather than a general audience. Nevertheless, the paper, destined to be a landmark, is well worth study by those interested in the details of climate modeling. Among many other important results, the paper establishes that the same model can produce different sensitivities to carbon dioxide, varying by a factor of three in terms of global average warming, depending on the treatment of clouds and their effects on radiation.

Silver, Cheryl Simon. *One Earth, One Future*. Washington, D.C.: National Academy Press, 1990.

A primer of global-change science, based on the Forum on Global Change and Our Common Future held in 1989. Easily readable and nonmathematical.

Socolow, Robert H., C. Andrews, F. Berkhout, and V. Thomas. *Industrial Ecology and Global Change*. Cambridge: Cambridge University Press, 1994.

A fascinating and thought-provoking collection of papers by participants at a two-week summer institute held in Colorado in 1992. Industrial ecology is a new field seeking to analyze interactions between human activities and the environment. In particular, it views industrial design and manufacturing not as isolated processes, but as part of a system that includes the environment. Thus, for example, it seeks to optimize the manufacturing cycle, from raw material to product to waste disposal, taking effects on the environment into account. Participants came from several countries, and their expertise varied from economics to climate theory.

Stevens, Payson R., and Kevin W. Kelley. *Embracing Earth*. San Francisco: Chronicle Books, 1992.

Simply the best collection of views of the Earth from space, combined with intelligent, sensitive, informed commentary. Visually stunning. If you think that science and art are incompatible, read this book. Astronaut and physicist Sally Ride said it all: "The view from overhead makes theory come alive."

Trenberth, Kevin E. (ed.). *Climate System Modeling*. New York: Cambridge University Press, 1993.

Twenty-three chapters totaling almost 800 pages, covering the field of climate modeling. This is a text by leading scientists, intended for graduate students, with the expectation that it will introduce people from one discipline to the several other disciplines that are important to climate. Topics include the atmosphere, the ocean, land surfaces, terrestrial ecosystems, atmospheric and marine chemistry, and the detailed structure of and results from a wide variety of climate models. An authoritative and up-to-date survey of the subject.

Turco, Richard P. *Earth under Siege: From Air Pollution to Global Change*. New York: Oxford University Press, 1997.

This book breaks new ground in integrating traditional topics of atmospheric science with the modern concerns of global change. The author, a distinguished UCLA professor, has all the credentials to attempt such a synthesis. From his own wide-ranging research experience, he has acquired a rare degree of interdisciplinary expertise, and he writes exceptionally clearly. This is a long-needed, authoritative, readable, up-to-date, one-volume global-change text.

Washington, Warren M., and Claire L. Parkinson. *An Introduction to Three-Dimensional Climate Modeling*. Mill Valley, Calif.: University Science Books, 1986.

A standard text on climate modeling, this book concentrates on the basics and, therefore, will not quickly become out of date. The book is especially strong on the mathematical foundation and computational techniques of climate modeling.

Weiner, Jonathan. *The Next One Hundred Years*. New York: Bantam Books, 1990.

A masterful account of global change by a gifted science writer, this book is especially good at painting the personalities of many of the scientists involved. It brings out clearly the interaction between science and politics. Of the recent books on global change for general audiences, this one is among the very best.

Wilson, Edward O. (ed.). *The Diversity of Life*. Cambridge, Mass.: Belknap Harvard, 1992.

Wilson is that rare combination: a superb scientist and a captivating writer (two Pulitzer Prizes). Highly recommended as a readable and authoritative account of the threat of loss of biodiversity due to human activities.

Wyman, Richard L. (ed.). *Global Climate Change and Life on Earth*. New York: Chapman and Hall, 1991.

The proceedings of a 1989 conference of the same title, this book contains 16 chapters, with emphasis on the effect of climate change on the world of living things and related policy alternatives. The individual chapters are brief but contain extensive references to the literature.

ORIGINAL SOURCES

Readers who wish to consult scientific publications in the research literature might begin with the following works; all are classic references that advanced our understanding of topics discussed in this book. Be forewarned: jargon and mathematics await the unwary here.

Arrhenius, S., 1896: "On the influence of carbonic acid in the air upon the temperature on the ground." *Philosophical Magazine* 41, 237–276. This paper was the first attempt to calculate the climatic effect of an increasing concentration of atmospheric carbon dioxide.

Farman, J. C., B. G. Gardiner, and J. D. Shanklin, 1985: "Large losses of total ozone in Antarctica reveal seasonal ClO_x/NO_x interaction." *Nature* 315, 207–210. This paper announced the discovery of the Antarctic ozone hole.

Lorenz, E. N., 1963: "Deterministic nonperiodic flow." *Journal of the Atmospheric Sciences* 20, 130–141. This paper is the Rosetta stone of atmospheric predictability theory.

Manabe, S., and R. J. Stouffer, 1980: "Sensitivity of a global climate model to an increase of CO_2 concentration in the atmosphere." *Journal of Geophysical Research* 85, 5529–5554. This paper initiated modern computer simulation studies of climate sensitivity to carbon dioxide, using global models of the coupled atmosphere-ocean climate system.

Molina, M. J., and F. S. Rowland, 1974: "Stratospheric sink for chlorofluoromethanes: Chlorine atom-catalyzed destruction of ozone." *Nature* 249, 810–812. This is the original publication of the theory that CFCs can cause stratospheric ozone depletion.

Ramanthan, V., 1975: "Greenhouse effect due to chlorofluorocarbons: Climatic implications." *Science* 190, 50–52. This paper showed that CFCs are powerful greenhouse gases.

Revelle, R., and H. E. Suess, 1957: "Carbon dioxide exchange between atmosphere and ocean and the question of an increase of atmospheric CO_2 during the past decades." *Tellus* 9, 18–27. This paper is a landmark in the study of carbon dioxide exchange between the atmosphere and the ocean.

Richardson, L. F., 1922: *Weather Prediction by Numerical Process.* London: Cambridge University Press (reprinted 1965 by Dover Publications, New York). All computer models of the global climate system, like all attempts to forecast weather with global atmospheric models, trace their origins to this visionary book.

INDEX

Richard C. J. Somerville

Since 1979, Richard Somerville has been professor of meteorology at Scripps Institution of Oceanography, University of California, San Diego. There he is a member of the Climate Research Division, an interdisciplinary group of scientists studying the variability and predictability of Earth's climate.

Dr. Somerville's major research interests are the greenhouse effect and global climate change. He is a specialist in computer modeling of the climate system. His current research is aimed at improving our understanding of the role of clouds in climate.

Dr. Somerville earned a B.S. degree from Pennsylvania State University in 1961 and a Ph.D. from New York University in 1966, both in meteorology. He has lectured extensively on climate change and has published more than 100 technical papers. His honors include election as a Fellow of both the American Association for the Advancement of Science and the American Meteorological Society.

Designer: U.C. Press Staff
Compositor: Braun-Brumfield, Inc.
Text: 10/13 Galliard
Display: Galliard
Printer: Braun-Brumfield, Inc.
Binder: Braun-Brumfield, Inc.